Colonial Industrialization and Labor
in Korea

The Onoda Cement Factory

Harvard East Asian Monographs, 181

The Harvard-Hallym Series on Korean Studies

The Harvard-Hallym Series on Korean Studies, published by the Harvard University Asia Center, is supported by the Korea Institute of Harvard University and by Hallym University in Korea. It is committed to the publication of outstanding new scholarly work on Korea, regardless of discipline, in both the humanities and the social sciences.

Professor Carter J. Eckert
Director
Korean Institute, Harvard University

Dr. Dahl-Sun Han
President
Hallym University

Colonial Industrialization and Labor in Korea

The Onoda Cement Factory

SOON-WON PARK

Published by the Harvard University Asia Center
and distributed by Harvard University Press
Cambridge (Massachusetts) and London
1999

Printed in the United States of America

The Harvard University Asia Center publishes a monograph series and, in coordination with the Fairbank Center for East Asian Research, the Korea Institute, the Reischauer Institute of Japanese Studies, and other faculties and institutes, administers research projects designed to further scholarly understanding of China, Japan, Vietnam, Korea, and other Asian countries. The Center also sponsors projects addressing multidisciplinary and regional issues in Asia.

Library of Congress Cataloging-in-Publication Data

Park, Soon-Won, 1949–
    Colonial industrialization and labor in Korea : the Onoda cement factory / Soon-Won Park.
       p.   cm. -- (Harvard East Asian Monographs ; 181) (Harvard-Hallym series on Korean studies)
    Includes bibliographical references and index.
    ISBN 0-674-14240-3 (alk. paper)
    1. Onoda Semento Kabushiki Kaisha--History. 2. Labor--Korea--History. 3. Cement industries--Korea--History.   I. Title.
II. Series. III. Series: Harvard-Hallym series on Korean studies.
HD9622.K640567   1999
331.7' 66694' 095195--dc21   99-24359
                                             CIP

Index by the author

    ∞   Printed on acid-free paper

Last figure below indicates year of this printing
08 07 06 05 04 03 02 01 00 99

To my parents

Young-Don Park and Wha-Rae Song Park

Acknowledgments

I acknowledge with gratitude the help of my professors at Harvard University whose guidance and encouragement made this work possible. Professors Albert Craig and Edward Wagner and Dr. Karl Moskowitz deserve special thanks for their help at the dissertation stage. They have been interested in my research subject from the beginning and have followed my work closely for several years with patience and support. Their thoughtful criticisms at many stages of the work sharpened the argument and shaped my approach in important ways.

Many individuals in Japan and Korea were also important in my research. As my research advisor at Tokyo University, Professor Totsuka Hideo was extremely helpful in introducing me to people and documents. He also read and commented on my outline, and I have profited from this. I owe particular thanks to Professor Takeda Haruhito of the Faculty of Economics of Tokyo University for introducing me to the Onoda Cement Company archives. Without his help, I could not have found the right material for my case study. Maeda Hiroshi, archivist at Onoda Cement Company, was generous beyond any expectations with his time, knowledge, and concern for the materials. Special thanks go to both Korean and Japanese interviewees who shared their time with me, talked about their experiences, and gave me the benefit of their knowledge of the colonial period.

Professor An Pyŏng-Jik of Seoul National University and the members of the Naksŏngdae Economic Institute also deserve special thanks for letting me join their monthly seminar on modern Korean economic history from 1990 to 1995. The contents of the seminar were extremely valuable for understanding historiographical trends and new issues in the socioeconomic history of Korea. Professors Hori Kazuo (Kyoto University), Carter Eckert and Andrew Gordon (Harvard University), Bruce Cumings (University of Chicago), Michael Robinson (Indiana University), Gi-Wook Shin (UCLA), Dennis McNamara (Georgetown University), and Sŏn Chae-Won (Tokyo University) have earned the gratitude of all of us who work in this field for their enduring passion and commitment to the development of the history of the late colonial period. Their work has given me great insights and inspired me to rethink and re-examine the Onoda workers' experience in the larger context of colonial modernity. Of course, I alone am responsible for the views expressed here.

I am very grateful for financial support from the Fulbright-Hays Dissertation Fellowship and the Korea Institute of Harvard University, which allowed me to do research in Seoul and Tokyo for two years. Sam Kidder of the Foreign Commercial Service/Tokyo was very thoughtful and patient in editing the manuscript at the dissertation stage. John Ziemer of the Harvard University Asia Center Publications Program has been wonderfully effective and productive in the final revision of the manuscript. Yi P'yŏng-Han of the Ch'ugye University of Fine Arts in Korea was also very gracious in producing computer graphics for the book on short notice. Finally, a special thanks to my husband, Ted Kloth, who has endured and supported my stubbornness on the topic with gentle affection, patience, and a sense of humor.

S.-W. P.

Contents

Tables, Figures, and Maps

Tables

Figures

Maps

Colonial Industrialization and Labor in Korea

The Onoda Cement Factory

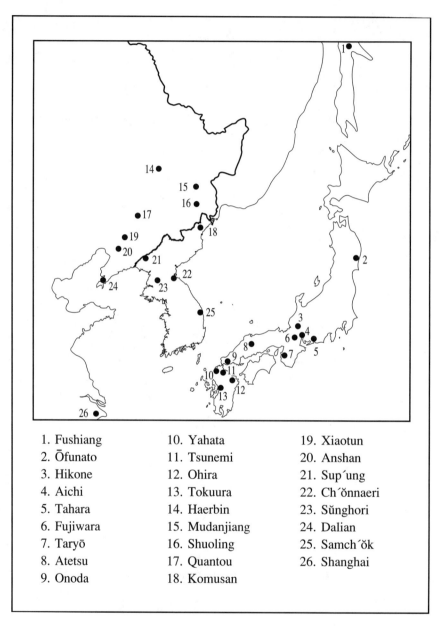

1. Fushiang	10. Yahata	19. Xiaotun
2. Ōfunato	11. Tsunemi	20. Anshan
3. Hikone	12. Ohira	21. Sup´ung
4. Aichi	13. Tokuura	22. Ch´ŏnnaeri
5. Tahara	14. Haerbin	23. Sŭnghori
6. Fujiwara	15. Mudanjiang	24. Dalian
7. Taryō	16. Shuoling	25. Samch´ŏk
8. Atetsu	17. Quantou	26. Shanghai
9. Onoda	18. Komusan	

Map 1 Branch factories of the Onoda Cement Company, 1945. Source:
Onoda semento kabushiki kaisha 1981: 397.

Introduction

This book is the story of the first generation of skilled workers in Korea. Overwhelmingly rural in origin, they met Japanese managers and workers and confronted the colonial experience in modern factories. These workers were not just passive victims, however. They were active players who formed their own individual identity amid the larger historical forces of the colonial period. Certainly, they led complex and hard lives. Their self-portraits are often colored with the resentful bitterness of hearts hardened by oppression and injustice, known in Korea as *han* (恨). These workers saw themselves as an unfortunate, exhausted generation who survived all the turmoils and ordeals of Korea's modern history—colonialism, liberation, occupation, war, division of the country, and rapid industrialization. This book is one step toward a detached portrait of these workers, the "colonial generation," as the succeeding generations have called them. Through the life experiences of these factory workers in the colonial and the post-colonial eras, we will see the emergence of the Korean industrial workforce as a part of the modern transformation of the Korean people.

Until the 1980s, the socioeconomic historiography of colonial Korea was deeply influenced by Japanese Marxist historians, because their anti-imperial viewpoint suited the nationalistic sentiments of Koreans in general and Korean academics in particular. These conventional master narratives generally present ideologically oriented, black-and-white interpretations of the colonial period as a monolithic confrontation between Japanese imperialism and the Korean struggle for national liberation. With their themes of anticolonialism and national-liberation struggles, these narratives see colonial history in binary terms and emphasize Japan's political repression, economic exploitation, and destructive assimilating cultural policies. Ordinary Korean people of the colonial period are viewed in terms of the same dichotomizing image—passive and impersonal victims of oppressive Japanese rule.

Scholars of the socioeconomic history of colonial Korea, including Kajimura Hideki (1977, 1981), Chŏn Sŏk-Tam (1978), Shin Yong-Ha (1982, 1987), and Kobayashi Hideo (1969, 1973), have described industrial growth in the 1930s as an "enclave style" wartime industrial development that exploited Koreans to the limit and had "no linkage effect" to the local economy or society.[1] Korean labor historians of the 1970s such as Kim Yun-Hwan (1982), Kwon Tu-Yŏng (1979), Kang Tong-Chin (1979), and Pak Hyŏn-Ch'ae (1979) studied and interpreted colonial labor and labor movements in the context of the national-liberation struggle of poverty-stricken, exploited workers. In their analyses, the Korean workforce has the following characteristics: (1) a cheap, abundant, colonial workforce was exploited by a discriminatory labor system; (2) Korean workers were limited to unskilled work because the Japanese monopolized skilled work for themselves; (3) a labor surplus continued until 1937, and the workforce mobilized during the war disappeared after 1945; (4) labor turnover and absenteeism rates were high because of workers' rural links and the poor working conditions; and (5) the colonial labor movement was typically an anti-Japanese nationalist movement.

Since the early 1980s, these earlier studies have been challenged and re-examined with iconoclastic vigor. Several factors both inside and outside the South Korean academic community affected these revisionist movements. First, South Korea's economic success and its growing reputation as a model newly industrializing country (NIC) led to an upsurge in national self-confidence. Second, this impressive economic performance attracted the attention of both economists and social scientists from the modern economic growth school and dependency theorists in America and Latin American countries. This in turn led Korean scholars to probe the growth of Korean capitalism from a more objective historical perspective.[2] Third, un-

---

1. See also Suh 1978; and, for North Korean work, Ri 1960.

2. Among the numerous studies along this line, a pathbreaking project was the eight-volume series Studies in the Modernization of the Republic of Korea: 1945–1975, published by the Council on East Asian Studies of Harvard

derstanding the nature of colonial modernity became a prerequisite for understanding the increasingly complex and diverse modernity of present-day Korea. And fourth, the development of a higher education system oriented toward graduate schools under the Chun Doo-Hwan government in the early 1980s brought about a surge in graduate-level research and Ph.D. dissertations in South Korea, which intensively explored all the major topics in modern Korean history from a new point of view.[3]

Many younger historians, who had a more objective scholarly attitude as well as faith and confidence in the modern development of the Korean people, started to re-examine and analyze the reception of modernity itself in the Korean colonial experience in a more balanced and open-minded manner. As Gi-Wook Shin and Michael Robinson (1999) summarize in their introduction to *Colonial Modernity in Korea*, nationalistic scholars were reluctant to examine modernity in the colonial context. For these scholars, colonialism produced at best a "distorted" modernity, hindering the creation of a "true" modernity. In the value-laden nationalist perspective, the colonial state as agent of change delegitimizes the "modern" itself.[4] The new trend of historical thinking, however, pointed out that one cannot (and should not) avoid colonialism in discussing Korean modernity and sought to articulate the mutually interlocking relations between colonialism and modernity as well as to discuss the complex nature of colonial modernity.

The concept of colonial modernity has become a useful conceptual tool in recent studies for illuminating Korea's unique path to modernity and the complex ways in which present Korean identities have been formed and deformed. Scholars in both East and West such as An Pyŏng-Jik (1990), Nakamura Tetsu (1991; Nakamura et al. 1988), Kim Nak-Nyŏn (1994), Hŏ Su-Yŏl (1994), Carter Eckert

---

University in 1979–81. For the dependency development approach, see Evans 1987; and Sŏ 1990.

3. The most popular topics among graduate-student researchers in the 1980s were the contemporary historical issues, such as the post-liberation years, the Korean War, the 1950s, and the colonial period, especially industrial growth during the 1930s and its impact.

4. For recent debates in Korea, see the special issue "Han'guk kŭndae sahoe ŭi hyŏngsŏng kwa kŭndaesŏng munje" (Formation of modern Korean society and issues of modernity), *Ch'angjak kwa pip'yŏng* 21, no. 4 (1993); and Han'guksa yŏn'guhoe 1995.

(1991), Dennis McNamara (1990), Bruce Cumings (1984), Hori Kazuo (1995), and Sŏn Chae-Won (1996) have demonstrated in the past two decades that although colonialism intervened in Korea's path to modernity, this intervention did not automatically make Koreans mere passive recipients of modernity. Their studies sought to elaborate the intrinsically dual nature of colonial industrial growth, its diverse impact on social differentiation and fragmentation, and the colonial modification of modernization in Korea. Karl Moskowitz (1980), Michael Robinson (1988), and Gi-Wook Shin (1996) also studied colonial white-collar workers, intellectual elites and the urban middle class, and peasant farmers, respectively, and demonstrated that Koreans participated directly and indirectly in the construction of a unique colonial modernity—a modernity that created capitalism, modern technology-oriented cosmopolitanism, an urban middle class, and a consumer culture but without political emancipation.

The global intellectual atmosphere also encouraged the historical rediscovery under way within the field of modern Korean studies in the West as well as in Korea. In the past two decades, under the rubrics of post-modern, post-colonial, post-structuralist, post-feminist, there has been a worldwide intellectual compulsion to go beyond the Eurocentric, male-oriented, elitist master narratives. Foucaultian discourses and Gramscian concepts of hegemony and counter-hegemony in history have made social scientists in both hemispheres aware that the nationalist logic of the master narratives dominates our narratives and constricts our habits of thought to linear, binary terms and simple black-and-white, East and West, past and present, self and other, dichotomies.

As Prasenjit Duara (1995) and other post-colonial writers like Homi Bhabha (1994), Gayatri Spivak (1993), and Partha Chatterjee (1986) argued in their studies of post-colonial existence in China and India, an exclusive focus on the political repression of a colony leads us to ignore the complexity of the colonial modernization process—its liberating forces and transformative power, as well as its repression. The current theorization of nationalism as a fluid, mutable, and constructed conceptual category that is neither predetermined nor fixed on a unitary pathway of development is an important intellectual leap beyond the horizon of conventional historiography (see Anderson 1983; Geller 1983; Harris 1990; Hobsbawm 1990; and Hobsbawm and Ranger 1983).

By the 1990s, after a decade of iconoclasm in the social sciences, history was understood not simply as part of a national homogeneous culture, tradition, and nation-state, but as a more complex and pluralistic process. The heavily politically oriented bias of traditional historiography, Duara (1995) has argued, neglected or repressed the complexities of the historical process in which economic, social, and cultural changes intertwined. At the end of the twentieth century, the concept of history is undergoing a profound redefinition because of a radical revision in the concept of human communities as the complex, multicultural, and multiethnic post-modern world increasingly matures and becomes more sophisticated. Younger scholars have begun searching for and rescuing many ignored and silenced historical subjects of the colonial past; their efforts have resulted in a new counter-narrative, a sociocultural perspective with a focus on subaltern studies of previously understudied subjects such as peasant farmers, ordinary city dwellers, workers, women (both rural and urban), the men and women mobilized during wartime, the marginal poor, and migrating diaspora groups.

These studies asked how the mutually interlocking historical forces (or hegemonies in Gramscian term), such as nationalism, modernity, and colonialism, worked in the complex human communities of colonial families, classrooms, offices, markets, worksites, and factories, as well as in colonial society as a whole, not just in terms of anti-imperialism, but in relation to a more complex process of changes in social, economic, and cultural values fostered by the emerging colonial modernity. For example, these studies argue that the issue of cultural assimilation in colonial Korea should be viewed as more than a process calculated to destroy Korean identity in favor of an imposed metropolitan identity to which there were only two possible responses: resistance or collaboration. As Michael Robinson (1988) has demonstrated in his studies of urban colonial Korea in the 1920s, Japanese colonialism and its cultural policy produced multiple possibilities for cultural adaptation; the decision to learn Japanese and participate in Japanese-owned companies or Japanese-dominated bureaucracies was part of the process of constructing a modern identity, an entirely new way of relating to one's social context. Modernity itself was not an issue of being Japanese or Korean, but, for the colonial subjects, a process of negotiating, in Bhabha's (1994: 6, 38, 58) term, a hybrid identity.

In this new focus on the socioeconomic changes resulting from the intensive wartime industrial growth in the late colonial period, many studies used more sophisticated social-scientific research methods to re-examine the previous interpretation of growth as enclave-style development and redefined it as "colonial, dependent development."[5] The major research done in the past decade by An Pyŏng-Jik, Nakamura Tetsu, Hŏ Su-Yŏl, Hori Kazuo, and Sŏn Chae-Won used econometric methods and analyses on both official and private statistics, including the 1930 and 1940 government censuses; their breakthroughs uncovered several structural changes beneath colonial industrial growth and transformed the traditional agrarian Korean society and economy into a dependent, yet developing urban society and capitalist economy. During this period, Korea experienced the penetration of capital throughout the society, including the agricultural sector, a rapid change in occupational structure (male agricultural employment dropped from 80.6 percent in 1930 to 71.0 percent in 1945), a huge migration of peasant farmers into urban areas and industrial worksites both within Korea and overseas, rapid urbanization (the urban population rose from 4 percent in 1920 to 7 percent in 1930 to 14 percent in 1945), a substantial growth in the number of male industrial workers, and an increase in the number of small and medium-scale Korean capitalists and entrepreneurs at least until 1940.[6] Although the issue of the relationship between colonialism and modernity is a chicken-and-egg question, in the end, the current discussions of the nature of colonial industrial growth and its complex impact on modernization, especially during wartime, have been necessary for Korean historiography to liberate itself from conventional twentieth-century historical narratives and interpretations.

This book is a product of the revisionary energy in colonial historiography. By analyzing the Korean workers employed in the Onoda Cement plant in Sŭnghori, South P'yŏngan province, near P'yŏngyang, from 1917 to 1942, I hope to show concretely and in detail the

5. See An Pyŏng-Jik 1986, 1988, 1990, 1993. For a more comprehensive, balanced, and up-to-date work on colonial industrial growth, see Hori 1995; see also Hori 1986, 1993a, 1993b, 1994; Kim Nak-Nyŏn 1994; Kim Kyŏng-Il 1992; and Yu 1992.

6. More recent works include Matsunaga 1991; and Sŏn 1996. Sŏn's study used the Onoda Sŭnghori, Ch'ŏnnaeri, and Komusan factories as the cases in a comparison with the Onoda main company.

growth of a modern skilled workforce, despite colonial segmentation and oppression. The original case study was done in the mid-1980s, but its analytical themes and perspectives have changed and matured over the past decade, as I absorbed new studies and interpretations that removed the dichotomizing constraints of conventional views and emphasized the dynamism and multiple possibilities afforded by competing ideas of nation, modernity, colonialism, communism, and militarism in colonial Korea.

The Sŭnghori factory was selected as the subject of this study because a nearly complete set of personnel records for the factory between 1917 and 1942 still exists in Tokyo in the main office of the Onoda Cement Corporation of Japan and became available for the research. The Onoda Cement Company was one of the largest enterprises in Japan and expanded greatly by supporting the empire building of Japan. It had ten branch factories in Japan, five in Korea, six in Manchuria, and seven in other locations throughout the Japanese empire. Its main office in Tokyo retains records of all its colonial operations.

The study is composed of four chapters. In Chapter 1, "Structural Changes in the Workforce of Colonial Korea," I examine the general working environment by looking at demographic and labor force conditions and changes in them, both the day labor and the factory labor markets, and government labor policy, which defined the triangular relationship of government, business, and labor. Because industrial growth in Korea began when it was a colony of Japan, these labor conditions reflected not only the general patterns of the initial stage of industrialization but also the colonial situation, which complicated industrialization and workers' experiences. This chapter will provide an understanding of the larger historical context in which the colonial factory workforce took shape.

In Chapter 2, "Labor-Management Relations in the Onoda Sŭnghori Factory," the focus is on the growth of Korean factory workers within the Sŭnghori factory between 1917 and 1942 and changes over time. Through primary company documents, personnel records of the branch factories in Korea, official company histories, and personal interviews, labor-management relations in the Sŭnghori factory are analyzed from eight perspectives: organizational structure, the source of the labor supply, the educational level of the workers, disciplining of the workers, hierarchy among the workers, labor turnover, wage and other compensation systems, and labor disputes.

This analysis of labor-management relations examines four larger historical themes related to the colonial modification of modern labor-management relations in the factory. First, the process of creating a labor force is examined: Who were the people recruited, trained, and retained as the labor force? How did Japanese managers deal with the low skill levels of Korean laborers and succeed in training and keeping a stable workforce in the plant? What was the Korean workers' attitude toward working in a large Japanese factory? To what extent did the colonial period represent a break with Korea's past and result in the establishment of new patterns of labor relations and state-society interaction?

Second, the workings of several mutually interlocking and reinforcing historical forces in the colonial factory are addressed: In what way and to what extent did colonialism, nationalism, communism, and modernity intertwine and interact with one another in the formation and growth of the factory labor force and labor relations in the Sŭnghori plant? How did specific political issues, such as oppression, discrimination, alienation, and collaboration, emerge? How did Korean workers respond to them? How were the individual identities of the workers formed and influenced by the larger historical forces of the colonial period?

Third, the responses of laborers are examined: To what extent and in what ways did working in the factory change the lives of farm youth? How different was life in the factory from the traditional Chosŏn dynasty rural working environment? Were there any labor organizations and labor disputes, and what was the impact of the Communist movement in the plant? What kind of class identity (here "class" is used in the sense of identity analogous to race, gender, or nation rather than in the classical Marxist sense) emerged as a response to tensions and contradictions caused by working in the Sŭnghori plant and how was this connected to national identity? Did colonialism and modernity merge to create a hybrid identity? Did the Sŭnghori workers share a working-class culture?

Changes in the nature and role of the labor force in the colonial economy after the war broke out in 1937 are dealt with in Chapter 3, "The War and Korean Workers: Disintegration of the Colonial System," because of the war's significant impact on industry, the labor force, and state-labor relations. Militarism in the late 1930s significantly influenced and changed the nature of colonial modernity, once more engendering further complications and change in the colonial society. This chapter examines in what way and to what extent the rapid industrialization and the mobilization for war after 1937 influenced the labor force and labor-management relations in colonial Korea in general and in the Onoda Sŭnghori factory in particular.

Chapter 4, "Workers in Liberated Korea: The Onoda Samch'ŏk Factory," addresses some larger historical questions relating to the impact of the colonial legacy on twentieth-century Korean labor by looking at changes in the labor force and labor relations in the southern half of liberated Korea after 1945 (a detailed examination of North Korean workers, including the Sŭnghori workers, is impossible because of the division of the country). Despite its limited nature, this chapter examines several historical themes concerning workers in the Onoda Samch'ŏk Factory, the only cement plant in the southern half of liberated Korea and a plant that later became a major cement manufacturer in South Korea: What was the legacy of the "colonial labor experience" in the violent political upheavals and divisions among the workers in the post-1945 period and South Korea after the 1960s? What was the relationship among the state, business, police, and workers in this period? To what extent did patterns of labor mobilization and control in South Korea after the 1960s differ from those of the colonial period? What was distinctive about South Korea's labor force as it developed in this period, compared with that of Japan or the West during their period of modern labor formation? What did the colonial birth of the workforce mean for the history of Korean labor in the twentieth century?

The answers to these questions not only correct the stereotypical image of cheap, surplus, unskilled colonial labor, but also elaborate on the complex nature of colonial industrial growth, its diverse impact on social differentiation, and the colonial complication of modernization in which the Korean workers were active participants, shaping and developing themselves as a part of a modern Korean people, despite the fragmented and alienating circumstances of colonial modernity. To be sure, this study has its own limits as a case study based on a Japanese-owned cement factory, which was a "strategic" industry, especially during the war years. The analysis in the following chapters pays attention to what is distinctive to this particular case compared to the general colonial labor situation as well as to how the findings of the study can be generalized. The strength of any case study lies, however, in its detailed descriptions and concrete analysis, which show the diversity, subtlety, and complexities of human communities much better than general, theoretical studies can. This analysis seeks to paint a more accurate and realistic portrait of the colonial generation of workers in Korea by showing the density, richness, and complexities of human communities and to add depth to our understanding and theorization of Korea's paths to modernity.

ONE

Structural Changes in the Workforce of Colonial Korea

In order to understand workers at the Onoda Sŭnghori plant, it is essential to examine the nature and structure of the labor force in the larger colonial context. Thanks to several important studies since the late 1980s, the previously accepted picture of static colonial demography has gradually been corrected, and the structural changes in colonial demography and labor force composition in the post-1930 period have been uncovered. The earlier studies, done in the 1960s and 1970s (see, e.g., Kim Ch'ŏl 1965), had stressed three points as characteristic of colonial demography: (1) the static nature of rural-urban migration within Korea, (2) a low rate of domestic migration, and (3) a high rate of overseas migration of the rural population. These interpretations reflected contemporary concerns as South Korea struggled with the problems of a huge surplus population and a high unemployment rate. Researchers generally viewed colonialism itself as the origin of these demographic problems. The first and second points were questioned and more or less corrected by studies in the 1990s (see, e.g., Hori 1995: 116–17; and Sŏn 1996: 41–57). The new interpretations highlighted the changes in demographic structure and the labor force in the fifteen years after 1930 and showed that the three characteristics previously thought to apply to the entire colonial period in reality fit only the pre-1930 period. By comparing the two censuses of 1930 and 1940 in a more comprehensive manner and by using other statistical materials, the new studies provided a fuller and more accurate picture of the changes in the Korean labor force before and after 1930 (Hori 1995: 116–27; and Sŏn 1996: 39–57).

The outstanding econometric studies by Hori Kazuo (1995) and Sŏn Chae-Won (1996) clarify developments in the Korean population and the occupational/regional structures of the labor force in the post-1930 period. They make several points important for understanding the emerging working class. (1) Under the growing demands for labor, the agricultural-sector population rapidly found nonagricultural employment both in Korea and overseas (mainly Manchuria and Japan). (2) A large number of farmers in the southern provinces migrated to the northern provinces and became employed in nonagricultural jobs, especially in the factory, mining, and construction sectors. (3) Rural out-migration to these provinces was concentrated in certain industrial centers, particularly Kyŏngsŏng (Seoul), P'yŏngyang, Pusan, Hŭngnam, Ch'ŏngjin, and Inch'ŏn. This phenomenon accelerated urbanization in the colony. (4) The factory labor market expanded and developed, absorbing day laborers into its workforce (Hori 1995: 98–128; Sŏn 1996: 57–84). The following sections examine these changes in detail as the background for the formation of factory labor force, focusing on the rural exodus and the change in occupational structure, migration northward and urbanization, the out-migration of laborers overseas, and the expansion of the labor market in general and the factory labor market in particular. At the end of the chapter, I examine the development of the colonial government's labor policy in order to study the effects on labor relations of the government's intervention and its ability to influence the labor market.

Rural Exodus:
The Shift to the Nonagricultural Sector

The government census of 1930 shows that colonial Korea was still an agricultural society: as of 1928, 9.8 million or 80.6 percent of the employed population worked in agriculture and only 0.6 million or 2.1 percent were engaged in mining and factory work. Hori Kazuo's (1995: 93–98) detailed study of colonial census statistics indicates, however, that this rural population was rapidly changing and disintegrating in the 1920s. The same census reveals that there were 1.75 million wage-earning workers in colonial Korea, divided between over a half-million agricultural workers and 1.16 million nonagricultural, mostly unskilled free laborers.

In other words, a half million people employed in agriculture, or almost 7 percent of the total population, were landless laborers.

These bankrupt self-cultivators or tenant farmers are called *mŏsŭm* in Korean, and had existed from the seventeenth century. Their numbers increased steadily, however, in the late nineteenth century and further accelerated after the annexation of Korea in 1910, particularly in the southern rice-paddy areas, because the colonial government maintained the premodern land tenure system in rural areas, even after its land survey of 1911–18, and despite the penetration of the capitalist market economy into the agricultural sector following the opening of the country in 1876. Between 1910 and the late 1920s, the number of mixed self-cultivator/tenant households decreased by 300,000, and the number of households in the tenant farmer category increased by 550,000. According to Hori, agricultural wage-earners emerged because of the land survey, the penetration of the rural sector by the market economy, and the impoverishment and dissolution of the traditional rural system.

Yi T'ae-Jin (1989) and Cho Kyŏng-Man (1987) have shown that, under these circumstances, traditional community customs like *dure* or *p'um-assi* collective work sharing were disappearing quickly from rural Korea and being replaced by a transitional labor management/control system for these laborers. For example, *kochiche*, an agricultural contract-labor system, was extensively practiced in the Chŏlla and Ch'ungch'ŏng regions, where rice cultivation was widely undertaken by contractors who hired and managed agricultural laborers within a very personalized labor control system (Hisama 1932; Hori 1995: 96). In addition to these agricultural wage-earning laborers, there were another 500,000 or so half-rural / half-urban free laborers, who floated between the urban and rural labor markets desperately seeking any income.[1] In other words, the traditional rural system and the rural population were fast disintegrating by the late 1920s, contrary to the picture of a dominantly agricultural society in the government census statistics.

The existence of this surplus labor force of almost a million workers in rural areas, especially in the southern six provinces, was only a part of the larger, serious rural crisis in colonial society by the end of the 1920s. Economic historians like Nakamura Tetsu, Miyajima Hiroshi, and Chang Shi-Wong explain this rural crisis as the result of a combination of interrelated factors: the deep penetration of the rural sector by the commercial market economy because of the Rice

---

1. Hori (1995: 95) counts 775,000 tenant farming households whose members supplemented their income with wage-earning jobs.

Production Promotion Plan and the Water Utilization Union system; the disappearance of the traditional work-sharing labor practices and the compartmentalization of rural households; the trend toward smaller-scale, labor-intensive rice cultivation using wage laborers; the rapid dissolution of the rural sector in the pre-1930 period due to the rapid impoverishment and bankruptcy of both self-cultivators and tenant farmers; and the accumulation of these landless bankrupt farmers in rural areas because of the lack of a pulling factor in the industrial urban sector (see Nakamura et al. 1988: chap. 1; Hori 1995: 91–97).

As for the nonagricultural wage-earners in the late 1920s, the government's 1930 national census and the government-run Railway Bureau's 1928 survey of urban wage-earners provide revealing and useful information. Most of the 1.16 million urban workers reported in the 1930 census were "miscellaneous workers" — by and large free day laborers, domestic household workers, and factory and mine workers.[2] Free day laborers, at 40.4 percent (468,000) of the total number of urban workers, were the largest group. This group consisted of casual laborers, transport workers, A-frame porters, and longshoremen (baggage men), all of whom can be categorized as workers in the informal urban labor market who floated widely searching for employment. Full-time and half-rural/half-industrial workers were lumped together under this rubric, and differences in working conditions and wages were ignored. They received very low wages and were often unemployed for long periods. Domestic workers, at 27.6 percent (319,000) of urban workers, formed the second largest group.[3] The third group, factory and mine workers, was extremely small. The two fields together accounted for only 5.4 percent (40,000 factory workers, 23,000 mine workers) of all nonagricultural workers. Factory workers were engaged mainly in food-processing industries, like rice mills and breweries, and in textile mills; their employment reflects the elementary level of industry at the time. This larger picture highlights the higher status of workers at the Sŭnghori plant, who were hired as early as 1920, in the national labor hierarchy.

2. The 1930 census reported 2.04 million workers engaged in nonagricultural-sector employment; half of these workers were thus employed in the urban sector.

3. They were categorized as *sendō* (Korean boy) and *senjō* (Korean girl) in the census.

Overall, Korean wage-earners remained a huge, frequently un-employed, floating population of job seekers, concentrated in the southern provinces. Until the early 1930s, urban industry provided few jobs for them. Inevitably, these urban and rural marginal poor or floating informal-sector workers suffered from a vicious circle of ex-tremely low wages, job insecurity, and long periods of unemploy-ment. These conditions were probably behind the image of an abun-dant, cheap, surplus pool of colonial labor.

The frequent reports in the press and in Communist publications from the mid-1920s on about the starvation-level living conditions among bankrupt peasant households and the urban poor, often de-scribed as "spring starvation," or "the barley hills," especially in the rice-paddy area of Kyŏngsang and Chŏlla provinces, engendered se-rious social concerns in the society at large and among colonial ad-ministrators, who were haunted by fears of communism. During the 1920s, the Government General of Korea on the one hand displayed indifference toward the huge pool of surplus labor and on the other hand pursued an aggressive and authoritarian labor policy focused on uprooting radical Communist elements and protecting the labor supply for large Japanese factories. This selective, dual policy dem-onstrates the self-serving economic policy of the colonial authorities even under the seemingly more moderate "Cultural Policy" of the 1920s. Rural bankruptcies and unemployment rates reached new peaks in the years after 1929, when the Great Depression hit the Japanese and Korean rural sectors hard, forcing colonial policymak-ers to treat the rural crisis and the labor surplus problem as serious concerns (see G.-W. Shin 1996: chap. 4).

The labor surplus soon ceased to be a problem, however. Indus-trial growth in the 1930s, especially after 1937, created a great demand for labor. With this new pulling force from the industrial sector, the scale of out-migration from the rural sector escalated re-markably, averaging 60,000 men per year during 1930–35, and in-creasing to 220,000 men per year during 1935–45. This large-scale and long-distance migration to both urban colonial Korea and other parts of the Japanese empire led to a drop in the percentage em-ployed in the rural sector from 80.6 percent in 1930 to 74.8 percent in 1940 to 71 percent in 1945.[4]

---

4. Hori (1995: 110–14) estimates that if the overseas Koreans are in-cluded, the ratio was 69.5 percent in 1945.

Within Korea, formal-sector jobs in industry and mining increased from 2.1 percent of the entire employed population in 1931 to 7.2 percent in 1942. For the first time in the colonial period, rural out-migration was absorbed into factory, mining, and construction jobs concentrated in new industrial centers such as Kyŏngsŏng, P'yŏngyang, Pusan, Inch'ŏn, Chinnamp'o, Hŭngnam, Najin, and Ch'ŏngjin. This concentrated movement to industrial centers also led to rapid urbanization, as the urban population rose from 3.4 percent of the total population in 1920 to 7.0 percent in 1935 to 13.2 percent by 1944. This percentage of the population in urban areas may not seem so great when compared to Japan's rate of 41.9 percent in 1944 and is barely comparable to Japan's 1908 level (18 percent) at the initial phase in Japanese urbanization. Nevertheless, it was a considerable growth in its own terms and remarkably rapid compared to urbanization in Korea in the pre-1930 period (Hori 1995: 110–12). The demand for labor came from both within and without Korea. Roughly half of this rural exodus was directed toward domestic urban industrial centers; the other half went to meet rapidly increasing demands from Japan and Manchuria (Hori 1995: 112–14).

South to North Regional Migration and Urbanization

In addition to its rapidity, another characteristic of the rural out-migration was that it moved from the poor southern provinces to the urban and industrial centers of the northern provinces, as well as Kyŏnggi province in the center of the peninsula. According to Hori's analysis of the 1930 and 1940 census statistics, most of the provinces, with the exception of Hwanghae and South Chŏlla, where the rural population increased 10 percent, lost more than 10 percent of their agricultural-sector employment; Kyŏnggi and four northern provinces lost more than 20 percent. Kyŏnggi and North and South Hamkyŏng provinces recorded the highest increase in nonagricultural-sector employment, with more than 100,000 workers in all three cases. By 1940, the nationwide average for nonagricultural-sector employment was 25.2 percent; Kyŏnggi province, however, recorded 47.6 percent, and North Hamkyŏng province 60.6 percent, indicating the concentration of migrating workers from the southern agricultural sector in these regions, in which industrial complexes were developing rapidly around Kyŏngsŏng-Inch'ŏn, Ch'ŏngjin-Najin, P'yŏngyang-Chinnamp'o, Hŭngnam-Hamhŭng, and Pusan.

This change also shows that interprovincial long-distance migration increased in this decade, in contrast to the intraprovincial migratory pattern of the 1920s (Han 1963: 124).

Another characteristic of the northward urbanization movement was the exceptional growth of the colonial capital, Kyŏngsŏng. The population of Kyŏngsŏng increased more than threefold from 343,000 in 1925 to 1,114,000 in 1940. There were two reasons for this expansion: a continuous inflow of new migrants to both Kyŏngsŏng and its environs and the consequent expansion of the administrative boundaries of the city in April 1936 (it is difficult to sort out how much of the population increase resulted from the administrative expansion; the territory of Kyŏngsong increased by a factor of 3.8 and the population by a factor of 1.7 as a result of the redrawing of the boundary lines [Hashiya 1990: 135]). Kyŏngsŏng's growth as a large industrial urban center was by far the most phenomenal and impressive of any city in Korea. It is also a fascinating example of a growing, modern urban space, and colonial life in the 1930s, with an infrastructure of a budding urban population, popular culture, and the penetration of modern technology and values through modern education (Hori 1995: 154–86).

As at the national level, industrial-sector jobs in Kyŏngsŏng also increased rapidly. Although this Chosŏn dynasty capital had a unique industrial structure of its own even during the pre-1930 period, with rice- and other food-processing operations, textile and household goods manufacturing, and printing as the main industries, Kyŏngsŏng's industrial structure developed further and rapidly in the post-1930 period, in a unique pattern centered around the cotton textile, printing, and machine and machine tools industries, as well as a variety of consumer goods manufactures. The rapid development of the machine industry was a response to the need to manufacture, repair, and maintain machines for the textile and consumer goods industries. By 1940, 70 percent of Korea's printing plants and 76.4 percent of the machine and machine tools factories were concentrated in Kyŏngsŏng. This industrial development was quite different from that in other industrial complexes in the north, such as Hŭngnam, Ch'ŏngjin, and Najin, whose rapid industrial growth depended heavily on military-related heavy chemical, metallurgical, and machinery industries (Hori 1995: 169–78).

Most important, this trend clearly suggests the expansion in consumer demand behind urban industrial growth in Kyŏngsŏng, which cannot be explained solely by the theory that industrial growth in this period was driven by the demands of the military. The case of Kyŏngsŏng certainly implies an increasing gap between the booming capital and the depressed rural areas. On the other hand, however, it also reveals that the enclave-theory approach, which stresses the self-serving nature of the wartime industrialization and absence of linkage effects of this industrial growth to Korean society and economy in the war years, has largely ignored or failed to uncover the socioeconomic changes occurring beneath the wartime industrial growth.[5]

Although the task is formidable due to the scarcity of personal or qualitative materials, more research on urbanization in the 1930s is needed. Urban groups—such as informal-sector workers, including household industry workers, both male and female, squatters, and miscellaneous workers—and their concrete responses to colonial modernity in the expanding urban space should be studied to shed light on the complexities of colonial working-class communities, their life-styles, and their subcultures.

Overseas Migration to Manchurian and Japanese Labor Markets

Another change in the labor force in colonial Korea in the 1930s was the large-scale out-migration of Korean workers to Manchuria and Japan. Overseas migration was common throughout the colonial period. In the pre-1930 period, Manchuria was the favored destination of Korean immigrants; in the post-1930 period, migration extended to all of the Japanese empire. The pattern accelerated from 1932, and migration exploded during 1938–40, but cooled abruptly after 1940. Roughly 1.3 million workers, 700,000 to Japan and 600,000 to Manchuria, voluntarily out-migrated from 1930 to 1940 in a search for industrial employment and higher wages than could be found in the Korean labor market. In addition, another one million Koreans were compulsorily mobilized for labor (0.72 million men for industrial la-

5. Among the negative legacies of this dual industrial development for contemporary Korean capitalism, Hori (1995: 186) singles out the Korean economy's abnormally high degree of reliance on the import-export trade, the strong reliance on Japanese production technology, the inferior position of small- and medium-size enterprises, and the almost total absence of industries in rural areas.

bor and 0.24 million men and women as civilian personnel for the military) after 1939 (Hori 1995: 114–16).

Korean migration to Manchuria, mostly of rural people from the northern provinces who crossed the Yalu and Tumen rivers, increased rapidly until the late 1910s but slowed by the late 1920s, as the Chinese warlord government and Manchurian Chinese came to view these Korean migrants as civilian front units carrying out the economic penetration policy of the Japanese Kwantung Army. There were many conflicts between Chinese and Korean settlers by the late 1920s, over Korean rights for education, residence, tenant farming, and community organization, in various places (Matsumura 1970).

Migration picked up after the Manchurian Incident in September 1931 and the establishment of the Japanese puppet state of Manchukuo by the Kwantung Army in 1932. The number of Korean residents in Manchuria increased from 600,000 in 1930 to 1.3 million in 1940. In contrast to the earlier immigrants from the Hamkyŏng and P'yŏngan regions, migrants during this period tended to come from southern rural areas and spread throughout Manchuria over the railways. Hori (1995: 113–15) correctly argues that this change reflects the emerging industrial relationship between Korea and Manchuria and their overlapping labor market as the two regions became important heavy-industrial supply bases for Japan's military expansion on the continent.

The migration of Koreans to Japan began during World War I, when Koreans from the southern provinces started to cross over to Japan. The colonial authorities attempted to restrict this Korean migration until 1939, because of concern over unemployment and social disorder in Japan.[6] In reality, however, migration increased con-

6. The major concern of the Government General was the tremendous expansion of emigration of bankrupt peasants to Japan beginning in the late 1910s. The massive influx of Korean laborers became a social issue in Japan as the unemployment rate increased during the economic recession of the early 1920s. In 1922, the Osaka Social Bureau surveyed Korean workers in the Osaka area, the largest Korean community in Japan, and concluded that the presence of large numbers of Korean workers was an important cause of Japanese unemployment. These problems undoubtedly fed racial hostility, which was revealed by the massacre of 6,000 Koreans following the Great Kantō Earthquake in September 1923. After October 1925, in response to the Peace Preservation Law passed by the Japanese Diet earlier that year, the Government General started to control Korean travelers. The Police Bureau

tinuously, except for a temporary slowdown after the 1923 Tokyo earthquake, and the number of Koreans in Japan grew from 40,000 in 1920 to 410,000 in 1930.

Better wages and more employment opportunities in the booming Japanese wartime industrial economy attracted a great number of Korean workers. Migration became massive in the 1930s, as 800,000 Koreans crossed over the Korea Strait between 1930 and 1940. By 1940, 1.24 million Koreans resided in Japan. More than three-quarters of these migrants were engaged in lower-end jobs in day labor, construction, unskilled factory work, and mining. Even these jobs, however, paid more than work in Korea. As for origins of the Korean migrants, 87 percent of them were from Kyŏngsang and Chŏlla provinces, and 7 percent from the Ch'ungch'ŏng region. Hori (1995: 116-17) argues that at this point even educated rural youth were drawn into the Japanese labor market.

This explosive overseas migration of Korean workers was a result of the yen-bloc labor market formed in the Japanese wartime empire. The economic autarky of the yen bloc created a new demand for labor by integrating all the peripheral colonial labor markets. Unlike the colonies of Great Britain or other European countries, as Lewis Gann (1984: 502–4) noted, Japan's military security policy resulted in endless military and colonization campaigns in East Asia, beginning with Taiwan (1895) and continuing with Korea (1910), Manchuria (1931), and finally deep into China (1937) until it overstretched itself in the self-destructive Greater East Asia Co-Prosperity Sphere (1941). Japan was not unmindful of the economic potential of these regions, but its primary reason for acquiring them was assumed strategic necessity.

For colonial workers, this continuous expansion and integration of labor markets meant not only increased opportunities for employment but also constant overcompetition in the multiply segmented, borderless labor market in the Japanese empire, as Sŏn Chae-Won (1996: 37) argues. In this imperial labor market, Japanese workers occupied the core, not only in the physical sense by occupying the center of the empire but also in a hierarchical sense by

---

of South Kyŏngsang province ordered the Pusan police to reduce the number of Korean passengers to Japan by checking especially for alcoholics, drug addicts, and pennyless floaters. This policy in turn led to the policy of transferring the surplus population from the south to the north.

taking most of the urban, modern-sector jobs throughout the empire. Workers from the colonies participated as the peripheral, middle, and lower-end workforce. This overlapping of domestic labor markets in Japan with those overseas in Manchuria and Korea complicated demographic movements and labor market developments in the Japanese empire.

The imperial labor market exhibited a peculiar duality. The push factors for local colonial labor were not only rural poverty and surplus labor but in-migrating Japanese workers who forced Korean or Manchurian job seekers out to the lower, peripheral layers of the labor market (the number of Japanese residents in Korea increased from 527,000 in 1930 to 713,000 in 1940 to 750,000 in 1945; Ch'oe Chin-Ho 1981). In the same manner, the pull factor for colonial labor was the number of low-level industrial jobs in the domestic as well as the overseas labor market. This phenomenon was a reflection of the military characteristics of Japanese colonialism.

The Labor Market Structure of Colonial Korea

Day Labor

The labor market structure of colonial Korea exhibits the general patterns of the early stage of industrialization, with some colonial characteristics and complications. Like all other late-developing traditional economies, for example, Japan in the 1890s or the first decade of the twentieth century, a large intermediate layer in the form of an informal-sector labor market emerged between the traditional rural-sector and the capitalistic modern-sector labor markets in Korea (Sŏn 1996: 29).[7] The transition from farmers, to nonagricultural, industrial workers in the labor market was hardly a smooth, straight movement from rural to industrial worksites. The *Chōsen no kosaku kanshū* (Customs in tenant farming in Korea), published by the colonial government in 1929 (Yoshio 1929b), allows us to glimpse how the rural population entered the labor market in the 1920s. The survey examined the destination of 1,600 rural out-migrants as of 1925. The survey results—44 percent of these migrants found miscellaneous day labor jobs, 15 percent found commercial jobs, 16 percent moved to Japan, and 10 percent moved to factory or other jobs in

---

7. Sŏn follows Sumiya Mikio's (1964) discussion of Japanese day laborers in the early twentieth century.

Korea—show the existence of a huge day labor market in the colonial Korea at the time (Yoshio 1929b: 40–41).

The Chōsen Railway Bureau (Chōsen tetsudō kyoku) surveyed day laborers at the national level as of July 1928 and published the results in *Chōsen ni okeru rōdōsha sū oyobi bumpū jōtai* (Numbers and distribution of laborers in Korea). Out of a total of 2.19 million day laborers surveyed, 43.7 percent could also be categorized as half-rural / half-industrial laborers (see Sŏn 1996: 75–77).[8] The survey confirms the intraprovincial, short-distance nature of rural-urban migration of workers until the late 1920s. In the majority of the provinces, day laborers came from nearby rural areas, which suggests that many of these day laborers were members of a half-rural / half-urban floating labor force (see Table 1.1). Only South P'yŏngan, South Hamkyŏng, and Kyŏnggi provinces had sizable numbers of day laborers who came from other provinces (Sŏn 1996: 78). This also suggests that the northern provinces had more full-time industrial day laborers, whereas the southern provinces below Hwanghae and Kangwon provinces had more half-rural / half-industrial laborers. Kyŏnggi was an exception among the southern provinces, probably because of the presence of the capital, Kyŏngsŏng (Sŏn 1996: 77).

The colonial characteristics of the labor market were most apparent in its compartmentalized composition. It was a multilayered, segmented labor market in which the subgroups differed by skill level, educational background, sex, and, most of all, nationality. Above the informal-sector day labor market, which consisted mostly of Koreans, Japanese dominated modern formal-sector employment in the bureaucracy, the professions, commerce, transportation, factories, and mines. Koreans dominated the agriculture, forestry, and fishery sectors. The Japanese developed a separate labor market for themselves, with its own wage scales and recruitment, promotion, and retirement systems.

8. The survey covered Japanese, Korean, and Chinese day laborers in Korea (around 190,000 workers working in mining or on government worksites were not included), surveying their work, working conditions, and hometown. See Chōsen sōtokufu, Tetsudō kyōkai 1929. Other statistical sources for factory and mining workers are Chōsen sōtokufū, Shakaika 1933 (survey date June 1931); Chōsen shōkō kaigisho 1936; and Chōsen sōtokufu, Rōmu kyōkai 1943 (survey date 1942).

Table 1.1
Regional Distribution of
Day Laborers, July 1928
(*as percentage of total number of*
nonagricultural workers in province)

Province	Full-time In-prov. (a)	Out-prov. (b)	a+b	Half-rural/half-urban	Unem-ployed drifters	Total (000s)
N Hamkyŏng	49.0%	27.5%	76.5%	21.8%	1.7%	61
S P'yŏngan	52.5	20.9	73.4	22.9	3.8	98
S Hamkyŏng	50.9	18.4	69.3	27.4	3.3	125
Kyŏnggi	51.5	15.1	66.6	26.6	6.8	162
N P'yŏngan	47.6	12.7	60.3	37.4	2.3	93
Kangwon	44.1	15.2	59.4	37.2	3.5	90
N Ch'ungch'ŏng	47.2	5.2	52.4	43.1	4.5	90
N Chŏlla	44.5	5.6	50.1	46.9	3.0	291
S Kyŏngsang	44.6	5.0	49.6	45.1	5.3	367
Hwanghae	36.3	11.3	47.6	46.1	6.3	110
S Chŏlla	38.8	2.6	41.5	54.6	3.9	341
N Kyŏngsang	34.6	5.5	40.1	53.6	6.3	255
S Ch'ungch'ŏng	34.4	4.8	39.2	57.6	3.3	107
NATIONAL TOTAL	43.2	8.7	51.8	43.7	4.4	2,191

NOTES: Due to rounding, figures may not total to sums shown. "In-province" refers to workers working within their province of origin; "out-province" to workers from other provinces working in the province indicated.
SOURCE: Sŏn Chae-Won 1996: 77.

The female labor market developed its own rules for recruit-ment, wages, and working conditions. Although it was also divided by nationality, the age factor was more important than it was in the male labor market. Employment among Korean female workers was concentrated in the 15–24 age group, because of patriarchal strictures against married women working outside the household and the custom of early marriage (63.6 percent of Korean female workers in the 15–19 age group and 96.9 percent of the 20–24 age group were married, according to a 1932 report; the comparable numbers for Japanese women workers were 9.0 percent and 61.9 percent, respec-tively). As a result, rice mills, textile factories, match makers, knit-ware concerns, and rubber shoe factories had to recruit farm girls continuously, and managers had to depend upon go-between labor recruiters for their supply of low-paid farm girls (Lee 1980: 54–56).[9]

The colonial labor market was also segmented by a kind of contract system (group vs. individual), by length of the contract (day labor, temporary, or full-time employment), by work site (rural area, transportation, construction, mining, and factory), and by economic sectors (formal vs. informal). Under these circumstances, as Son Chae-Won (1996: 37–38) pointed out, male Korean youths entering the job market experienced intense competition in each compartmentalized subgroup of the labor market with other Korean male workers, at a fiercer level than in a normal labor market situation.

This diversified and segmented labor market engendered various hybrid, transitional labor relations that combined traditional labor control methods with industrial management methods in the colonial worksites. Like the *oyabun/kobun* (*oyagata*) system of labor relations in Meiji Japan, or coolie leader / coolie system in the Manchurian labor market, the Korean day labor market also developed labor contractor groups. A *sipchang* (head of 10 people) was a manager-contractor between employer and the workers who controlled 10–50 day laborers in places like dockyards or construction worksites. Mine owners also used a contracting system by hiring a *tŏkdae*, a system that had existed since the late Chosŏn period (Nam 1991).

A similar labor-management system was also found in the agricultural labor market. The *kochi* contracting system emerged as a method to control the *mŏsŭm*, the rural-sector wage-earning day laborers. As noted above, the increasing practice of the *kochi* system implies the gradual disintegration of traditional communal work customs and their replacement by subcontracting systems in the rural area (see Yun 1990; and Kang Man-Kil 1987).

The labor surplus that had existed in the colonial labor market before 1930 disappeared abruptly by the mid-1930s. The acute labor shortage, especially of skilled workers, accelerated with the drafting of skilled Japanese workers from colonial factories after 1937. The driving force behind this change was a sudden upsurge in large-scale Japanese industrial ventures into colonial Korea and changes in the industrial structure in the post-1930 period. The labor market expanded and Korean workers moved up within the labor market hierarchy. Many day laborers in the informal sector began to move

9. For recent studies on colonial female labor, see Yi Jeong-Ok 1990; and Kang Ih-Su 1991.

into formal-sector jobs in industry from the mid-1930s on. Within the formal-sector labor market, the number of Korean female workers in light industry increased steadily, and both Korean and Japanese male workers became increasingly drawn into the large-scale factories in the heavy chemical, metallurgical, machine and machine tools, and ceramics industries, especially after 1937.

Factory Labor Market

The *Kōba oyobi kōzan ni okeru rōdō jōkyō chōsa* (Chōsen sōtokufu, Shakaika 1933) provides a picture of the factory labor market as of June 1931, on the eve of the 1930s industrial growth. There were three main industries in Korea at the time of the survey: textiles, food processing, and chemicals. Kyŏnggi province had the largest market for factory labor, and the Kyŏngsŏng-Yŏngdŭngp'o industrial complex played a central role in this. As Table 1.2 shows, the provinces of Kyŏnggi, South Kyŏngsang, South P'yŏngan (where the Onoda Cement Company was located, near the provincial capital of P'yŏngyang), and South Hamkyŏng had many more workers than the southern provinces. This is directly related to the existence of large industrial centers in these provinces, like Kyŏngsŏng, Pusan, Hŭngnam, and P'yŏngyang (Sŏn 1996: 83).

The distribution of industries varied by province. Kyŏnggi province had the most diverse and balanced distribution of the three major industries. Nevertheless, the printing and machine and machine tools industries were concentrated there, probably because of its urban, metropolitan consumer culture and life-styles. Second, the most industrialized province, South Kyŏngsang, had many textile and food-processing factories. The distribution in South P'yŏngan was balanced, in the order food processing, chemicals, and textiles. The chemical industry was dominant in South Hamkyŏng province, because of the existence of the huge Chōsen Nitrogen Fertilizer Company, which was established at Hŭngnam in 1929. The metallurgical industry was concentrated in Hwanghae province, due to the Mitsubishi Steel Mills in Kyŏmip'o, and the ceramics industry was strongly represented in Kyŏnggi, South P'yŏngan, and South Hamkyŏng provinces, a direct reflection of the Onoda Cement branch factories at Sŭnghori and Ch'ŏnnaeri, in the last two provinces (Sŏn 1996: 82).

The distribution of labor was also segmented by nationality.

Table 1.2
Distribution of Factories and Workers
by Province and Number of Employees, June 1931
(*as percentage of total numbers of
factories and workers in province*)

| Province | Number of employees | | | | | | |
	10–29	30–49	100–50–99	200–199	500–299	999	1,000+
Kyŏnggi							
factories (361)	64.8%	15.0%	11.1%	6.6%	1.7%	0.3%	0.6%
workers (17,808)	21.7	11.4	15.2	22.5	11.9	3.0	14.1
N Ch'ungch'ŏng							
factories (15)	40.0	53.3	–	–	6.7	–	–
workers (727)	17.9	37.6	–	–	44.6	–	–
S Ch'ungch'ŏng							
factories (35)	57.1	17.1	8.6	11.4	2.9	2.9	–
workers (2,457)	14.0	8.5	8.3	24.7	14.5	29.9	–
N Chŏlla							
factories (88)	59.1	18.2	15.9	3.4	3.4	–	–
workers (3,869)	23.6	14.1	25.5	8.7	28.1	–	–
N Kyŏngsang							
factories (93)	72.0	14.0	8.6	1.1	–	4.3	–
workers (5,369)	19.0	8.9	10.2	2.0	–	59.9	–
S Chŏlla							
factories (157)	72.6	17.2	5.7	2.5	1.3	0.6	–
workers (5,812)	33.8	16.9	11.5	12.3	13.3	12.2	–
S Kyŏngsang							
factories (140)	66.4	14.3	12.9	3.6	1.4	0.7	0.7
workers (7,362)	20.0	10.1	15.3	10.9	9.5	8.1	26.0
Hwanghae							
factories (33)	51.5	12.1	24.2	6.1	3.0	–	3.0
workers (13,061)	9.3	4.7	17.2	10.9	15.8	–	42.1
S P'yŏngan							
factories (115)	63.5	12.2	7.8	11.3	3.5	1.7	–
workers	15.4	6.7	10.1	28.7	19.0	20.1	–
N P'yŏngan							
factories (70)	55.7	18.6	18.6	2.9	1.4	2.9	–
workers (3,738)	19.6	12.9	23.1	6.1	10.8	27.5	–
Kangwon							
factories (21)	81.0	9.5	9.5	–	–	–	–
workers (474)	55.3	16.5	28.3	–	–	–	–

Table 1.2, continued

Province	10–29	30–49	100– 50–99	200– 199	500– 299	999	1,000+
			Number of employees				
S Hamkyŏng							
factories (57)	66.7	14.0	8.8	5.3	1.8	1.8	1.8
workers (6,892)	8.9	4.1	5.2	6.0	6.1	8.0	61.6
N Hamkyŏng							
factories (14)	71.4	14.3	14.3	–	–	–	–
workers (373)	49.1	19.3	31.6	–	–	–	–
TOTAL							
FACTORIES (1,199)	65.1	15.6	10.9	5.1	1.80	1.1	0.4
WORKERS (65,374)	19.8	10.4	13.8	14.8	12.41	3.6	15.2

NOTES: Due to rounding, figures may not total to sums shown. Figures in parentheses following "factories" and "workers" indicate total numbers in province.
SOURCE: Chōsen sōtokufu, Shakaika 1933: 18–19; cited in Sŏn Chae-Won 1996: 83.

Japanese workers were concentrated in the chemical industry in South Hamkyŏng and Kyŏnggi provinces. Large numbers of Koreans, both male and female, were found in the textile and food-processing industries in Kyŏnggi, South Kyŏngsang, South P'yŏng-an, South Chŏlla, and North Kyŏngsang provinces. Chinese workers were concentrated in the lumber industry, carpentry, and wood-products manufacturing in North P'yŏngan province (Sŏn 1996: 82). In terms of distribution by factory size, Kyŏnggi, South P'yŏngan, and North P'yŏngan provinces showed a balanced distribution of small (10–29 employees), medium (30–99), and large-size (over 100) factories, whereas South Kyŏngsang, Hwanghae, and South Hamkyŏng provinces had more large factories with over 1,000 employees because of Japanese investment in this area.[10]

10. The Chōsen Textile Company in Pusan, South Kyŏngsang, had 1,913 employees; the Mitsubishi Iron Mill in Kyŏm'ip'o, Hwanghae, had 1,288; and the Chōsen Nitrogen Fertilizer Company in Hŭngnam, South Hamkyŏng, had 4,246 in 1931 and 20,000 by 1940. Kyŏnggi province had the three largest government-owned factories: Yongsan Machinery Plant (1,318 employees), a division of the Railway Bureau; the Tobacco Factory (1,203 employees), which was run by the Monopoly Bureau; and the Kyŏngsŏng

The 1942 survey of factory workers and the labor market, *Chōsen rōdō gijutsu tōkei chōsa hōkoku, Shōwa 17 nen* (Results of the statistical survey of Korean laborers and technicians, 1942), published by the colonial authorities, is an invaluable source for comparing and evaluating the changes in the labor market during the 1930s. During the wartime industrial mobilization, the number of factory workers in Korea increased continuously until 1945. The change occurred rapidly until 1937 and then explosively after 1937, changing the composition of the whole labor force. The number of industrial workers grew to approximately 1.75 million by 1942 (including transportation workers and day laborers). From 1933 to 1942, the number of factory, mining, and construction workers increased 3.3 times, from 223,115 to 744,023 (see Table 1.3 and Fig. 1) The number of factory workers increased 3.9 times. The number of miners grew fourfold, and that of construction workers increased a remarkable 8.7 times. Factory, mining, and construction workers, generally regarded as the full-time, regular, core group of industrial workers, accounted for more than half of the whole group by 1945, although another half remained in the informal sector, including day laborers (An Pyŏng-Jik 1990).

Two points become apparent when the statistical surveys of 1931 and 1941 are compared. First, the numbers of both Japanese and Korean male workers increased continuously in heavy industries such as the chemical, metallurgical, machinery, and ceramics industries. Second, the number of Korean female workers decreased in food processing, while increasing rapidly in the textile and chemical industries; women workers were heavily concentrated in rubber products manufacturing (Hori 1995: 98–127; see Table 1.4).

The ratio of Japanese to Korean factory workers also changed and fluctuated throughout the 1930s. The number of Japanese factory workers doubled during the 1930–36 period, from 5,826 to 11,337, accounting for a constant 10–11 percent of the entire factory workforce in this period. The Japanese, mostly skilled workers, were strongly represented in the heavy industries, such as the metallurgical, machine and machine tools, chemical, ceramics, and electric and gas industries. This picture started to change after 1936. Although

---

Printing Office (1,500 employees), under the Government General (Sŏn 1996: 82).

Table 1.3
Growth of the Working Class, 1933–1943
(000s of workers)

Type of worker	1933	1943 (%)
Factory workers	99.4	390 (22.3%)
Mineworkers	70.7	280 (16.0)
Transportation workers	n/a	170 (9.7)
Construction workers	43.6	380 (21.7)
Miscellaneous workers	n/a	530 (30.3)

SOURCES: *1933: Shokugin chōsa geppō*, no. 38 (1933): 3–4; *1943*: Nippon tei-koku gikai 1943, vol. 1: 70.

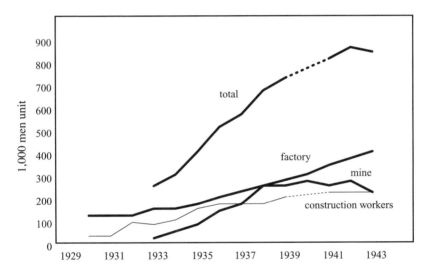

Fig. 1. Changes in the number of workers in Korea, 1929–1943. Sources: *factory workers*: Chōsen sōtokufu 1930–43 (1941 ed.); *mineworkers*: Chōsen sōto-kufu 1944; *construction workers*: Masahisa 1941b: 3–4; *for 1941–43*: Chōsen sōtokufu, Rōmu kyōkai 1944.

Table 1.4
Growth in Number of Factories and Workers
by Industry and Size, 1931–1941

Industry	Workers (000s)	Factories Total	Number of workers 5–29	30–100	101–999	1,000+
Textile						
1931	18.2	270	183	55	31	1
1941	65.0	1,680	1,360	227	84	9
Metal						
1931	4.5	244	230	13	0	1
1941	17.7	364	298	44	20	2
Machine						
1931	2.9	235	216	14	5	0
1941	33.4	940	745	148	42	5
Chemical						
1931	17.9	677	633	29	14	1
1941	72.4	1,523	1,072	319	125	7
Food						
1931	27.6	2,173	2,037	115	21	0
1941	41.9	2,201	1,885	260	56	0
TOTAL (FACTORIES)						
1931		4,613	4,202	318	90	3
1941		9,566	7,865	1,276	402	23
TOTAL (WORKERS, 000S)						
1931	86.4		38.8	15.8	24.4	7.4
1941	282.5		81.0	66.0	86.3	49.3

NOTE: Figures shown do not include government-run factories except those employing under 100 workers in 1931.
SOURCE: Hori 1995: 101.

the absolute number of Japanese workers increased from 11,337 in
1936 to 21,370 in 1941, the ratio of Japanese workers to the total
number of factory workers decreased from 11.4 percent to 7.1 percent over the same period. This ratio further decreased during the
1941–43 period to under 7 percent, as many Japanese workers were
drafted for military service (Hori 1995: 102).

Another qualitative change among industrial workers in the 1930s was the rapid increase in the number of male workers in large-scale heavy industrial factories, mines, or construction sites in the five northern provinces. More than 50 percent of industrial workers were engaged in factories with more than 100 workers by 1939. This phenomenon accelerated when industrial development became focused on the war-related heavy industries. In terms of output, the food-processing industry, for example, came to rank far below the textile, chemical, machine and machine tools, and metallurgical industries. In contrast to this quantitative and qualitative improvement in the male factory workforce, the ratio of female workers, who were mostly employed in light industry, peaked in 1932 at 34 percent of the total factory workforce and then decreased to 30 percent from the mid-1930s on (Lee 1980: 89). Because of the concentration of female factory workers in nonmilitary light industries, the wartime industrial mobilization did not influence the female labor market as much as it did the male labor market.

The government's wartime labor statistics, although not complete, reveal a ratio of skilled to unskilled factory and mine workers of roughly 1:4. Table 1.5 shows the years of employment of factory and mine workers in four categories (less than one year, one-three years, three-five years, more than five years) in 1943. These statistics reveal that around half of the Korean factory and mine workers were new recruits with less than one year's experience, and more than 30 percent were workers with 1–2 years of experience. Only around 20 percent had more than 3 years of work experience. We may regard the workers in this last category as full-time, steadily employed workers with enough skills and discipline to be considered modern skilled industrial workers (An Pyŏng-Jik 1993).

This division of the workforce between skilled and unskilled labor explains why many scholars are still cautious about recognizing the positive impact of the wartime mobilization and are concerned more about the negative elements of this change. They argue that although some upper-level skilled Korean workers had intensive work training and moved rapidly upward to more responsible and even supervisory positions because of the shortage of skilled Japanese workers, these opportunities were quite limited. Further, even for this top layer of workers, there was an uncrossable upper boundary, and the industrial workforce was still tightly controlled by a

Table 1.5
Distribution of Male Workers
by Years of Work Experience, 1943

Years of experience	All workers no. (%)	Korean no. (%)	Japanese no. (%)	Others no. (%)
	Factories			
0–1	61,616 (44.0)	57,533 (46.8)	3,784 (23.6)	299 (28.5)
1–3	44,326 (31.6)	38,707 (31.5)	5,306 (33.1)	313 (29.8)
3–5	18,346 (13.1)	15,049 (12.2)	3,157 (19.7)	140 (13.3)
5+	14,705 (10.5)	10,613 (8.6)	3,795 (23.6)	297 (28.3)
Day laborers	1,082 (0.8)	1,073 (0.9)	9 (0.1)	0 (0.0)
TOTAL	140,075 (100.0)	122,975 (100.0)	16,051 (100.0)	1,049 (100.0)
	Mines			
0–1	34,834 (44.1)	34,360 (44.6)	355 (26.2)	119 (20.7)
1–3	25,955 (32.9)	25,344 (32.9)	423 (31.3)	188 (32.6)
3–5	11,202 (14.2)	10,757 (14.0)	252 (18.6)	193 (33.5)
5+	6,895 (8.7)	6,500 (8.4)	319 (23.6)	76 (13.2)
Day laborers	50 (0.1)	46 (0.1)	4 (0.3)	0 (0.0)
TOTAL	78,936 (100.0)	77,007 (100.0)	1,353 (100.0)	576 (100.0)

SOURCE: Chōsen sōtokufu, Rōmu kyōkai 1943. The survey was limited to businesses employing more than 30 employees.

small minority of Japanese workers and engineers (Yi Hong-Rak 1994; Sŏn 1995).

However, several empirical case studies (see, e.g., An Pyŏng-Jik 1988; Chŏng Chae-Chŏng 1989; Sŏn 1995; S.-W. Park 1985, 1990; Kim Tong-Uk 1989) of changes in the upper layer of skilled workers during the colonial period confirmed not only that there had been an upward, qualitative movement of Korean workers but also the fact that the liberation in 1945 furthered this upward movement by promoting the upper layer of Korean skilled workers to the ranks of technical workers, engineers, and sometimes even managers, in South Korean industry. Some scholars argue that the historical impact of this growth of skilled workers in the war years was more significant in the post-liberation and post–Korean War era, when their experience made them valuable human assets.[11] This issue touches upon what is probably the most subtle yet essential element of colonial modernity — the mutually interlocking and reinforcing nature of colonialism and modernity. In the following chapters, we will explore the meaning and implications of the upward mobility of these workers.

The Labor Policy of the Japanese Colonial Government

Labor Market Policy

Conventional narratives of colonial labor policy depict Korean workers as cheap, abundant, silent, passive victims with no legal protections or channels for grievances except spontaneous labor disputes. The labor policy of the colonial state in Korea is portrayed as authoritarian and self-serving, focusing only on Japanese interests, the uprooting of radical, Communist elements, and the protection of the labor supply for large Japanese factories. They also emphasize the government's total neglect of the problem of rural surplus labor until the early 1930s versus its active, interventionist policy to meet the demands of the wartime labor mobilization in the late colonial period (see, e.g., Chŏn and Ch'oe 1978; Kobayashi 1969; Kim Yun-Hwan 1982; Kwon Tu-Yŏng 1979; and Pak Hyŏn-Ch'ae 1979).

Many studies of the past decade have, however, castigated these conventional interpretations as totalizing, politically biased narratives that repress and cover up the richness and complexities of the colonial drama by projecting a simple, binary exploitation-resistance view of colonial Korea. These studies have re-examined and reevaluated colonial history, including the interwar years, as a product of the society's own complexities and dynamics, which involved Korean as well as Japanese social groups (see, e.g., Kwon Hyŏk-T'ae 1991; Kim Nak-Nyŏn 1994; Cho Sŏng-Won 1993; Shin Yŏng-Hong 1984; G.-W. Shin 1996; McNamara 1990; Eckert 1991; and G.-W. Shin and M. Robinson 1999).

In 1921, 1936, and 1938, the Government General called major conferences to examine its socioeconomic policies for colonial Korea, and policy suggestions from these meetings generally guided the government's subsequent political, socioeconomic, industrial, and

---

11. Mason et al. 1980 explains this point in terms of physical facilities, educational zeal, and the demonstration effect in the post-colonial period.

labor policies.[12] The first conference, the Chōsen sangyō chōsa iinkai (Commission to survey Chōsen industry), was called by newly arrived Governor-General Saitō Makoto in September 1921 to reexamine colonial policies in the wake of the March First movement era. Japanese government and military officials, Japanese businessmen, directors of related offices, and a few Korean social and business leaders were invited to discuss new socioeconomic policies for Korea in tune with Saitō's new Cultural Policy (see Chōsen sōtokufu 1935: 315). The committee presented its comprehensive economic and industrial policy suggestions to Governor-General Saitō in 1922, and these became the basic policy-planning guidelines until the 1936 conference.

It is clear from these guidelines that "cultural" rule was still authoritarian, but based on more sophisticated, divide-and-rule policies. The Rice Production Promotion Plan, which had been launched in 1920, was continued, and railway construction remained the major economic goal of the coming decade. The economic policy of the previous decade of developing Korea as a rice supplier and restricting industrial development in Korea so as to use it as a market for Japanese manufactured goods was reconfirmed without much change. There was no mention of labor training or a labor market policy, with the exception of a strong demand from Japanese businessmen to deal with the anti-Japanese social atmosphere and social turmoil, including labor strikes and the labor movement, by force if necessary. Accordingly, the issue of social order and stabilization in both rural and urban areas became a new concern of the colonial government, and government officials had to tackle the difficult task of applying modified versions of selected Japanese social legislation to the colonial setting (Sŏn 1996: 180).

The situation was similar in Japan. The Taishō government had to adopt policies oriented more toward social order and control; this was reflected in the system of social control practiced in the 1920s under the Factory Law and the Peace Preservation Law. Table 1.6 illuminates the problems and national policy responses of the interwar years. A comparison of Japanese and Korean legislation reveals

12. In addition to these three major policymaking conferences, there was one minor conference called by Governor-General Ugaki Kazushige in 1933. The names and dates of these conferences are Chōsen sangyō chōsa iinkai, Sept. 1921; Chōsen sangyō kondankai, May 13–14, 1933; Chōsen sangyō keizai chōsakai, Oct. 1936; Jikyoku taisaku chōsakai, Sept. 1938.

the selective, filtered-down nature of the application of the Japanese legal framework to colonial Korea in these years. Liberal political legislation such as the new election law and universal manhood suffrage (1925) and the Labor Dispute Mediation Law (1926) was never applied to Korea, and social legislation like the Tenant Dispute Mediation Law (1924) was not promulgated in Korea until eight years later. The restrictive Peace Preservation Law (1925), however, was applied immediately. The 1923 Factory Law was applied in modified form to the highly industrialized province of Kyŏnggi and an extension of the law throughout the colony was planned, although in the end it was never put into effect and officially abandoned after the 1936 policy-planning conference.

The Saitō government established a new office, the Social Affairs Section (Shakaika), in the Internal Affairs Bureau (Naimukyoku) of the Government General in July 1921, to handle such matters as social disputes, labor disputes, increasing Communist activities, and tenant disputes. In July 1922, the Social Affairs Section launched a survey of the labor situation in factories and mines, hiring more than ten full-time employees, as the first step toward modified application of the Factory Law to Korea (Chōsen sōtokufu, Shakaika 1923: 4–5; Chōsen sōtokufu 1935: 514).

During the interwar years, the colonial government neglected the education of Koreans and kept vocational training to a minimum, leaving the educational level of colonial workers extremely low until the 1930s. The revised Educational Law of 1922 illustrates the limited nature of even elementary education and vocational training. Comparison to the situation in Japan clarifies this point. In 1886, at a time when Japanese capitalistic development had barely started, the Meiji government instituted compulsory education with three–four years of elementary education. In the first year of compulsory education, 62 percent of school-age males were enrolled in elementary school. In contrast, the enrollment rate for males in Korea was only 19.7 percent in 1935, 50 years later, even in the midst of rapid industrial growth (An Pyŏng-Jik 1990: 395–96) (See Fig. 2).

The principle of the labor market policy, which was exclusively for Japanese-owned, large-scale enterprises, was to use Japanese workers to fill all the engineering, technical, and skilled jobs, and to use cheap, abundant Korean workers for unskilled or semiskilled labor. This approach was possible because of the geographical proximity of Korea to Japan, which was only an overnight ferry ride

Table 1.6
Social Legislation in Japan and Korea in the Interwar Years

Japan	Korea
1911 Promulgation of Factory Law	
1916 Implementation of Factory Law	
1918/7 Rice riot	
1919 Nihon rōdō sōdōmei reorganized (25,000 members)	1919 March First movement
	1920 First national labor organization established
	1920 Governor-General Saitō arrives
	1920/12 Rice Production Promotion Plan launched
	1921/7/7 Social Affairs Section established in Internal Affairs Bureau of Government General
	1921/9 Saitō calls policymaking conference
	1922/2 Factory Control Regulation only for Kyŏnggi province
	1922/7/7 Social Affairs Section conducts factory survey
1922/11 Social Affairs Section established in the Interior Ministry	
1923/6 Revised Factory Law	1923/8 Survey results published
1923/9 Tokyo Earthquake	
1924/7 Tenant Dispute Mediation Law	
1924/10 Labor survey started	
1925/4 Peace Preservation Law enacted	1925/4 First Korean Communist party (KCP) organized
1925/5 Universal manhood suffrage enacted; Lower House of Diet election	1925/10 Peace Preservation Law applied to Korea in revised form; KCP dissolved
1926/4 Labor Disputes Mediation Law enacted	
1927 Bank Crisis	1927/2 Sin'ganhoe established
	1928 Special Higher Police Force formed for thought control in Korea, Manchuria, Siberia

Table 1.6, continued

Japan	Korea
1929 Implementation of the revised factory law; Great Depression	1929 Peace Preservation Law revised and applied to Korea; Wonsan General Strike
1930 Shōwa Depression	
1931 Major Industries Control Law	1931/5 Sin'ganhoe dissolved
1931/9 Manchurian Incident	1932 Tenant Arbitration Ordinance promulgated
	1934 Agricultural Lands Ordinance promulgated

SOURCES: Nihon rōmukan 1987; Andō Ryoō 1979: 199–207; Nakamura et al. 1988: 228–31; Sŏn Chae-Won 1996: 176–77.

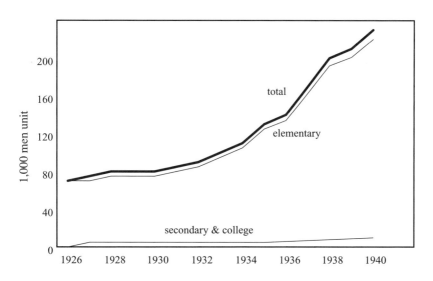

Fig. 2 Changes in the number of school graduates in Korea, 1926–1940.
SOURCE: Chōsen sōtokufu 1941: 115–16.

away. Under these circumstances, Japanese managers could create a dualistic, discriminatory labor-management system by placing a certain number of skilled Japanese workers on the shop floor. These Japanese workers had daily contact with Korean workers, controlling and supervising their work as lower-level managers. The Onoda Sŭnghori case in the following chapters will illuminate colonial labor relations in the large-scale Japanese factories, as well as the racial tensions that resulted.

In the early 1930s, several new problems led to more visibly authoritarian policies in the Japanese empire and the end of the Cultural Policy in Korea. One of the major problems was the Shōwa Depression and the upsurge of radical tenant disputes resulting from the long-term rural depression and tension between landlords and tenant farmers (80 percent of the population lived in rural areas, and 78 percent of the farmers were tenant farmers). Governor-General Ugaki in Korea arrived in June 1931 (he served until 1936) and began implementing a new agricultural policy, the Rural Revitalization Campaign (Nōson shinkō ūndō). It was also during this period that Korea and Manchuria became the largest and most competitive market for investments following promulgation of the Major Industries Control Law in Japan in 1931 (Kobayashi 1969: 115–22).

Regarding the continued tenant activism as a reflection of rural economic deterioration and a serious hindrance to Japan's need to mobilize Korean labor and resources for "total war," Governor-General Ugaki was determined to reform the agricultural land system with the Rural Revitalization Campaign and the new land laws. In this context, the Ugaki government promulgated the Tenant Arbitration Ordinance in 1932 and the Agricultural Lands Ordinance in 1934. These acts were a surprising development in colonial land policy and instrumental in the decline of the landlord class in the next two decades (for a detailed study, see G.-W. Shin 1996: chap. 7).

The early 1930s also witnessed a fundamental change in government labor policy to an active intervention in the labor market as an acute labor shortage, first of unskilled workers but later of skilled workers as well, developed in this period. The government had simultaneously to mobilize unskilled Korean workers on a large scale, to improve their skills, and to maintain labor stability by means of authoritarian suppression. It launched its first labor-mobilization policy for the unskilled labor force in April 1934, in the name of a "policy to transfer the surplus southern population to the northern provinces" (*nansen kajō jinkō hokuisaku*), as a part of the "out-of-province employment promotion policy" (*dōgai shokugyō assen seisaku*). The majority of those affected were construction workers sent from the five southern provinces to northern construction and industrial sites. This program was implemented by the Social Affairs Section of the Internal Affairs Bureau and the internal affairs sections (*naimuka*) of each provincial administration; later, in 1941, the newly created Labor Affairs Section (Rōmuka) assumed sole responsibility for the program. A private organization, the Kyŏngsŏng Civil Engineering and Construction Association (Keijō dōboku kenchiku kyōkai, later renamed the Chōsen dōboku kenchiku kyōkai), also actively supported this labor mobilization (Hirose 1995).

The second national-level socioeconomic policy-planning meeting, the "Chōsen sangyō keizai chōsakai" (Commission to survey the industrial economy of Chōsen), was called by newly arrived Governor-General Minami Jirō in October 1936 in order to mobilize colonial elites to support the new policies for the upcoming total war in China. The main concern of the conference was how to apply the revised Major Industries Control Law to Korea (it was implemented in Korea in March 1937). The importance of government direction and control increased tremendously as the economy was put on a wartime footing. Both the government and business showed increased interest in the promotion of labor productivity by training workers, because a shortage of skilled workers endangered wartime industrial operations.

The close cooperation between the government and big business, characteristic of the period 1931–37, was replaced between 1937 and 1945 by tight control of both business and labor by the wartime government. A unique labor-management system (labeled "Japanese paternalism" or "Japanese employment system" in the 1950s) stressing triangular cooperation among government, business, and labor to support the war in China took shape during these intensive war years. The wartime labor system is addressed in greater detail at the end of this chapter.

Labor Control Policy

In contrast to its neglect of the surplus labor problem, the colonial government became increasingly rigid and authoritarian throughout the 1920s in dealing with labor and social militancy. The number of labor disputes and participants doubled throughout the 1920s, and disputes became more radical and militant by the end of the decade (as shown in the Wonsan General Strike, which lasted four months in 1929). Three factors are generally seen as the political and economic causes of this spurt in labor militancy and activity: (1) the series of economic crises during the interwar years, including the post-WWI economic recession, the 1923 Tokyo Earthquake, the 1927 bank crisis in Taiwan and Japan, and the Shōwa Depression following the Great Depression in 1929; (2) the Cultural Policy of the 1920s; and (3) the Communist movement and Communist infiltration of the workplace (Kim Yun-Hwan 1982: chap. 3; see also Kim Kyŏng-Il 1987, 1992).

The Saitō administration remained authoritarian but became more sophisticated in the 1920s, developing a new state-society relationship as well as new social policies. The March First movement had stirred up the nationalist consciousness of the Korean people, and the subsequent introduction of Communist ideology helped make the late 1920s a period of active mass movements with improved organizational effectiveness and militancy. In response, the government concentrated on preventing Communist agents from penetrating factories and other industrial worksites and lent full support to Japanese managers through extensive and efficient police actions. The Police Bureau (Keimukyoku) in the government became more powerful and actively cooperated with the Social Affairs Section. If workers became uncooperative, the police were always there to see that the employer's will was obeyed, in the name of the Cultural Policy of Governor-General Saitō in the 1920s.

Legal measures for rationalizing authoritarian police suppression of labor and social resistance were first instituted in Japan, when the Diet passed the Peace Preservation Law in April 1925. Unlike liberal legislation such as the Factory Law or the Labor Dispute Mediation Law, which were either carefully studied and evaluated for modified application or never applied to Korea, this law was immediately applied to Korea beginning in October 1925, when the colonial police raided the first Korean Communist party office (Kobayashi 1969: 110–15). This selective approach to implementing Japanese laws illustrates the issue-by-issue pragmatism of the colonial government in the interwar years. The government dealt with each policy issue by carefully studying, evaluating, and considering the colonial situation and the Korean response. For example, the Factory Law was carefully studied and evaluated for modification, delaying actual implementation, whereas the Peace Preservation Law was applied to the colony immediately and even expanded in the late 1920s. As mentioned earlier, for example, the police bureau of South Kyŏngsang province applied the law by ordering the Pusan police to reduce the number of Korean migrants to Japan by preventing alcoholics, drug addicts, and the indigent from embarking. Before the Communist party was ordered to disband in 1928, there were three more rounds of extensive raids and arrests of party leaders in Korea on charges of violating the Peace Preservation Law (Kim Yun-Hwan 1982: 277–88).

The Kōtō keisatsu, the Special Higher Police Force, was formed in 1928 by the Government General for thought control and suppression of radical elements in Korea, Manchuria, and Siberia. A further revision of the Peace Preservation Law the next year gave the government the authority to execute the leaders of the independence movement by hanging. The Sin'ganhoe, the only remaining organization of national-level political elites, was dissolved in May 1931 by the Special Higher Police Force (Sueji 1949: 53–91; Kim Yun-Hwan 1982: 193–96, 211–12).

The Communists were, however, equally determined and tireless in attaining labor and peasant support in colonial Korea. Communist tactics were re-examined after the dissolution of the Korean Communist party in late 1928. Two major international Communist conferences, the Propintern (1930) and the Pacific Comintern (1931), blamed the disintegration of Korean Communist groups on the failure of the bourgeois intelligentsia leaders to obtain massive labor support and ordered a change in tactics to attract factory workers and peasants rather than petit bourgeois intellectuals. Many Korean agitators, trained by Siberian and Manchurian Communist groups, were sent to the peninsula to organize left-wing labor unions among the rapidly growing pool of male workers, especially in the northern industrial areas of Hamkyŏng and P'yŏngan provinces, or Red peasant unions.[13]

In parallel with growing tenant-landlord disputes in the rural areas, labor disputes in colonial Korea reached a record high in 1930–32, during the Shōwa Depression. There were five waves of mass

---

13. In 1934, the police closed night schools for rural youth and urban workers. These night schools had been useful networks for the Communist activists (Kim Yun Hwan 1982: 141–48; Chōsen sōtokufu, Keimukyoku 1933: 146–47).

arrests of leaders of underground left-wing labor or peasant unions, starting with the arrests in 1931 of some 1,800 people allegedly associated with the Hŭngnam Red Labor Union. These actions took place in the industrial cities of Hŭngnam, Sinŭiju, P'yŏngyang, Wonsan, and Chinnamp'o (in addition to Chŏlla and Kyŏngsang provinces) and resulted in the imprisonment of the majority of agitators and almost crushed the underground labor and peasant movements.[14] The contest between the two determined ideological adversaries — the imperial police and Communist activists — ended in the bloody defeat of the Communists, at least in the short run. Labor agitation decreased decisively after 1934 and finally went underground after 1937 under the wartime emergency rule and compulsory assimilation policies of the Naisen Ittai (Japan and Korea as one body) and the Kōminka (Japanization of the colonial subjects as equal imperial subjects) movements (Ogle 1990: 3–7; Chou 1996).

Ironically, the government's authoritarian labor-control policy assisted the cause of the Communists in the 1930s. The mass suppressions built up the image of the Communists, because the authorities designated every instance of labor trouble a Communist plot. The Japanese sought to instill a fear of communism to bind Koreans to the colonial system. The results were the exact opposite: an overly politicized labor movement. The prestige of the Communists was so enhanced that they became known as the heroes of the underground and could lead an intense, though short-lived, labor movement in the immediate post-liberation period, until the newly arrived U.S. Military Occupation Government crushed these activities in early 1947 (Pak Chi-Hyang 1992: 130–35). (The experiences of workers in the Onoda Samch'ŏk factory, discussed in Chapter 4, illuminate the overly politicized, ideological nature of labor affairs and the labor movement in the post-liberation era.)

Wartime Labor Policy

During the eight years following the war in China in July 1937, the government's labor policies became increasingly active and inter-

---

14. The majority of those arrested were confined to prisons until the liberation, when they were released and became leaders of the left-wing labor movement. Many were also executed by hanging, committed suicide, or died of tuberculosis, malnutrition, or mental disorders during their terms in colonial prisons (Kim Kyŏng-Il 1994; Kobayashi 1969: 115–22).

ventionist. They were complicated by adoption of two new ideologies and the subsequent ideological mobilization of the workers: spiritual Japanization, officially called the Kōminka movement, and the Sanpō movement (abbreviation of Sangyō hōkokutai ūndō, or "Movement of the great patriotic corps of industrial workers"), a Japanese-style labor-management system that emphasized voluntary cooperation between labor and management for the war effort.[15]

In line with these imperial ideological campaigns, the third official policymaking conference, the Jikyoku taisaku chōsakai (Commission to investigate countermeasures for the current situation), was held in September 1938 to discuss socioeconomic issues related to wartime industrial demand. The commission's advisory report made three major recommendations; for the first time since annexation in 1910, the improvement of labor productivity and a worker-training program became the focal points of industrial policy.

The report recommended (1) an expansion of military-related industries such as metal processing, machine and machine tools, and mining; (2) reorganization of the Korean labor force for military purposes through the training of technicians and skilled workers and mobilization of unskilled workers; and (3) transformation of small- and medium-size factories into subcontracting workshops for large-scale military industries (Chōsen sōtokufu 1938: 103-22). When we compare these recommendations to those of the 1936 conference, the drastic change in labor policy becomes clear. This 1938 meeting stressed labor-management cooperation and preservation and mobilization of labor for wartime industrial development. Both the government and business now showed increased interest in the promotion of labor productivity by training workers, because the shortage of skilled workers was impeding the war effort. Labor affairs even received special bureaucratic support. The Social Affairs Section, which had moved back to the Internal Affairs Bureau from the Education Bureau (Gakumukyoku) in 1936, spawned a new Labor Affairs Section (Rōmuka) in 1940. The new section was devoted to labor mobilization and other labor affairs and immediately launched a

15. The Kōminka movement in colonial Korea promoted three major campaigns: prohibition of the Korean language and the substitution of Japanese; mandatory Shintō worship not only in official places but also in schools; and the Japanization of Korean names. Koreans deeply resented these campaigns as evidence of Japan's fanatical determination to destroy Korean identity. See Hŏ 1985.

new survey of factory labor for extensive mobilization of the labor force for the war effort. The survey results were published during 1941–43, as the *Chōsen rōdō gijutsu tōkei chōsa kekka hōkoku* (Results of the statistical survey of the Korean laborers and technicians).

Education became the inevitable tool for the compulsory mobilization. The Education Law was revised twice in a haphazard manner, in 1938 and 1943, to support the spiritual mobilization of the colonial peoples as loyal subjects of the Japanese emperor and to address the wartime demand for trained, qualified workers. Under the 1938 law, education was reorganized in a military-style regimentation centering on Shintō ideology. Korean-language classes became elective from 1938 on and were eventually eliminated. The Japanese terminology of *sho* (primary), *chū* (middle), and *kōtō jogakkō* (female secondary) schools was imposed. Under the 1943 Education Law, middle school was shortened from five to four years to meet the urgent labor shortage, and students were mobilized for compulsory labor (*Gakudō kinrorei*) (Yi Kwang-Ho and Chŏn Myŏng-Ki 1994: 245–53).

In April 1937, the government started an aggressive Official Employment Promotion Policy (*Kan assen shokugyō seisaku*) at the national level to supply Korean laborers to strategic industrial projects. A long list of regulations relating to both unskilled and skilled workers was hastily issued (Chōsen sōtokufu 1940: 546–48). For example, mine workers were included in the official labor mobilization program beginning in November 1938, after the Ordinance on Korean Gold Production (*Chōsen sankinrei*), promulgated in September 1937, started a gold rush. Under the program, 12,000 workers in 1937, 20,000 in 1938, and an average of 40,000–50,000 every year from 1939 to 1944 were mobilized (Hirose 1995: 120–25).

Government labor mobilization became compulsory in 1939 with the promulgation of the Ordinance on the National Draft (*Kokumin jōyōrei*) and intensified in 1941 with the extension of the age of those eligible for mobilization from 20–45 years to 18–45 years, as the demand for workers from the mining, transportation, and construction sectors all over the Japanese empire became desperately urgent. The government also launched the Patriotic Labor Corps for National Support (Kinrō hōkokutai) campaign for more extensive labor mobilization of students, women, and older males within Korea (Sŏn 1995: 56–57).

In late 1941, as the labor shortage intensified with the outbreak of the Pacific War, the Association for Korean Labor Affairs (Chōsen rōmu kyōkai) was established and made solely responsible for labor mobilization. Within the colonial government, the Labor Affairs Section was also hurriedly established. As of 1945, almost three-quarters of a million workers had been mobilized. By occupational breakdown, these workers included 340,000 coal miners, 200,000 factory and other workers, 110,000 construction workers, and 67,000 metallurgical workers. An additional 240,000 Koreans were mobilized as civilian workers for the Japanese military, including the comfort women, beginning in 1943. In other words, one million Korean men and women were mobilized by force from 1939 to 1945.[16]

The government also intervened actively in industrial job training at the national level. In 1937, it established the Skilled Worker Training Center (Jukurenkō yōseisho), in affiliation with the Chōsen Industrial Association (Chōsen kōgyō kyōkai), to promote the training of Korean technicians and skilled workers. The center had two bureaus, the electrical bureau and the machinery bureau, and trained approximately 100–300 Korean youths as skilled workers every year through 1945 (An Pyŏng-Jik 1988: 172–76). As the labor shortage worsened with the drafting of Japanese skilled workers from colonial factories after 1938, the government responded by issuing a series of make-shift laws, such as the Regulations Limiting Hiring of New Graduates (September 1938), Regulations on In-company Training of Technicians (June 1939), and Regulations Limiting the Hiring of New Employees (September 1938) (Hŏ 1985: 104).

To carry out these compulsory labor policies, the government and military imposed a new kind of labor relations on industrial worksites. They directly intervened in labor management in large factories in 1938 by launching the Sanpō movement, which was an ideological campaign to encourage emperor worship among colonial workers. The campaign instituted patriotic industrial units (*aikoku-*

16. These mobilized workers, their sociocultural experiences, their level of modernity as an uprooted and floating urban population, and their whereabouts after liberation are topics awaiting imaginative and innovative research and interpretation. Recently the teenage Korean girls who were mobilized by force as "comfort women" have received wide attention from the Korean public, feminist groups, and the international human rights movement. The comfort women, estimated to number approximately 100,000, were mobilized as part of the civilian support personnel for the military under the name *teishintai* (volunteer corps).

han) in factories in Japan, Korea, and Manchuria, and called for greater sacrifice and increased productivity and output to be achieved by industrial managers and workers cooperating in the imperial war efforts. Each unit in the firm chose representatives to form a workers association. The association was given office space inside the plant and provided with funds to carry out programs for the war effort. Full-time officers of the association were paid by the company. Together the association and employer established programs for educating workers, making the production process more efficient, and preventing disputes among the workers.

Whether the Sanpō system helped the Japanese war effort or whether Korean and Japanese workers responded voluntarily is uncertain, but one thing is sure: this wartime industrial relations system, particularly the *aikokuhan* and the Sanpō movement as a company-oriented labor-management council system, had a deep impact on Korean labor practices. Again, the enclave-theory approach to the wartime experience proves inadequate as an explanation. Rather, the wartime experience bequeathed a continuing legacy to Korean labor in several areas: (1) the politicization of labor, (2) a tradition of government intervention in labor-management relations and a strong bond between government and business, (3) the company union system, and (4) the labor-management council system. Many historians of Japanese labor, including Sumiya Mikio (1964) and Andrew Gordon (1985: 299–305), argue that these wartime labor relations, especially the Sanpō system and the *aikokuhan*, were the origins of the uniquely Japanese labor-management council system and the company union system, which is still practiced in Japan as well as Korea even today.[17]

Of course, Korean labor practices and industrial relations again changed and were complicated by new elements during the U.S. Occupation (U.S.-style economic unionism), the Korean War (anti-communism), and, most recently, the rapid economic growth and authoritarian labor suppression during the military dictatorships of

---

17. These practices resurfaced during the 1960s economic growth period and have continued. The Chun Doo-Hwan government further reinforced them by making the labor-management council system mandatory in any plant with over 100 workers. The Sixth Republic continued this practice, until the 1996 labor reforms. The practice of companies' paying union officers is still the custom in Korea and is cited as an obstacle to worker autonomy and independence at the bargaining table.

Park Chung-Hee and Chun Doo-Hwan. Although present-day Korean labor relations and practices are a blend of all these historical experiences, most observers of contemporary Korean labor emphasize the strong influence of the colonial practices, including the company union system and the labor-management councils, on contemporary Korean labor relations, especially during the Park and Chun eras.

The demographic structure, the workforce, the labor market situation, and government labor policy in colonial Korea changed before and after 1930. Labor conditions reflected the general patterns of the initial stage of industrialization, with some colonial characteristics and modifications. These patterns were complicated in many ways during the forced wartime industrial mobilization. The image of abundant, cheap, surplus labor in colonial Korea is valid only until the early 1930s. Critical change occurred during the 1930s, and the intensive wartime experience from 1937 to 1945 transformed colonial industry, labor, and society.

These wartime changes had a significant effect on the development of the Korean labor force. The number of industrial workers increased, and many informal-sector, unskilled workers were absorbed into the formal sector. Many Korean workers responded aggressively to the new job openings as opportunities for socioeconomic advancement. Many received intensive training due to the wartime demand for educated and trained workers. The upper layer of Korean workers rapidly improved their skills and sometimes advanced to higher-level jobs due to openings caused by industrial expansion and positions left vacant by drafted Japanese workers. Recent studies confirm the quantitative increase in Korean industrial workers, both formal- and informal-sector workers, and also the qualitative, upwardly mobile movement of these new industrial workers. With this background in mind, we can now turn to the specific case studies of the Onoda Sŭnghori and Samch'ŏk factories.

TWO

Labor-Management Relations in the Onoda Sŭnghori Factory

This chapter focuses on changes in the Korean workforce at the Sŭnghori factory between 1917 and 1937. Company documents and personal interviews with surviving Onoda employees allow us to reconstruct colonial working-class life from the point of view of skilled workers. The Onoda Sŭnghori factory was selected for study because of the availability of primary documents preserved in company files. This was the only company among the twelve contacted that retained a complete set of records on its colonial ventures.[1] The main office of the Onoda Cement Company in Tokyo received semiannual reports from the engineering departments in the five branch factories in Korea at Sŭnghori, Ch'ŏnnaeri, Komusan, Samch'ŏk, and Sup'ung. The reports contain a wealth of information on the workers, including their numbers, length of hire, absenteeism, training, injuries, wages and other forms of compensation, special activities, and labor problems. These sources do not cover the workers' lives outside the workshop, since they were compiled by management in the form of reports. Nevertheless, their detailed and accurate information on the internal organization, work, and overall changes in

1. The other eleven companies were the Kyŏngsŏng Textile Company, Chōsen Leather Company, Chōsen Textile Company, and Chōsen Silk Reeling Company (all located in Korea), and the Kirin Brewery, Ōkura Zaibatsu, Mitsubishi Steelworks, Nihon Steelworks, Tōyō Textile Company, Nihon Chissō Company, and Kanebō Textile Company (Japanese companies with branch factories in Korea).

the composition of the workforce permit us to track the transformation of rural youths into regular skilled workers.

In addition, a pamphlet on worker regulations in the Onoda Company, three official company histories (published to commemorate the fiftieth [1931], seventieth [1951], and hundredth [1981] anniversaries of its establishment), the memoirs of a manager of the Sŭnghori factory, and interviews with five Koreans (three workers, one clerk, and one engineer) and one Japanese (a manager of the Sŭnghori factory and later president of the Onoda Cement Company) who worked in the Sŭnghori or Samch'ŏk factories provided useful insights beyond the written records. Materials in North Korea, if any, were not available for this study.

The labor-management situation in the factory is analyzed from the points of view of (1) organizational structure, (2) sources of the labor supply, (3) educational level of the workers, (4) disciplining of the workers, (5) the hierarchy of the workers, both on the shop floor and outside the factory, (6) labor turnover, (7) wages and other forms of compensation, and (8) labor disputes. Four historical themes guide the analysis and reveal colonial modifications of modern labor-management relations in the factory. First, several questions regarding the process of creating a labor force are addressed. What sort of people were recruited and trained? What sort of person remained committed to work in the factory? How did Japanese managers deal with the low skill levels of the Korean recruits and succeed in training and keeping a stable workforce in the plant? What was the Korean workers' attitude toward working in a large-scale Japanese factory? To what extent did the colonial period represent a break from Korea's past and result in the establishment of new patterns of labor relations and state-society interaction?

A second group of questions deals with the existence and workings of several historical forces in the colonial factory. In what way and to what extent did colonialism, nationalism, communism, and modernity intertwine in the formation and growth of the factory labor force and labor relations in the Sŭnghori plant? How did specific political issues of colonialism, such as oppression, discrimination, and collaboration, interact, and what was the Korean workers' response? Were there any labor organizations and labor disputes, and if there were, what impact did the Communist movement have on them?

A third consideration is the human aspect of the responses of individual workers to their transformation from peasant to factory worker. To what extent and in what ways did working in the factory change the life of a farm youth? How different was it from the traditional rural working environment? Did workers identify as a group and, if so, did that identification lead to labor organizations and collective actions? What kind of class identity—here "class" in the modern identity sense of race, gender, or nation rather than the classical Marxist sense—emerged in response to the tensions and contradictions caused by working in the Sŭnghori plant, and how did this identity relate to workers' national identity? Did colonialism and modernity merge to create a hybrid identity? Did the Sŭnghori workers have a shared working-class culture and identity? How were the individual identities of the workers formed and influenced by these larger historical forces of the colonial period?

The fourth group of questions concerns changes in the nature and role of the labor force in the colonial economy after war broke out in 1937 (these are discussed separately in Chapter 3, because of the war's significant impact on industry, the labor force, and state-labor relations). Militarism in the late 1930s significantly influenced and changed the nature of colonial modernity, once more engendering further complications and flux in the colonial society. Chapter 4 examines in what way and to what extent the rapid industrialization and mobilization for war after 1937 influenced the workforce structure and labor-management relations in colonial Korea in general and in the Onoda Sŭnghori factory in particular.

This study belongs to a series of empirical case studies of colonial workers begun in the 1980s to probe these historical questions and concepts. Several key studies, all of them case studies of large-scale, Japanese-owned industrial plants, such as the Chōsen Nitrogen Fertilizer Company at Hŭngnam, the Chōsen Oil Refinery Plant at Ulsan, and the Yongsan Machinery Plant for the government-run Chōsen Railway Bureau in Seoul, provide a picture of the growing skilled labor force during the period of industrial growth in the 1930s (see An Pyŏng-Jik 1988; Chŏng Chae-Chŏng 1989; S.-W. Park 1990; Hŏ 1994; Kang Man-Kil et al. 1994; Hori 1993b; Sŏn 1996). These studies agree on several general points. First, the ratio of Korean workers to Japanese workers increased in all the large-scale industrial plants in the 1920s and the 1930s. The speed of the increase was gradual in the 1920s but escalated rapidly during the 1930s and exploded after 1939. In 1944–45, the ratio between Korean and Japanese skilled workers reversed in large factories. A minority of Korean workers improved their skills throughout the 1930s, and some became low-level foremen or low-level technicians after the late 1930s. Other case studies, such as Carter Eckert's (1991, 1996) and Dennis McNamara's (1990) studies of Korean entrepreneurs and Karl Moskowitz's (1980) study of white-collar bank workers during the colonial period, confirm the colonial origins of Korean capitalism and modern human capital and show in detail that this upward movement was not limited to the industrial workforce but widespread in other modern-sector jobs in schools, companies, banks, and even government offices (see also Hŏ 1994; Chu 1994; and on workers, An Pyŏng-Jik 1988; Chŏng Chae-Chŏng 1989; S.-W. Park 1985; and Sŏn 1996). These studies also agree, however, that the hierarchical, segmented labor pattern of a minority of Japanese managers, engineers, and skilled workers on the one hand and a majority of unskilled Korean free laborers on the other hand did not completely disappear even during the wartime emergency and collapse of the colonial administrative system in late colonial Korea. The case of Onoda Sŭnghori workers illuminates these points in a concrete context.

The Cement Industry and Colonial Development

South P'yŏngan province was the second most developed province in colonial Korea, after Kyŏnggi province, in terms of the scale, capital, and number of employees in the mining and manufacturing sector when the Onoda Cement Company's Sŭnghori branch began operations near P'yŏngyang in December 1919 (P'yŏngan namdoch'ŏng 1975: 531). There were 75 industrial and mining companies, including rice mills, ironworks, food-processing plants, knitware manufacturers, and producers of miscellaneous household items, in the province employing more than ten permanent employees by mid-1922 (Chōsen sōtokufu, Shakaika 1923: 29–39). Japanese companies had developed large coal and iron mines in the 1910s to exploit the rich iron and coal deposits in the province. The four largest were the Meiji Mining Company's Daesŏng Coal Mine (151 employees) and Anju Coal Mine (555 employees), the Nihon Iron and Steel Company's Kaesan Iron Mine (276 employees), and Mitsubishi's Chōsen Anthracite Mine (366 employees) (Chōsen sōtokufu, Shakaika 1923: 39–40). The area was also traditionally famous for its household weaving industry, which produced regional cotton and silk specialties (P'yŏngan namdoch'ŏng 1975: 531).

Of these factories and mines, 30 companies employed more than 50 workers and of these 9 employed more than 100 workers. The composition of hiring at these large-scale factories reflected the unsophisticated rice-mill-oriented employment pattern of industry as a whole. There were four rice mills, two iron works (Chōsen Commercial and Industrial Ironworks, 133 employees; and P'yŏngyang Ironworks, 130 employees), and the Dai Nihon Sugar Refinery (123 employees). The Onoda Cement Sŭnghori factory (624 employees) and the Anju Coal Mine of the Meiji Mining Company (555 miners) were the only companies employing more than 500 workers (Chōsen sōtokufu, Shakaika 1923: 38–39).

As for Korean-owned industrial concerns, the hosiery and the rubber shoes industries had developed rapidly in the P'yŏngyang area since the early 1920s and were financed and run exclusively by Korean capital and management. Cotton socks and rubber walking shoes first appeared in the local market around 1920 and immediately became popular items among Koreans. The small- and medium-size Korean manufacturers in these two industries met the increasing demand from the national market. The majority of the factory owners were Korean Christians in South P'yŏngan province, which was the country's largest Presbyterian community at the time. The P'yŏngan area traditionally had weaker links to elite *yangban* traditions because the Chosŏn dynasty had discriminated against the region. One result was that commercial activity was much more developed here than in other parts of the country with the exception of the capital, since ingrained in the *yangban* tradition were anti-work, anti-commercial biases (see Kajimura 1977: 162–75).

The capital of the province, P'yŏngyang, was traditionally the administrative and commercial center of the northwestern part of the peninsula. P'yŏngyang was opened to foreigners in 1897 and became an important station along the Kyŏngsŏng–Sinŭiju railway in 1907. As P'yŏngyang developed rapidly not only as the administrative but also as the commercial, educational, and industrial center of South P'yŏngan province, its population increased from 57,878 in 1917 to 89,423 in 1925 to 140,703 in 1930. By 1939, it had reached 249,185. In 1921, P'yŏngyang passed Pusan to become the second largest city in Korea. The number of Japanese residents in P'yŏngyang also increased rapidly, from 6,443 in 1910 to 20,073 in 1930 (P'yŏngan namdoch'ŏng 1975: 1103; Chōsen sōtokufu 1934, vol. 9: 2).

The May 1920 opening of the Onoda branch factory in Sŭnghori was a pioneering event in many ways. The Sŭnghori plant was the largest and most up-to-date factory in the province and also the first cement manufactory in the country. It was part of the boom in colonial ventures following the economic expansion during World War I in Japan.

Beginning in the late 1890s Korea started to import Japanese cement as the construction of modern facilities was launched on a large scale after the Sino-Japanese war. Cement and steel were essential materials for the construction of railroads, roads, barracks, large buildings, bridges, harbors, and dams. The building of the Yongsan train station and Yongsan military base was followed by the construction of the Kyŏngsŏng–Inch'ŏn railway starting in 1897. Shortly thereafter, the Han River Bridge was completed in 1900. Construction of the Kyŏngsŏng-Pusan railway was begun in 1901 by the Japanese military railway bureau. The demand for cement increased continuously as the Japanese military in Korea pushed railways and road construction in preparation for the war with Russia (Tongyang shiment chushikhoesa 1967: 60). After the Russo-Japanese war in 1905, the Protectorate government undertook construction of the Pusan-Masan railway (begun in 1905) and the Kyŏngsŏng-Sinŭiju railway (begun in 1907). All these projects increased the demand for cement and steel.

The earliest extant record on cement imports into Korea dates from about 1904. In that year, Korea imported 37 percent of Japan's total exports of cement and limestone, and 30 percent the next year (Tongyang shiment chushikhoesa 1967: 61). As Table 2.1 shows, the Korean demand for cement increased steadily after the annexation in 1910. Public works such as railways (the P'yŏngyang coal mine railways in 1910, the Yalu River railway in 1911, the Seoul-Kwangju railway in 1914, and the Seoul-Wonsan railway in 1914), highways between regional centers throughout the country, the repair and expansion of port facilities, and major buildings in the cities were part of the policy of the Government General to develop a modern infrastructure in Korea. Railway construction was the largest user of cement, accounting for an average 20 percent of total cement consumption in these years.

The cement industry in Japan began in 1872, when the Meiji government set up the government-run Asano Cement Company to

Table 2.1
Korea's Cement and Limestone
Imports, 1906–1919

Year	Imports (10,000 *kin*)*	Price (¥)
1906	3,972	454,610
1907	4,301	746,638
1908	2,167	267,694
1909	n/a	323,851
1910	2,581	381,384
1911	3,618	541,000
1912	4,764	659,000
1913	5,010	701,000
1914	4,678	490,000
1915	7,060	645,000
1916	7,979	790,000
1917	9,733	1,685,000
1918	8,488	1,816,000
1919	7,442	1,606,000

* 10,000 *kin* = 6 metric tons
SOURCE: Tongyang shiment chushikhoesa
1967: 61.

meet the demand of construction projects required for Japan's initial industrialization. In the 1880s, private cement factories were also established by pioneering entrepreneurs, and these factories were able to export cement to Korea and China by the time of the Sino-Japanese War in 1894 (Onoda semento kabushiki kaisha 1931: 512). The Onoda Cement Company was established in 1881 in a limestone mine in Onoda, Yamaguchi prefecture, by several former samurai from Chōshū *han* led by Kasai Zumpachi (first president, May 1881–Nov. 1901). The company grew rapidly during the initial industrialization of Japan in the period between the Sino-Japanese War and the Russo-Japanese War. Three years after the Russo-Japanese War, the company undertook its first overseas venture by establishing a branch factory in Dalian, aimed mainly at supplying cement for construction of the South Manchurian Railway, which Japan took over from Russia after the war (Onoda semento kabushiki kaisha 1981: 153–54). This was the beginning of Onoda's colonial ventures in

Manchuria and Korea, which lasted until the end of the Japanese empire in 1945.

When the Government General of Korea undertook a survey of natural resources and industrial raw materials in Korea after the annexation, it found limestone deposits near the border between Kyŏnggi and Hwanghae provinces. This information was made known to an executive director of the Onoda Cement Company, Kasai Shinzō (fourth president of the company, July 1918–July 1939), a grandson of the company's founder, when he stopped at Kyŏngsŏng in September 1913 on his way to Mukden in Manchuria (Onoda semento kabushiki kaisha 1981: 207). Kasai's entrepreneurial instincts were stimulated, and he persuaded the executive committee of the main company to consider the potential of a quarry in the area. By 1915, the company had huge expansion projects under way due to the export boom of World War I. It dispatched an engineering team in January 1916 with the approval of the Government General. After five months of surveying in Kyŏnggi, Hwanghae, and South P'yŏngan provinces, the team selected a limestone deposit in Sŭnghori, five miles east of P'yŏngyang, as the best site for the plant. Sŭnghori was well endowed for cement manufacturing. It was located at the foot of Mount Mandal, a high-quality limestone deposit, and it was near the Taedong River, which provided abundant water and good access to the sea. In addition, the nearby Sadong Coal Mine afforded easy railway access to the essential fuel supply (Onoda semento kabushiki kaisha 1951: 514).

In October 1916, Kasai came to Korea and received the approval of Governor-General Hasegawa Yoshimichi (October 1916–August 1919) to establish a branch plant in Sŭnghori. The Government General welcomed the production of cement in the colony. Kasai's request for official support from the Railway Bureau to build a simple freight railway from the Sadong Coal Mine to Sŭnghori was immediately approved.

Onoda began to buy land around Mount Mandal for a plant and railway site in early 1917. The company bought 40,000 *p'yŏng* of land for a plant site and 800,000 *p'yŏng* for the limestone quarries (1 *p'yŏng* = 3.95 square yards). Sŭnghori, an obscure village with only several dozen households, suddenly became the largest plant site in the province and quickly attracted many farmers into construction work on railways, the plant buildings, and company housing. Many work-hungry newcomers surged into this area as word spread throughout the province (Onoda semento kabushiki kaisha 1951: 527).

The construction work took a full three years, twice the amount of time estimated in the original plan. The land purchases took longer than expected, and the arrival of equipment from Europe was delayed because of the war there. After the necessary capital equipment had arrived (a boiler from Britain, an electrical generator from Switzerland, an iron board for the revolving kiln from the United States), the first fire was lit in the kiln in December 1919. The initial production capacity of this first modern cement factory in the colony was 60,000 tons/year (250 tons/workday). The plant had one revolving kiln at this time (Onoda semento kabushiki kaisha 1981: 210).

The demand for cement increased in the 1920s with the launching of the fifteen-year Rice Production Promotion Plan in 1920. Water utilization associations were organized in rice-growing areas of the country in order to construct reservoirs and irrigation channels. In 1924, the Government General helped underwrite expansion of the Onoda Sŭnghori plant by ordering provincial governors to use Onoda cement on all government construction projects, including the water utilization projects. In addition, the Government General allocated 10 percent of the ¥900 million budgeted for major irrigational facilities projects to purchase cement, an area in which Onoda enjoyed a monopoly. Demand grew as the Pujŏn River Dam, the Hŭngnam Chōsen Nitrogen Fertilizer Company plant, and Sinhŭng railroad projects began in South Hamkyŏng province in 1926 (Onoda semento kabushiki kaisha 1951: 513).

At the time of the plant's construction in 1919, the estimated annual demand for cement in Korea was 45,000 tons; actual use was more than double this amount by 1922 and triple it by 1923. As Table 2.2 shows, the use of cement by the water utilization associations expanded suddenly in 1923, outstripping the amount of cement used in railway construction that year. By 1924, the output of the Sŭnghori plant could barely meet half the total demand in the peninsula, and cement imports increased until 1928 (see Tables 2.3 and 2.4). The Japanese suppliers of this imported cement were the Onoda Cement Company, Toyokoku Cement Company, Oita Cement Company, Ube Cement Company, and Nihon Cement Company (Tongyang shiment chushikhoesa 1967: 67).

From the government's standpoint, an active colonial venture allowed the Onoda Cement Company in Japan to cope with a serious slump in the Japanese cement industry during the post–World War I economic recession of the early 1920s. Japanese cement companies organized cartels, first in 1924 and again in 1929, to prevent over-production of cement during the recession and to block domestic expansion. The cartel also established price controls for cement in 1931. Naturally, many companies in Japan competed fiercely for ex-port markets in Korea, Manchuria, and China. Until the mid-1930s, however, only the Onoda company ventured directly into the colony (Tongyang shiment chushikhoesa 1967: 67).

The Korean operations of the Onoda Cement Company expanded rapidly throughout the 1920s, in close relationship with the colonial government. The Sŭnghori factory expanded its production capacity three times during this decade, in 1923–24, 1927–28, and 1928–30. By 1924, the factory had installed an additional kiln and increased ca-pacity to 150,000 tons/year. At the end of 1930, another kiln was added, and the production capacity increased to 320,000 tons/year, surpassing the production of Onoda's main factory in Japan (Onoda semento kabushiki kaisha 1981: 287–95).

Onoda also constructed a new factory in Ch'ŏnnaeri, near Won-san in South Hamkyŏng province, in 1929. As the Onoda manage-ment was planning the second and third expansions of the Sŭnghori plant in spring 1926, it learned of the Pujŏn hydroelectric power de-velopment planned by a fast-growing new *zaibatsu*, Nihon chissō (Japan Nitrogen Fertilizer Corporation); an estimated 150,000 tons of cement was required for the dam construction alone. At the same time, the Government General informed the managers of the existence of limestone deposits north of Wonsan not far from the Pujŏn River and the Hŭngnam area. Thus, the Onoda management, which was looking for new ventures outside Japan, immediately ap-proved plans for a second factory in colonial Korea (*Andō shōmon-roku*: 97–98).[2]

An engineering team headed by Andō Toyoroku was dispatched from the Sŭnghori plant, and the team chose a site at Ch'ŏnnaeri, Doch'o *myŏn*, Munch'ŏn *kun*, South Hamkyŏng province, in late 1926 after three months of surveying. This site had a good harbor,

---

2. This was an informal pamphlet published by the Onoda Cement Company. Andō, a former manager of the Onoda Sŭnghori plant and the seventh president of the Onoda Cement Company, gave a talk to the business historians who wrote the *Onoda semento hyakunenshi*.

Table 2.2
Cement Sales by Category of Use from the Sŭnghori Plant, 1920–1930, and the Ch'ŏnnaeri (Ch) Plant, 1929–1930
(*metric tons*)

Year	Railways	Electricity	Ports	Roads and bridges	Construction	Miscellaneous	Cement goods	Water utilization	Total
1920	2,764	521	414	1,460	3,862	3,928	1,517	5,594	20,060
1921	3,051	3,344	49	3,469	4,605	12,822	1,359	5,831	34,530
1922	13,438	n/a	218	4,755	7,679	14,180	392	2,838	43,500
1923	12,153	n/a	955	6,852	6,840	10,932	1,751	13,467	52,950
1924	14,270	n/a	709	8,663	7,179	14,105	911	6,603	52,440
1925	11,471	n/a	4,247	13,581	7,116	10,389	587	2,999	50,390
1926	27,741	1,452	2,306	14,521	4,557	9,823	750	17,610	78,760
1927	29,662	17,352	401	16,826	21,117	15,184	942	20,786	122,270
1928	24,368	27,642	2,797	11,640	10,064	37,273	632	14,794	129,210
1929	16,898	20,270	180	7,785	3,585	45,715	150	12,747	107,330
Ch:	8,532	38,446	3,082	2,001	12,726	5,263	473	9,541	80,064
1930	27,908	5,181	355	5,413	7,675	42,830	1,449	10,542	101,353
Ch:	1,469	55,026	5,463	787	n/a	5,518	n/a	9,428	77,691

SOURCE: Onoda semento kabushiki kaisha 1981: 239, 304–5.

Table 2.3
Sales of the Sŭnghori Factory by Regional Destination, 1920–1924
(*metric tons*)

Year	Korea	Japan	Manchuria	China	Taiwan	Total
1920	20,060	n/a	7,970	3,280	n/a	31,310
1921	34,530	1,120	7,390	13,320	2,240	58,600
1922	43,500	n/a	8,520	2,630	n/a	54,650
1923	52,950	320	2,800	n/a	56,070	n/a
1924	52,440	5,420	9,620	1,850	n/a	69,330

SOURCE: Onoda semento kabushiki kaisha 1981: 239.

Table 2.4
Supplies of Cement in Korea, 1922–1931
(*metric tons*)

Year	Domestic supply				Imports (%)		Total (%)	
	Sŭngho	Ch'ŏnnae	Total	(%)				
1922	44,775	—	44,775	(42.2)	61,225	(57.8)	106,000	(100)
1923	52,277	—	52,277	(35.6)	94,440	(64.4)	146,717	(100)
1924	53,627	—	53,627	(56.9)	40,675	(43.1)	94,302	(100)
1925	48,311	—	48,311	(56.8)	36,704	(43.2)	85,015	(100)
1926	77,554	—	77,554	(52.5)	70,172	(47.5)	147,726	(100)
1927	124,165	—	124,165	(59.7)	83,826	(40.3)	207,991	(100)
1928	133,335	—	133,335	(51.3)	126,375	(48.7)	259,710	(100)
1929	109,488	80,428	189,916	(63.2)	110,746	(36.8)	300,662	(100)
1930	104,210	77,942	182,152	(63.1)	106,434	(36.9)	288,586	(100)
1931	107,853	61,460	169,313	(70.2)	71,996	(29.8)	241,309	(100)

SOURCE: Onoda semento kabushiki kaisha 1981: 305.

accessible water resources, and a ready source of energy in a nearby coal mine. A rail line between the Ch'ŏnnaeri plant site and Yongdam Station on the main Hamkyŏng Railway was completed in November 1927. Factory construction was finished within a year. The new plant had a production capacity of 130,000 tons/year. The two Onoda plants could supply 70 percent of the total cement demand of the peninsula by 1930. The combined production of the two plants surpassed production at the main factory in Japan by 1930, and the

Korean branches became the two largest factories among the eight Onoda factories (see Table 2.5).

With the construction of the Ch'ŏnnaeri factory, the Onoda management was trying not only to expand capacity but also to rationalize production. Given the increasing labor shortages in Japan, they anticipated wage increases and eventual labor shortages in the colony as well in the near future. The goal of the production rationalization program was to reduce expenditures on raw materials, fuel, labor, and packing. The Ch'ŏnnaeri plant had more up-to-date machines, including advanced pulverizers, revolving kilns, turbines, and boilers. Paper bags replaced hemp bags to reduce packing costs (Onoda semento kabushiki kaisha 1981: 297).

In the 1930s, the Onoda Company had to consolidate its colonial ventures as expansion in Japan became more difficult when the Japanese government began to control major industries to support the military. The Major Industries Control Law was implemented in Japan in 1931, but the policy was not enforced in Korea and Manchuria until 1937, and the two colonies became major capital investment markets for Japanese industry in these six years. Even though demand for cement increased in Japan shortly after the Manchurian Incident in 1931, cement companies resumed competitive overproduction, which engendered formation of the third cement cartel in 1934 to control production and sales in Japan. The Onoda branch factories in Dalian, Sŭnghori, and Ch'ŏnnaeri were officially separated from the parent company to escape restrictions on expansion by the Major Industries Control Law. In 1932, the Dalian plant was renamed the Kwantungshu Cement Company and the Korean operations became the Chōsen Onoda Cement Company.

Under these circumstances, the Onoda company naturally came to emphasize its ventures in Korea and Manchuria as they became the most promising in terms of not only profits but also market potential. The demand for cement increased rapidly in Korea and Manchuria in the 1930s as these areas industrialized. Approximately half of the company's total profits, helped by cheap electricity and fuel, as well as low labor costs, was generated by the Sŭnghori and Ch'ŏnnaeri factories by 1932 (see Tables 2.6 and 2.7).

Major expansions of the Ch'ŏnnaeri factory in 1934–35 and again in 1935–36 increased its annual production capacity to 400,000 tons by 1937, giving the Ch'ŏnnaeri branch the largest production capac-

Table 2.5
Production Capacity of the Onoda Cement Company,
by Factory, 1923–1932
(*000 metric tons/year*)

Factory	1923	1924	1925	1928	1929	1930	1931	1932
Main plant	129	190	248	248	255	255	268	276
Dalian	136	136	136	250	250	250	250	250
Sŭnghori	50	155	155	220	220	320	320	320
Aichi			60	60	60	70	70	70
Ch'ŏnnaeri				130	130	130	130	130
Yahata					95	95	96	98
Atetsu							100	100
Fujiwara								170
TOTAL	315	481	599	908	1,010	1,120	1,234	1,414

SOURCE: Onoda semento kabushiki kaisha 1981: 297.

Table 2.6
Contribution of Factories in Each Region to
Total Profits of the Onoda Cement Company, 1931–1937
(*in 000 ¥ and as percentage of total profits*)

Year	Japan		Korea		Manchuria		Total	
1931	222	(42.5%)	169	(32.4%)	131	(25.1%)	522	(100%)
1932	193	(21.6)	432	(48.4)	268	(30.0)	893	(100)
1933	534	(35.9)	592	(39.8)	362	(24.3)	1,488	(100)
1934	476	(29.0)	708	(43.1)	458	(27.9)	1.642	(100)
1935	625	(36.0)	795	(45.7)	318	(18.3)	1,738	(100)
1936	665	(40.0)	755	(45.4)	244	(14.6)	1,664	(100)
1937	619	(38.5)	724	(45.0)	266	(16.5)	1,609	(100)

SOURCE: Onoda semento kabushiki kaisha 1981: 366.

ity among all Onoda factories that year. The adoption in the 1936 expansion of the Lepol kiln method, invented in Germany in 1930, halved fuel costs by allowing the Ch'ŏnnaeri factory to use cheap electricity from the Changjin Hydroelectric Power Company, making it the most profitable branch by 1937 (Onoda semento kabushiki kaisha 1981: 361).

Table 2.7
Onoda Cement Company Production
by Area, 1942–1945

Year	Japan (%)	Dalien (%)	Korea (%)	(%)	Total (metric tons)
1942	45.8	25.0	29.2	100	1,796,273
1943	41.9	24.1	34.0	100	1,859,915
1944	34.4	27.8	37.8	100	1,725,156
1945	50.7	32.2	17.1	100	528,234

SOURCE: Onoda semento kabushiki kaisha 1981: 387.

As militarism became more influential in decision-making in the Japanese government, Onoda expanded its business further north in Korea as well as in Manchuria. The company decided to open a third branch factory in Korea, at Komusan, Sŏsang *myŏn*, Puryŏng *kun*, North Hamkyŏng province in 1933, to meet increasing demand in this area, as eastern Manchuria and the northeastern part of Korea developed rapidly following the establishment of the Japanese puppet government in Manchuria. This plant was completed in June 1936, with a production capacity of 150,000 tons/year. Two other factories were set up in Anshan and Quantou to meet demand in Manchuria (Onoda semento kabushiki kaisha 1981: 361).

Other Japanese cement companies started to venture into Korea after formation of the third cement cartel in 1934. In 1935, the Ube Cement Company established a branch factory in Haeju, Hwanghae province. This facility, the Chōsen Cement Company, had a production capacity of 540,000 tons/year. The Asano Cement Company set up a branch factory in Sariwon, Hwanghae province, with a production capacity of 180,000 tons/year in 1936. The fourth branch factory in Korea was established at Sajikri, Samch'ŏk *kun*, Kangwon province in 1937 to supply cement to the southern area of Korea. The completion of the Samch'ŏk factory took almost five years due to difficulties in obtaining machinery and construction materials during the war. The factory was completed in June 1942 with a capacity of 84,000 tons/year. A cement-pulverizing plant was also erected at the Sup'ung Dam construction site on the Yalu River at the special request of the Nihon Chissō leader Noguchi Jun, the Government General of Korea, and the government of Manchukuo for the Joint Yalu River Water Power Development Project (Onoda semento kabushiki kaisha 1981: 392). Thus, six cement factories were in operation in colonial Korea by 1945. The four Onoda factories (not counting the Sup'ung Dam plant) supplied 60 percent of the total consumption in Korea.

The Japanese government's decision not to designate the cement industry an essential wartime industry in 1937 restricted its expansion. Production at Onoda factories throughout the Japanese empire declined gradually after 1939, when output peaked at approximately 1.9 million tons that year. The decline was caused by shortages of coal, other raw materials, and skilled laborers, as well as the difficulties of transporting materials during the war (Onoda semento kabushiki kaisha 1981: 387). The Association of Cement Industries was created in 1940 to control the production and sales of cement in Japan. In 1941 all industries were combined into 25 major industrial groups, and many small-and medium-scale companies were merged with larger businesses as the economy of Japan and the Japanese empire was mobilized for war in China and in the Pacific. In December 1943, the government and military assumed control of 683 major industrial companies under the Munitions Company Law (Onoda semento kabushiki kaisha 1981: 367–368). Onoda's colonial ventures in Korea and Manchuria, however, continued to grow between 1937 and 1945 because of demands from war-related industries and construction in the area. By the end of World War II, the Onoda Company controlled 29 branch factories: 10 in Japan, 7 in Manchuria, 5 in Korea, and 7 in other locations (see Map 1, p. xvi). In April 1944, the Onoda Company was designated a war-related company and began producing alumina clinker by crushing alum, which was used as a substitute for bauxite from Southeast Asia, the supply of which had been cut off since 1941. In December 1944, the Sŭnghori, Ch'ŏnnaeri, Komusan, and Samch'ŏk factories were similarly designated and also started to produce alumina clinker with their limestone pulverizers (Onoda semento kabushiki kaisha 1981: 389).

Labor Relations in the Onoda Sŭnghori Factory

Organization

At the time the Onoda Cement Company established its Sŭnghori branch factory in 1919, three types of factories could be distinguished in colonial Korea in terms of manufacturing technology. The first was the typical colonial pattern of multi-worker units engaged in the simple processing of raw materials. Workers in this type of factory did not need particular skills. More sophisticated finishing work was usually done in the metropolitan country. In colonial Korea, rice processing, silk reeling, cotton ginning, leather processing, and metal refining fell into this category. The second type comprised factories with somewhat more developed technology. Some skilled workers were needed to operate this kind of factory, although the majority of workers were unskilled. Most plants of this type used simple technology to provide services such as printing or to produce daily necessities for the domestic market, such as foodstuffs, tobacco, socks, rubber shoes, bricks, ceramics, and many other miscellaneous commodities. The third type consisted of up-to-date, large-scale factories with modern industrial technology operated by steam or electric power and producing industrial products. Highly trained engineers, technicians, and machine operators were required to run this type of factory. Typical industries in this category are cotton textiles, chemicals, metals, machine and machine tools, gas and electricity utilities, sugar, cement, and breweries.

Each type of factory developed its own methods of recruiting, training, and organizing its labor force. Probably only the managers of the third type of factories were concerned with labor management in the modern sense of training and maintaining a qualified labor force in the workshop, because it was important for the productivity of this type of factory. The operation of the first and second types of factory was not as dependent on the literacy, skills, and commitment of workers, and unskilled hands were always available in the colonial surplus labor market. Until the late 1920s, all the factories in colonial Korea, except several dozen large, capital-intensive, Japanese-owned factories and two Korean-owned factories, the Kyŏngsŏng Spinning and Weaving Company and the Chosŏn Silk Reeling Company, established during the World War I economic boom between 1917 and 1919, belonged to the first and second types.

By the time the Onoda Cement Company, a representative of the third type of factories, established the Sŭnghori plant in 1919, it already had a highly developed labor-management system formulated through 38 years of management experience in the main company since 1881 and 12 years of experience managing Chinese workers at its Dalian plant since 1907. Labor management at the Sŭnghori factory was the most advanced in the colony in the 1920s, a time when both Korean and Japanese employers were free to choose the pattern of work organization they desired. In principle the Sŭnghori managers applied the main company's labor-management regulations to their Japanese workers, but in reality they modified these regulations in managing both Korean and Japanese workers in the colonial situation.

A pamphlet with the regulations for workers (*Shokkō kisoku*) was given to each new recruit. The pamphlets were first printed by the main company in 1912, 30 years after the company's formation, and were quite advanced. The regulations included details on factory life such as the internal hierarchy of workers; rules and qualifications for entry, leave, promotion, leaves of absence and retirement; instructions for daily duties; explanation of policies on wages and other forms of compensation; and fines and punishments. Regulations on relief in cases of injury, sickness, and death while on duty were added to the *Shokkō kisoku* following implementation of the Factory Law in 1916 in Japan, which made companies responsible for compensating workers suffering from work-related injuries or illnesses. These regulations were applied to Korean workers at the Sŭnghori factory in modified form because the Factory Law was applied only in Japan and thereby only applicable to Japanese workers at the Sŭnghori factory (interview with Andō Toyoroku).

Given the hierarchical juxtaposition of Japanese and Korean workers at the Sŭnghori plant, the management of the factory developed a colonial pattern. The organization of the plant basically followed the same form as that in the main factory. It also adopted the organizational pattern used successfully for ten years at the Dalian factory. Heading the plant were four or five executives sent from the head office. Below them were the white-collar staff of the company, who were divided into three departments: Engineering, Accounting, and Sales.

Engineers, who were university graduates, planned and supervised the manufacturing process at the factory. The number of engineers at the Sŭnghori factory increased from 8 in 1917 to 11 in 1919 to 16 in 1923 and to 24 in 1929, remaining at that level until the 1930s. By 1929, five Korean engineers, out of the total of 24, were working in the plant. Kim Won-Pong, hired in 1923, was the first Korean engineer. In 1927 and 1928, two more Koreans, Ch'oe Hwang and Im Myŏng, entered the Engineering Department. Two Korean engineers were transferred to the Ch'ŏnnaeri factory in 1930. In the 1930s, the number of Korean engineers remained steady at six or seven, but increased markedly after 1941. A few of these Korean engineers worked in the Onoda factories more than 20 years (*Onoda shokuinroku* 1923-45).

The Accounting and Sales departments were composed of university graduates who oversaw administrative matters in these areas. In 1920, these two departments had six Japanese clerks and one Korean clerk, an accountant who specialized in calculating Korean workers' pay. This part of the staff grew to 20 members by 1927 and remained the same size, although factory production and sales expanded rapidly in the next two decades (*Kokajō* 1920). In addition, there was a five-to-seven member intermediary team of supervisors in the Security Section to handle general affairs for the workers, such as recruitment, dismissal, morale, evaluations of work performance, reports to the engineers, and aid for workers (*Shokkō kisoku*).

All the Japanese white-collar office workers and engineers in these three departments were brought from the main office in Japan. Most of them were recent graduates of the commercial or engineering faculties of prestigious universities (*Andō shōmonroku*, p. 20). Skilled Japanese workers, who were responsible for the principal tasks in the manufacturing process, were also transferred from the main factory. These workers were loyal Onoda men, usually in their late twenties or early thirties; most of them had had some elementary schooling and at least five years of work experience at the main factory.[3]

Koreans were recruited in their late teens or early twenties so that older Japanese skilled workers could train and supervise them with fewer conflicts. Older men were seldom recruited. The age structure of the Japanese and Korean workers in the Sŭnghori plant in November 1921 shows this policy clearly (see Table 2.8).

In the first five years of the plant's operation, some of these Korean recruits were sent to the main factory in Japan for intensive training; they were treated as a select Korean group who could play an intermediate role between the Japanese and Korean workers. The managers of the Sŭnghori factory initially selected 21 Korean youths who could speak Japanese, as well as two Japanese youths, and sent them to the main factory for six months' training in three groups

3. Based on an unpublished manuscript written by Haruhito Takeda, who wrote the section on the years 1914–23 in Onoda semento kabushiki kaisha 1981. He is now teaching in the Faculty of Economics, Tokyo University. I deeply appreciate his guidance.

Table 2.8
Age Structure of Japanese and
Korean Workers at the
Sŭnghori Plant, 1921

Age	Japanese	Korean
< 14	0	1
15–19	6	130
20–24	7	192
25–29	22	141
30–34	31	97
35–39	20	44
40–44	11	5
45–49	7	3
50–54	2	1
55–59	1	0
TOTAL	107	614

SOURCE: *Kokajō* 1921, first half.

between January and June, June and November, and August and November, 1919. The Korean workers were paid less than Japanese skilled workers and were useful as a liaison group between Japanese managers and skilled workers on the one hand and Korean workers who could not understand Japanese on the other hand (interview with Andō Toyoroku).

Overall, upper management and shop floor workers coexisted, with no direct contact. Physically, the factory consisted of two separate sections: an office building for white-collar workers (*shokuin*), and factory workshops, where the blue-collar workers (*shokkō*) worked. *Shokuin* and *shokkō* were clearly separated by workplace, kind of work, and treatment. Only the engineers, who supervised the production process, and bureau and section chiefs moved back and forth between office and factory (interviews with Andō Toyoroku, Oh Pyŏng-Ho, and Lee Kŭn-T'ae).[4]

The production process consisted of four steps: (1) quarrying of the limestone; (2) pulverizing of the limestone and the mixing of it with clay, iron ore, stone, and sand; (3) baking of the mixture in a

4. All three were office workers and were ignorant of the details of factory workers' lives.

kiln and precipitation of it into semi-processed clinker; and (4) the addition of gypsum to the clinker and its repulverization into cement. The factory workshop was divided by function. The Engineering Department had four major bureaus (*bu*): Manufacturing, Maintenance, Packing and Shipping, and General Affairs. Each bureau was further subdivided into a number of sections (*kakari*). The main bureau, the Manufacturing Bureau, was divided into nine sections that controlled the steps in the production process: the Turbine, Boiler, Electricity, Coal, Clay, Mixing, Limestone, Kiln, and Cement sections. The Maintenance Bureau controlled eight sections: Lathe, Casting, Carpentry, Wooden Pattern, Finishing, Tin Plate, Tile, and Bricks. The General Affairs Bureau was composed of seven sections: Waterworks, Analysis, Steam Boiler Making, Storage, General Engineering Affairs, Security, and Preparatory Engineering. Besides the workers inside the factory, there were workers engaged in support activities, including miners, porters, and construction workers. These workers were recruited separately by the head of a temporary, ad hoc bureau set up for such tasks as collection of limestone, transportation of materials and finished goods, and expansion and additional construction work (*Kokajō*, Ch'ŏnnaeri section, 1927, second half).

The workers were divided into three categories based upon skill level and seniority: novice (*teigō*), apprentice (*minarai*), and regular workers (*honshokkō*). Newly recruited workers remained novices for one year. With the permission of his supervisor and approval by the company, a worker could then advance to a two-year apprenticeship. After three years of experience to gain a comprehensive understanding of the work he did and with the approval of his superior, usually a section chief, a worker became a skilled regular worker (*Shokkō kisoku*, p. 14).

Each section was headed by a chief who reported to the head of the Engineering Bureau. Each chief was a veteran skilled worker capable of supervising other workers as well as maintaining the machines and equipment in his section. He was also responsible for certain personnel matters in the section, including illnesses, injuries, retirement, leaves of absence from work due to mourning, tardiness, and so forth. In reality, the section chiefs exercised power and discipline in the workshop instead of the more remote upper-management group. There was also a deputy section chief to take over the responsibilities of the section chief when the chief was absent.

In addition, there were two shift foremen (one each for the night and the early morning shift) in each section of the Manufacturing Bureau, which instituted a twenty-four-hour, three-shift system beginning in November 1920 to replace the previous ten-and-a-half hour, two-shift system. The shifts ran from 7:00 A.M.–3:00 P.M., 3:00 P.M.–11:00 P.M., and 11:00 P.M.–7:00 A.M. The outgoing shift would brief the incoming shift foremen on what had been done during their shift and what was to be done during the next shift (*Shokkō kisoku*, p. 20; Andō interview).

The three-shift system was first introduced in the Kiln Section of the main Onoda factory in 1899 and was later extended to the entire Manufacturing Bureau by 1914 as a means of increasing production without increasing production costs. As the labor shortage increased and wages rose during and after World War I, this system was commonly implemented in large plants in Japan to raise labor productivity. Thus, even though the average daily wage of Korean workers rose from ¥0.55 to ¥0.86 Yen (compared with ¥1.72 to ¥2.40 for Japanese workers) after November 1920 because the previous wage had been given for a 10.5-hour day, productivity increased more than enough to cover the cost of the wage increase. Workers were less tired, and the accident rate for machine operators dropped (Onoda semento kabushiki kaisha 1951: 520).

Section chiefs and shift leaders, the mid-level managers between the workers and upper management, disciplined and trained the workforce through daily contact and supervision. The Onoda management structured its workforce so that this group of older skilled Japanese workers could train young Korean recruits in the operations of machinery and equipment in the factory. These skilled Japanese workers in supervisory positions received the highest daily wages in their respective sections. In addition, Japanese section chiefs in colonial factories received special post and overseas allowances that raised their pay 40 percent above that of skilled workers in the main factory (*Andō shōmonroku*, pp. 78–79). This labor-management pattern was characteristic of the Dalian, Sŭnghori, and other colonial branch factories. The managers did train local colonial recruits, but they brought in skilled Japanese workers as lower-level managers and used them to control and manage the colonial workers.

To be sure, these Japanese supervisors could make the workers' lives miserable. Often racial prejudice and tension between Japanese section chiefs and Korean workers intensified the instability and hostility of workshops, docks, construction sites, and mines in the colony. Only two labor disputes occurred between 1920 and 1941 at the Onoda plants in Korea, however. Why this was the case and why labor disputes were more frequent in Korean-owned small workshops are examined below in the section on labor responses.

The size of the workforce at the Sŭnghori factory did not change much between 1920 and 1941 (the period for which data are available). As Table 2.9 shows, the factory employed 30–50 white-collar office workers and approximately 700 factory workers. The ratio of Japanese factory workers to total workers ranged between 13 and 22 percent. In June 1920, 86 of the total 633 shokkō were Japanese; all of them were skilled workers specially selected and transferred from the main factory to fill positions as section chiefs, deputy chiefs, or shift foremen in the new factory. The 547 Korean workers employed in June 1920 included 21 workers who had returned from training as machine operators and barrel makers at the main factory in 1919 and could be regarded as skilled workers.

When the company started the three-shift system in late 1920, around 200 new workers were hired, but within five years the number of workers gradually stabilized at 650–700 and generally remained at that level until the early 1940s. Considering the productivity increase from 60,000 tons/year in 1920 to 320,000 tons/year in 1931, and the threefold expansion of factory facilities in this period, the static nature of the number of employees suggests a rationalizing effort by management to raise labor productivity. Management also controlled the size of the workforce by hiring temporary workers for short-term needs. The sudden increase in the number of workers to 982 (193 Japanese and 789 Koreans) in 1930 resulted from hiring workers temporarily for the factory expansion in 1930 (*Kokajō* 1930, second half). By 1931 the number of workers had dropped to 790, and by 1932 it had returned to its customary level (see Table 2.9). Even though we do not have data on the number of regular Korean workers until 1933, Table 2.9 shows that the Sŭnghori factory had 409 regular workers (62.4 percent of total workers) out of a total of 655 workers in the plant by 1933. Among the regular workers, almost three-quarters were Korean (108 Japanese; 301 Korean); these numbers imply that the company had been successful in training and keeping a substantial number of Korean skilled workers after a decade of operations.

The ethnic composition of the workforce changed in various ways after 1935. In general, the number of Japanese workers rose until 1935 and decreased rapidly thereafter, from 158 (21.5 percent) in 1935 to 123 (16.8 percent) in 1939 and 83 (12 percent) in 1942, even though the number of workers in this period was generally stable at 650–700. The decrease in the number of Japanese workers was equally distributed across all three categories of employees (regular workers, apprentices, novices). Conversely the total number of Korean workers increased steadily during this period, most notably in the apprentice and novice categories. In contrast, the drop in the number of regular Korean workers from 313 in 1935 to 248 in 1942 implies high labor turnover among Korean skilled workers in this period.

The drop in the number of Japanese workers was, according to company records, due mainly to the drafting of Japanese youths into the military after 1938, which caused a serious shortage of skilled workers throughout the Japanese empire. This also explains why Korean skilled workers left the Sŭnghori factory in increasing numbers as the demand for skilled workers increased rapidly after the industrial boom of the mid-1930s and accelerated after the drafting of Japanese skilled workers into the Imperial Army. In the case of the cement industry, the new factories set up in Haeju and Sariwon in the mid-1930s competitively recruited skilled laborers by offering better wages and other benefits. This accelerated the labor turnover rate despite government attempts to control it. The Sŭnghori factory also sent many skilled workers to the new Onoda branch factories at Komusan, Samch'ŏk, and the Yalu River. The Japanese monopoly over supervisory positions started to break down during the war, and important changes in worker composition occurred in the factory (see Chapter 3).

Table 2.9
Categories of Workers and Wages at the Sünghori Plant, 1920–1942
(data shown only when available)

| Year | White-collar workers | | Blue-collar workers | | | Japanese workers | | | Korean workers | | | Daily wages (¥) | | | Attendance rate (%) |
	Total	Korean	Japanese*	Korean	Total	Regular workers	Apprentices	Novices	Regular workers	Apprentices	Novices	Japanese	Korean	Average	
1920/6			86 (14)	547	633										
1920/10	22		110 (14)	673	783							1.72	0.55	0.715	90
1920/11			107 (13)	716	823							2.40	0.86	1.07	94
1921			107 (15)	614	721							2.26	0.86	1.07	90
1922			103 (17)	490	593							2.25	0.87	1.11	93
1923	31	1	101 (18)	477	578							2.27	0.88		95
1924	31	1	107 (18)	503	610							2.29	0.86	1.11	94
1925	35	1	103 (15)	569	672							2.27	0.86	1.09	
1926	37	1										2.28	0.84	1.08	
1927	52	2										2.27	0.82	1.06	95
1928	39	3										2.22	0.80	1.04	95
1929	44	5										2.29	0.78	1.01	
1930	44	5	193 (19)	789	982							2.18	0.84	1.06	95
1931	44	5	161 (20)	629	790							2.15	0.81	1.07	
1932	44	5	138 (20)	565	703							2.27	0.84	1.13	
1933	41	3	137 (21)	518	655	108	16	13	301	162	55	2.30	0.85	1.14	96
1934	38	6	143 (22)	495	638							2.30	0.88	1.20	
1935	35	4	158 (22)	542	700	101	12	45	313	88	141	2.32	0.88	1.19	97

Year														
1936	38	3	149 (21)	547	696							2.33	0.87	1.21
1937	34	3	128 (19)	533	661							2.46	0.92	1.26
1938	51	6	131 (19)	554	685	92	19	20	255	111	188	2.65	0.99	1.33	96
1939	48		123 (17)	605	728							2.75	1.03	1.37
1940	48		108 (17)	582	690							2.95	1.10	1.40
1941	46		92 (13)	596	688	62	14	16	220	149	227	3.18	1.26	1.53
1942	40		83 (12)	599	682	66	7	10	248	159	192	3.41	1.38	1.66

* Figures in parentheses indicate the percentage of Japanese blue-collar workers at the factory.

NOTE: No data are available for 1943–45.

SOURCES: *Kokajō* 1920, first half; 1920, 1923, 1924, 1925, 1926, 1927, 1928, 1929, 1930, 1933, 1935, 1938, 1941, 1942, second halves.

Sources of Labor for the Sŭnghori Factory

Traditional, clan-oriented community life in Korea declined rapidly in the 1920s as the capitalistic market economy and other modern systems penetrated deeply into rural areas. As rice, for example, became the major cash crop, rural work-sharing customs, such as the *dure* and *p'um-assi* systems, were fast replaced by contract labor systems. Much of labor on the rice crop came to be performed by agricultural workers (*mŏsŭm*) organized and controlled by subcontractors in the *kochi* system of rural contract labor.

Similarly, transitional labor practices began emerging in the nonagricultural sectors in the late Chosŏn period; examples are the new groups of labor recruiters and contractors called *sipchang* in the day-labor markets for dockworkers and construction laborers and *tŏkdae* among miners. The slow and gradual development of these systems is a sign of resistance and the continuing life of traditional, hierarchically based systems of human relations in the labor market during this transitional period. The arrangements in these systems were typically based on such traditional values of interpersonal relations as loyalty, personal obligations, and hierarchical relations rather than on equality, class consciousness, or legal contracts. Age and seniority in terms of work experience and membership in the group were important determinants of status in the group, because of the lack of modern-style standards of work efficiency, occupational categories, or job grades.

Such patterns were widespread in the early stages of industrialization not only in East Asia but also in the West. Similar transitional labor relations are Japan's *oyagata* system and the Manchurian and Chinese "coolie head" system. In modern factories, however, the disciplining and managing of workers were developed further through direct, formal, and contractual management techniques. The experiences of workers at the Sŭnghori factory illustrate the differences between the transitional practices in the day labor market and the new system based on rigorous rules in a modern factory, which were themselves a careful mixture of traditional Asian values of hierarchical interpersonal relations and Western-style contractual work relations. Colonialism further complicated the labor situation. The next three sections examine the intertwining of the larger historical forces of colonialism, nationalism, modernity, and even communism in the experience of rural youth entering a modern factory.

Unlike textile factories in urban areas that hired a special recruiter to gather young females from rural households, or the huge construction projects in North and South Hamkyŏng provinces that needed tens of thousands of male workers all at once during the late 1920s, the managers of the Sŭnghori factory did not encounter problems recruiting young Korean males from nearby rural areas to work at the factory until after 1937. In 1917, the news of employment opportunities at the factory spread rapidly among the work-hungry rural population. By 1924, Sŭnghori had become a factory town with a population of more than 5,000 drawn from throughout South P'yŏngan province.

According to the recollections of Andō Toyoroku (pers. interview), recruitment for work at the plant was initially accomplished by hiring the smarter-looking day laborers who had worked on construction of the plant during 1917–19. In the early 1920s, sons or younger relatives of workers were hired after simple interviews. From the managers' point of view, especially since they had a guaranteed supply of skilled workers from the main company in Japan, this hiring pattern was economical since there was no formal network for collecting information on potential employees at a distance. The hiring of acquaintances or relatives of existing workers also aided in labor control by strengthening the human ties that made quitting harder for the new recruits. Primary schooling was highly valued, but it was not a prerequisite for hiring.

Most of the recruits, the majority of whom were teenage boys, were eager to learn and readily adapted themselves to the routines and regulations of factory life. Even though most of these new employees had never seen a factory or even cement before, they understood that obtaining work experience and useful skills in a modern factory could be a valuable asset for their economic independence and advancement in the future. This attitude probably helped them overcome any shock and fear they may have felt in the beginning (Andō interview).

One special characteristic of the Sŭnghori factory was that its parent company had 38 years of experience in modern cement manufacturing and company management. It had developed highly sophisticated and detailed labor-management methods for securing loyalty and stability in its workforce. Modern factories need full-time, skilled workers year-round due to their advanced production process. It was essential for profitable operations at the factory that the workforce be stable and disciplined, and this could be accomplished only by careful training and management.

The introduction of more rational labor-management relations at the Sŭnghori factory had two effects on Korean labor relations. On the one hand, the Onoda managers were able to upgrade the quality of Sŭnghori workers in a brief amount of time. The Sŭnghori factory had an advanced and committed management compared to that found in small- and medium-size factories in Korea at the time, which followed arbitrary, nonprofessional labor-management methods. A new worker was thoroughly disciplined and transformed into a full-time factory worker instead of remaining a day laborer or seasonal, half-agricultural/half-industrial worker as was the case in construction or mining. In contrast to the experience of the overwhelming numbers of Koreans in the day labor market in the 1920s, those who found employment at the Sŭnghori factory were in a fortunate position.

On the other hand, because Japanese skilled workers surged to the colonial factories, traditional Korean handicraft artisans or experienced workers were pushed out to underemployment in the informal sector or complete unemployment. This discontinuity in human resources happened throughout the modern sector and resulted in a segmentation of the labor market in colonial Korea. Sŏn Chae-Won (1996: 36–38) has pointed out that this situation resulted in a fierce competition among Korean workers in their much more segmented and compartmentalized labor market.

Most of the workers at the Sŭnghori factory came from within South P'yŏgan province until the 1930s, further proof of the intraprovincial nature of population migration at the time, which we saw in Chapter 1. A late 1925 survey by the Engineering Department revealed that 190 (39 percent) of the 483 Korean workers who responded to the survey came from Sŭnghori and Nŭngsŏngri, a village located next to Sŭnghori (see Map 2). Another 208 (43 percent) were intraprovincial migrants from villages in South P'yŏngan province who had settled in a new village in front of the factory (see Table 2.10). Thus, five years after the opening of the factory, 82 percent of the Korean workers at the Sŭnghori factory were from South P'yŏngan province.

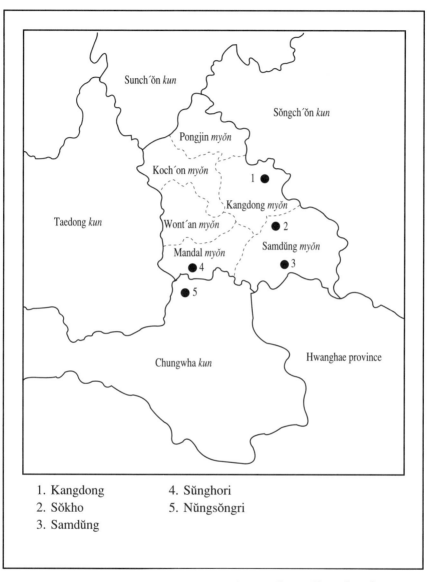

Sunch´ŏn *kun*

Sŏngch´ŏn *kun*

Pongjin *myŏn*

Koch´on *myŏn*

1 ●

Kangdong *myŏn*

Taedong *kun*

Wont´an *myŏn*

● 2

Samdŭng *myŏn*

Mandal *myŏn*

● 4

● 3

● 5

Chungwha *kun*

Hwanghae province

1. Kangdong   4. Sŭnghori
2. Sŏkho   5. Nŭngsŏngri
3. Samdŭng

Map 2 Sŭnghori, Kangdong *kun*, and Nŭngsŏngri, Chunghwa *kun*

Table 2.10
Geographical Origins of Korean Workers
at the Sŭnghori Plant, 1925

Geographical origin	Number	Percentage of total
Sŭnghori	147	30%
Nŭngsŏngri	43	9
South P'yŏngan province	208	43
Other provinces	85	18
TOTAL	483	100

SOURCE: *Kokajō* 1925, second half.

The pattern of intraprovincial migration of factory workers did not change much throughout the colonial period. A 1942 survey of the origins of workers at selected large-scale factories and mines undertaken by the Chōsen shokusan ginkō (Chōsen Industrial Bank) found the same pattern. This further confirms the limited nature of long-distance, interprovincial migration in Korea until the late 1930s. The geographical origins of Sŭnghori workers had become somewhat more heterogeneous by the early 1930s, but the majority were still from South and North P'yŏngan provinces. According to the Chōsen Industrial Bank (*Shokugin chōsa geppō*, Feb. 1942: 19) survey, the majority of workers in the surveyed factories were from nearby rural areas, and only a small minority were from outside the province, especially migrants from the southern provinces.

The Sŭnghori factory site was popular because it was a place where work was always available and a full-time worker could afford rice and beef and live in a heated room or house, all of which were rare in other areas. According to Kye Chi-P'ung (1915–91; pers. interview), a former Sŭnghori factory worker, Sŭnghori was famous as a "place for labor" (*nodong p'an*) among the work-seeking males of South P'yŏngan province in the late 1920s and early 1930s due to the continuous expansion of the factory in this period. Kye Chi-P'ung described himself as a quick-tempered, frank, and active youth from South P'yŏngan province who fit in well with his smart and aggressive Korean coworkers. Many such men and youths, including his father, had moved into the area from throughout South P'yŏngan province looking for work. Kye's father moved to Sŭnghori in 1926 with his wife and his then ten-year-old son and worked as a carpenter. Kye graduated from the Sŭngho common school in 1931 at the age of 16 and worked in the Manufacturing Bureau of the Sŭnghori factory during 1932–34.

Educational Level of the Workers

The teenage boys who formed the pool of recruits were neither graduates of a modern school system nor illiterates. They were for the most part frustrated rural youths who yearned for modern learning as a means of self-advancement in a colonial society in which modern education was limited to the colonizers and a tiny minority of the colonized. A modern school education, even primary schooling, and Japanese-language ability, were important assets for a Korean youth seeking a job in the modern sector. An elementary school diploma, or sometimes only Japanese-language ability, could qualify a teenage boy for a job as a clerk in local government, a clerical position in a Japanese store, or a local police post. And these jobs increased the status not only of the young man himself but also of his family. The father of a man who fled to the city in his early teens and returned to his country hometown as a policeman after several years of clerical work in a Japanese pastry shop, for example, was able to negotiate a favorable tenancy contract (*Tonga ilbo*, Nov. 1, 1924: 3).

It became clear to the colonial subjects that their social status could be enhanced through modern education and the new kinds of jobs in urban areas. Landlords eagerly sent their sons, occasionally even their daughters, to post-primary or post-secondary schools in major cities in Korea, particularly Kyŏngsŏng, and in Japan. Modern education was pursued even in the reformed version of the *sŏdang* (the traditional small schools for study of the Chinese classics), whose numbers increased radically in the 1910s and 1920s. Given the colonial government's total neglect of general education for Koreans, the modernized *sŏdang* helped meet the increasing demand for education among commoners, who would not have sought an education in the Chosŏn period (*Kokajō* 1927, second half; Ōno 1936: 26–27). In 1919, the Japanese literacy rate was 1.6 percent among Korean males and 0.2 percent among females. Only 340,000 Koreans out of a total population of 17.1 million understood Japanese by this point.[5]

5. The Japanese literacy rate grew from 0.6 percent in 1913 to 1.6 percent (340,000 people) in 1919 to 13.9 percent in 1939 to 15.6 percent (3.57 million

Unfortunately, data on the Korean literacy rate are not available. As Table 2.11 shows, the numbers of common (primary) schools increased from 355 in 1912 to 517 in 1919, with enrollments reaching just under 90,000 students. Nevertheless, even this number of schools meant less than one school per each four *myŏn*, and a primary-school education was available to only 3.9 percent of school-age children.

Even though the March First movement of 1919 ended in failure, it had far-reaching consequences. Among Koreans, it aroused national consciousness and presented them with practical strategies for achieving national independence. The movement also shook up the colonial government, which replaced its harsh military policies with more civilized and sophisticated "cultural" policies. The older generation came to realize that national independence would only be achieved by future generations with modern knowledge and with the ability to utilize modern industrial power. This realization led to the promotion of elementary schooling, and entrance into elementary schools became very competitive despite an increase in the number of schools after the new Educational Law of 1921. The age of elementary school students ranged from seven years to the late teens, reflecting both the zeal for education and acquisition of Japanese-language skills and the miserable state of educational facilities. Many *sŏdang* graduates went on to common schools, especially for Japanese studies and modern elementary school subjects (Ōno 1936: 26–27). The educational situation before the 1930s was one reason many Koreans felt alienated. They had heard of modernity but never experienced it in reality. Colonial modernity evolved with a painful time lag and a sense of "in-betweenness," to use Homi Bhabha's term.

It is not surprising that in 1922 over 80 percent of factory workers in the peninsula had no modern schooling. This is understandable given the low quality of labor demanded by industry, which was still dominated by small-scale production and unsophisticated management at the beginning of the 1920s. The first official factory survey was conducted by the Saitō government in 1922, and the results were published as the *Kaisha oyobi kōjō ni okeru rōdōsha chōsa* (A survey on workers employed in companies and factories) in 1923. Ac-

people) in 1940 (Ōno 1936: 72–73; Chōsen sōtokufu, Gakumukyoku 1941: 17–20).

Table 2.11
Modern Educational Facilities in Korea, 1912 and 1919

Type of school	1912 Schools	1912 Students	1919 Schools	1919 Students
Common schools	355(25)	44,638	517(33)	89,288
Higher common schools	3	917	12	3,841
Students abroad		550		678
Special schools	1	93	6	585
Vocational schools	19	1,456	22	2,034
Sŏdang	16,540	141,604	23,556	268,607

SOURCE: Ōnō 1936: 68.

Table 2.12
Educational Background of Factory and
Mineworkers in Korea, July 1922

Level	Number	Percentage of total
No schooling	25,192	59.0%
Sŏdang training	9,351	22.0
Common school dropouts	3,456	7.6
Common school graduates	4,446	10.0
Higher common school dropouts	330	0.7
Higher common school graduates	148	0.3
TOTAL	42,923	100.0

SOURCE: Chōsen sōtokufu, Shakaika 1923: 19.

cording to this survey (see Table 2.12), 57 percent of workers (approximately 42,000 were factory workers) in factories and mines that employed more than ten workers had no formal schooling at all, and 24 percent had only some *sŏdang* training. Some 18 percent had attended common schools, and of these only 10.3 percent (4,969) had graduated (Chōsen sōtokufu, Shakaika 1923: 19). The educational picture for South P'yŏngan province was not much different from the national pattern, except for the much higher ratio of *sŏdang* trainees (see Table 2.13). Common school graduates or dropouts constituted a minority of the workers, both nationwide and in South P'yŏngan province (approximately 17–19 percent).

Table 2.13
Educational Background of Factory and
Mineworkers in South P'yŏngan Province, July 1922

Level	Number	Percentage of total
No schooling	2,402	46.0%
Sŏdang training	1,892	37.0
Common school dropouts	432	8.0
Common school graduates	396	8.0
Higher common school dropouts	33	0.6
Higher common school graduates	21	0.4
TOTAL	5,176	100.0

SOURCE: Chōsen sōtokufu, Shakaika 1923: 19.

Six official statistical surveys, in addition to the census data published in 1930 and 1940 by the Government General, contain material on factory and mining workers: *Kaisha oyobi kōjō ni okeru rōdōsha no chōsa* (Survey of workers in companies and factories; Chōsen sōtokufu, Shakaika 1923), *Chōsen ni okeru rōdōsha sū oyobi bumpu jōtai* (The number and distribution of workers in Korea; Chōsen sōtokufu, Tetsudō kyōkai 1929), *Kōjō oyobi kōzan ni okeru rōdō jōkyō chōsa* (Survey of working conditions in factories and mines; Chōsen sōtokufu, Shakaika, 1933), *Chōsenjin shokkō ni kansuru ichi kōsatsu* (Investigation of Korean factory workers; Chōsen shōkō kaigishō 1936), *Keijō ni okeru kōjō chōsa* (Survey of factories in Seoul; Keijō shōkō kaigishō 1943), and *Chōsen rōdō gijutsu tōkei chōsa hōkoku* (Results of the statistical survey of Korean laborers and technicians; Chōsen sōtokufu, Rōmu kyōkai, 1941, 1942, 1943). An analysis of these surveys shows that the pattern of higher literacy among male workers in large-scale, heavy industries such as oil refineries, ironworks, chemical plants, ceramics factories, and railway machine shops continued until the end of the colonial period; this is a general pattern in all industrializing societies. Most of the common school graduates or dropouts were concentrated in the machine and machine tools, chemical, and metal industries, which required skilled male workers. The majority of small-scale, light industries such as textiles, rice milling, match making, food processing, and tobacco probably did not employ many common school graduates but instead depended heavily on cheaper, unskilled female laborers. According to the 1942 *Chōsen rōdō gijutsu tōkei chōsa hōkoku*, good physical condition and a personal recommendation remained basic considerations in the hiring process, except for several specific skilled fields in large-scale industries (*Shokugin chōsa geppō*, Feb. 1942: 22).

Although the low educational level of workers did not cause serious problems in most large Japanese factories, the educational level of workers increased gradually in such industries as the need for skilled Korean workers increased during the mid-1930s wartime industrial growth. The colonial government had to revise the educational law hurriedly twice, in 1938 and 1940, to meet the urgent demand for educated skilled workers (*Shokugin chōsa geppō*, May 1944: 113: see also Chapter 3).

When the Sŭnghori factory was built in 1919, educational facilities were as lacking in Kangdong *kun* as elsewhere in colonial Korea at the time. Mandal *myŏn* had only one private common school. Two public common schools existed in other *myŏn* in Kangdong *kun*, which had a population of 56,396 by 1925. The Samdŭng Public Common School in Samdŭng *myŏn*, the first modern school in the area, was first established in 1901 under the Elementary School Law. The Kangdong Public Common School in Kangdong *myŏn* was established in 1911 under the new policy of one common school in each *kun* (P'yŏngan namdoch'ŏng 1975: 1105). Two other private schools in addition to the one in Mandal *myŏn* were set up by Korean educators during the Protectorate period when leaders of Korean communities turned desperately to education and publication as the last hope to regain national independence and power. Basing themselves on the strong church organization in the area, Presbyterian missionaries as well as converted Korean Presbyterians in the P'yŏngan and Hwanghae areas were very active in this educational enlightenment movement between 1895 and 1910 under the leadership of elites such as Yun Ch'i-Ho, An Ch'ang-Ho, and Lee Sŭng-Hun (Min 1974: 204–14).

Given the lack of formal education in Kangdong *kun*, the management of the Sŭnghori factory could not require primary schooling as a basic condition for employment. Thus, recruitment at the Sŭnghori factory emphasized educational qualifications less than good physical condition, common sense, and reliable personal recommendations. Indeed, many sections within the factory required unskilled work, for example, the Waterworks Section or the Storage

Section in the General Affairs Bureau or the Packing, Barrel-making, and Shipping sections in the Packing and Shipping Bureau. There were, however, jobs that required some limited technical skills, and these positions were filled by common school graduates based on an entrance examination. Basically, all important production tasks and supervisory jobs were filled by skilled Japanese workers, most of whom had graduated from elementary schools in Japan.

The quality of recruits seemed to improve gradually in the Sŭnghori factory during the 1920s following establishment of the Sŭngho Common School for Korean children in 1924. As Sŭnghori's population increased to approximately a thousand households, or about 5,000 people by 1924, the need for a common school for children and teenage boys in the area became urgent. In May 1926, the Sŭngho Higher Common School, a secondary institution, was established for Korean and Japanese students in the area. At a time when the colonial government was barely fulfilling its plan to set up one school in every three *myŏn* (there were 2,521 *myŏn*s in the peninsula) by 1922, the presence of two schools in Sŭnghori was exceptional (Mandal *myŏn* also had a private common school set up by a Korean in 1920) (Chōsen sōtokufu 1940: 202; P'yŏngnan namdoch'ŏng 1975: 1103).

As mentioned above, the factory management also sent a small number of Koreans to Japan for training as an intermediate group between Japanese and Korean workers. In 1919, for example, they dispatched 21 teenage Korean boys who could understand Japanese to the main factory for training in production operations and barrel making. This program continued for nine years, until 1927, and involved a total of 49 Korean and eight Japanese workers.

The Sŭngho Common School immediately became the main source of recruitment of factory workers, and the educational level of new recruits rose accordingly. In 1927, approximately 80 percent of the workers in the Sŭnghori factory had had several years of elementary schooling; this was much higher than the average level of workers in general. As of late 1927, 502 out of the 633 Korean workers in the factory had received some formal education (see Table 2.14). The growing importance and availability of education is shown in the fact that all 134 new Korean recruits that year had some schooling (see Table 2.15).

The lower illiteracy rate in 1927 is an impressive change over the picture painted by the general factory survey of 1923 (I am assuming

Table 2.14
Educational Background of Korean Workers
at the Sŭnghori Factory, 1927

Level	Number	Percentage of total
No schooling	131	20.7%
Common school dropouts	428	67.6
Common school graduates	63	10.0
Higher common school dropouts and graduates	11	1.7
TOTAL	633	100.0

SOURCE: *Kokajō* 1927, second half.

Table 2.15
Educational Background of New Recruits
at the Sŭnghori Factory, 1927

Level	Korean (%)		Japanese (%)	
No schooling	0		0	
Common school dropouts	110	(82.1)	3	(9.1)
Common school graduates	23	(17.0)	26	(78.8)
Higher common school dropouts and graduates	1	(0.9)	4	(12.1)
TOTAL	134	(100.0)	33	(100.0)

SOURCE: *Kokajō* 1927, second half.

that workers with no schooling are illiterate and that schooling, however brief, conferred some degree of literacy). Moreover, the 20 percent of the workforce with no formal schooling more than likely were older workers born too early to receive a common school or *sŏdang* education. The large number of common school dropouts probably reflects several realities of colonial society in the 1920s. This high dropout rate implies a generally pragmatic attitude toward the common schools. Many boys who had no intention of advancing to secondary school dropped out after learning enough basic Japanese and arithmetic to qualify for employment. Given the grammatical similarities between Korean and Japanese and also the common elements in the writing systems because of the borrowing of Chinese characters, which would have been familiar to anyone with *sŏdang* training, it usually took only a few years for a Korean boy to learn enough Japanese to work in a modern job. Many boys could not enter common schools until their teens for financial reasons and were under pressure to make a living rather than stay in school for the full six years. Probably they were better motivated and better prepared to learn. Elementary schooling was important for these teenage boys not because of the diploma but because of the language training and basic modern knowledge they learned in the schools and needed for employment in modern-sector jobs in the colony.

According to Kye Chi-P'ung (pers. interview), who worked in the Sŭnghori factory during 1932–34, the Sŭngho Common School assisted job-seeking Korean youths by issuing false certificates of attendance, a document required of job applicants by the company in the 1930s. This practice was understandable because the Sŭngho common school could not accommodate all the local school-age children in the 1930s as the population in the area grew rapidly (*Tonga ilbo*, Feb. 28, 1936: 4). Kye recalled that an understanding of Japanese and arithmetic satisfied the company's requirements and common school dropouts could function in the workshop without much problem except in the more technical production sections.

The Sŭnghori factory also had an on-the-job training program for intelligent and diligent youths. Prior to 1927, the company conducted an on-site training program; it was believed that it was necessary to invest two or three years of training to produce efficient workers. The program included elementary-level training for Koreans with no schooling and courses in arithmetic, physics, and chemistry for common school dropouts or graduates. Basically, work skills were taught on the job, and the training program was used to upgrade the basic knowledge needed by workers to understand the factory process in more depth and to work more efficiently (*Kokajō* 1927, second half). The classes were conducted once a week between 3:00 and 4:00 P.M. during work hours in the workers' dining room and were open to anyone who wanted to join. Japanese supervisors often encouraged brighter Koreans to take the classes. Japanese and Korean engineers served as teachers and were paid for teaching (*Kokajō*, 1933, 1937, second halves). Class size ranged between ten and twenty students who were eager to learn or improve their Japanese-language skills and basic knowledge of factory operations and who used this opportunity to advance themselves.

The classes for Koreans with no schooling included Japanese and basic arithmetic at the second- or third-grade level—for example, the metric system and the writing of daily reports in the workshop. The advanced classes on mathematics, physics, and chemistry were open to both Japanese and Korean workers with elementary schooling. These classes used secondary-school textbooks and met once a week for an hour (*Kokajō* 1937, second half). Workers in the Analysis Section of the General Affairs Bureau were strongly encouraged to take this training program.

The management of the Sŭnghori factory also emphasized language training for both Japanese and Korean workers to try to alleviate communication problems, which posed a serious barrier to an efficient operation. The inability to communicate work instructions led to accidents, misunderstandings, and hostility between Japanese and Korean workers (*Kokajō* 1928, second half). Management encouraged Japanese office and factory workers to acquire enough basic Korean conversational skills to be able to talk with Korean workers; the response of Japanese workers is not known (*Kokajō* 1926, second half).

Labor market fluctuations beginning in 1926, however, led to a change of thinking about these training programs after 1927. In 1927, the Sŭnghori factory lost many Korean workers trained over the previous seven years, mainly because of the increasing demand for Korean male workers. The driving force behind this new labor demand was a huge hydroelectric development project in the northern areas of North and South Hamkyŏng provinces, launched by the ambitious Noguchi Jun (1873–1944), president of the Japan Nitrogen Fertilizer Corporation (hereafter Nihon Chissō). The project was unprecedented in colonial industrial history in boldness and scale. In spring 1926, Noguchi established the Chōsen suiryoku tenki kabushiki kaisha (Korea Water Power Corporation) with a capital of ¥20 million, the largest venture to date in the colonial capital markets. The new company immediately launched construction of the Pujŏn River Dam, which required around 2,000 construction workers daily for three years (Miyake 1937: 104–5; *Tonga ilbo*, Oct. 14, 1926: 6).

The following year, Noguchi formed the Korea Nitrogen Fertilizer Corporation (hereafter Chōsen Chissō), with capital of ¥10 million.

This was the first element in his ambitious master plan of a future electro-chemical industrial complex in the Hŭngnam area, hitherto an obscure fishing village on the coast of South Hamkyŏng province. In November 1929, the first part of the Pujŏn River Dam was finished, with an estimated annual generation capacity of 65,000 kilowatts. Two months later, in January 1930, the Chōsen Chissō plant in Hŭngnam started operations, using power from Pujŏn Water Power Station. By August 1931, the capital of Chōsen Chissō had increased to ¥60 million, a sixfold growth in only four years; thereafter it expanded rapidly and became the largest electrico-chemical industrial complex in both Japan and Korea until the end of the colonial period (Yoshioka 1962: 164–66).

From the standpoint of industrial development in Korea, the Pujŏn River project and the growth of Chōsen Chissō was a crucial stepping-stone for the large-scale industrialization of the 1930s. The success of Noguchi's enterprise proved that a large-scale chemical industry in Korea was technically feasible and financially attractive. Furthermore, within a decade after development of the Pujŏn River Dam began in 1926, all major suitable hydroelectric sites had been developed in close cooperation between Noguchi's Nihon Chissō conglomerate and the colonial government, then led by Governor-General Ugaki Kazushige, providing abundant and cheap power for the rapid industrial growth of the 1930s.

Penetration of the Noguchi group into the northern region also ignited a construction boom in the northern provinces and brought important changes in the labor policy of the Government General. Concurrent construction projects such as the Pujŏn River Dam and its related roads and railways, Hŭngnam harbor, and the Hŭngnam industrial zone required unprecedented numbers of workers. This spurt in labor demand forced the colonial government to confront a peculiar labor market problem: a shortage of labor in the north and a huge surplus of labor in the rural south (Yoshio 1929a: 13–14).

Analysis of Onoda company reports (*Kokajō*) for these years reveals the effect of this increased demand for labor on Sŭnghori workers. Many longtime Korean workers at the Sŭnghori factory whose lack of schooling prevented promotion to the status of regular worker began leaving the factory for these new worksites in 1926. In 1927, in response to this unexpected change in the labor market, the Sŭnghori management initiated a more intensive training program for the workers with no schooling to give them Japanese-language and math skills equivalent to those acquired in the second or third year of common school (*Kokajō* 1927, second half). The prohibition against promotion of workers without a formal education beyond the novice level was rescinded, and these workers could now acquire regular-worker status. In 1930, after the company had achieved its goal of giving all such workers an education, this training program was stopped (*Kokajō* 1931, second half).

The Sŭnghori factory itself was experiencing a greater demand for regular workers during this period because of the expansion of the Sŭnghori factory and the establishment of the new factory at Ch'ŏnnaeri. Many regular workers, both Japanese and Koreans, were transferred to Ch'ŏnnaeri to train new recruits and to supervise production in the new factory. Consequently, Onoda hired many new temporary workers after 1927 and felt a keen pressure to train them as regular workers to meet the increasing demand for productive and efficient workers in the two factories. In September 1927 the Engineering Department of the Sŭnghori factory adopted a new program of intensive training for recruits. Its main purpose was to give preliminary general training on factory operations and to screen novices before assignment to the various sections (*Kokajō* 1927, second half).

The Disciplining of the Workforce

Another form of worker education came about because of the demands of the work environment and the discipline it imposed on the lives of workers. The Korean youths recruited to work in the factory in the early 1920s were accustomed to a seasonal agricultural work environment, and the routines of factory life were a totally new experience and a source of tension and pressure. New social relations appropriate to modern forms of contractual industrial organization and a new hierarchy, new social groups, and new patterns of authority developed. All of these were strange and often contrary to the practices familiar to the new workers.

To begin with, factory work itself was a new experience. The year-round, eight-hour workday spent in one location with breaks only for meals caused much strain. Learning to observe exact starting and stopping times also required much effort. In addition, the workers had to overcome tensions and fears associated with working around frightening machines and complicated equipment. An added burden was the metric system of weights and measures, which was incomprehensible to those without common school education. The strain was heightened because of the mixing of Japanese and Koreans, who remained distrustful of each other—a problem exacerbated by the language barrier. Japanese section chiefs and foremen gave orders and instructions in Japanese. Koreans who could not understand Japanese had to rely on their compatriots who were able to understand Japanese to translate (*Kokajō* 1923, second half). Nevertheless, the Sŭnghori factory seemed to succeed in producing an efficient and productive labor force within roughly a decade. In its report (*Kokajō*) for the second half of the year 1933, the Sŭnghori factory informed the main office that the factory now had an efficient, well-disciplined, and stable labor force of 409 skilled regular workers, of whom 301 were Korean. The Sŭnghori plant's ability to expand production sevenfold between 1920 and 1942 with more or less the same size workforce and to train Korean workers sufficiently well enough that they could teach other Koreans is proof of Onoda's successful disciplining and development of skilled Korean workers.

From management's point of view, there were two steps in disciplining local recruits. The first task was to eliminate pre-industrial behavioral habits that lowered efficiency. The second was to transform these novices into stable regular workers loyal to Onoda Cement. In principle, Japanese managers adopted the labor-control techniques developed at the main company, using both an incentive system and strict rules to discipline Korean workers as well as locally employed Japanese workers. In reality, however, they developed a peculiar pattern of labor-management relations, which was characteristic of the Japanese-owned, modern, large-scale colonial factory and reflected the complex nature of colonial modernity.

The Sŭnghori management used four main types of sanctions to discipline workers (*Shokkō kisoku*, pp. 51–55): rebukes (oral as well as written), fines (up to 50 percent of daily wages), temporary suspensions (1–7 days), and dismissals. A system of bonuses was used to reward and encourage desirable habits.

Strict Rules. The primary requirement was to be present every day and to be on time. Tardiness and absenteeism lowered productivity considerably. The Sŭnghori factory used a time-card system to enforce punctuality for factory entry and exit. Sirens, one a half-hour before a shift began and another at the start of each shift, were used to alert workers, most of whom would not have had watches or clocks. Every worker had to carry a time card and stamp the card at the time clock in the security guard's box in front of the factory gate upon entering and leaving the factory. The time card was used to calculate wages, paid every two weeks (*Shokkō kisoku*, p. 15).

Management also provided an incentive for perfect attendance by paying bonuses to workers with no absences and no tardies for one full month. The company ordered the gate guards to be strict about time recording. For their part, the workers were careful to keep clear records on their time cards, for being one minute late only once resulted in the loss of the monthly bonus. This led to frequent quarrels between the security guards and workers. Failure to carry the time card or alterations of the data on it were punished by a fine of 10 percent of the worker's daily wage. The seminannual factory reports frequently mentioned that workers failed to line up in orderly rows to punch their time cards; this problem was also controlled by assessing a fine of 10 percent of daily wages (*Kokajō* 1923, second half; *Shokkō kisoku*, p. 55). This combination of strict controls and monetary incentives quickly transformed village youths into punctual, diligent factory workers (Kye interview).

According to the *Shokkō kisoku* (p. 56), the fine for being absent without prior notice was 40 percent of daily wages (in addition to the loss of wages for the time missed). A worker who was late for work more than twice in any two-week period was fined 50 percent of his daily wages for the days in question. Other misconduct frequently reprimanded or fined by section chiefs or shift heads included leaving work without the section chief's permission; sleeping, smoking, or eating during work hours, especially during the second and third shifts; drunkenness during work hours; pilferage; entrance or exit through the fence surrounding the factory grounds rather than through the gate; and urination in improper places. Fines and suspensions from work for these or other reasons rendered workers ineligible for the incentive bonuses.

More serious acts of misbehavior, such as the refusal to obey an order, damaging of company property, and arbitrary stoppage of work or absence without notice, were punishable by one to seven days of suspension from work. A worker who committed a crime, organized or participated in a strike, destroyed machinery or equipment, or stole company products was dismissed immediately (*Kokajō*, 1927, second half).

To be sure, it is an open question whether the elaborate and thorough schedule of punishments and fines specified in the *Shokkō kisoku* was enforced. According to the semi-annual reports of the Sŭnghori plant, however, by around 1927, seven years after the factory opened, these bad work habits had largely disappeared from the workplace (*Kokajō* 1927, second half). Probably these strict rules were necessary to eliminate the new workers' premodern, undisciplined behavioral patterns, but not sufficient to promote productivity and a fuller commitment to work. Like the main factory in Japan, the Sŭnghori plant adopted a seniority-oriented incentive system as a complementary tactic to discipline and stabilize colonial workers, although again the system was modified into a characteristic colonial pattern.

Incentive Systems. Besides strict rules, the management of the Sŭnghori factory also adopted the incentive systems used by the main company, which had been developed through 38 years of experience in training men and retaining them. Onoda's incentive system featured seniority-based compensation, regular bonuses, a continuous-service bonus, and retirement fund benefits, to encourage continued employment and a lifetime commitment to work and company.

There were four kinds of bonuses, both monetary and nonmonetary: the perfect attendance bonus, the diligence bonus, the special bonus, and the certificate of merit. The first two were clearly directed at reduction of absenteeism and tardiness among the workers (*Shokkō kisoku*, pp. 41–47). The perfect attendance bonus was given at the end of every month to workers who had had no absences and no tardies for twenty-eight days that month. The amount awarded was ¥1.68, or six *sen* per day, the equivalent of two days' wages for an average Korean worker in 1927 (*Kokajō* 1927, second half). The diligence bonus was given twice a year, in summer and winter, to workers who had not been absent, tardy, or left early for six consecutive months (see Table 2.16). This nonmonetary bonus was divided into a first-class award, which consisted of a suit, and a second-class award, which was a set of underwear. In 1935 and 1938, respectively, the unit price of the suit was ¥3.25 and ¥8.37 and of the underwear ¥1.35 and ¥2.95 (*Kokajō* 1935, 1938, second halves). A recipient of the first-class diligence bonus was also given a special shoulder stripe to wear; these stripes could be accumulated during their career with Onoda. This kind of visible award was a psycho-

Table 2.16
Recipients of Diligence Bonuses
at the Sŭnghori Factory, 1931–1935
(J = Japanese, K = Korean, T = Total)

Year		First category J	K	T	Second category J	K	T	Total	Rate*
1931	Winter	80	253	333	16	54	70	403	63%
	Summer	79	235	314	19	65	84	398	65
1932	Winter	93	266	359	12	56	68	427	70
	Summer	86	295	381	24	50	74	455	73
1933	Winter	95	311	406	9	42	51	457	76
	Summer	90	303	393	12	66	78	471	79
1934	Winter	80	270	350	14	59	73	423	73
	Summer	77	272	349	13	61	74	423	78
1935	Winter	67	242	309	25	81	106	415	77
	Summer	59	223	282	32	77	109	391	75

* As a percentage of the total workforce.
SOURCE: *Kokajō* 1935, second half.

logical stimulus and incentive to other workers in the workshop (*Shokkō kisoku*, p. 45). Approximately 65–80 percent of the Korean workers received awards in each six-month period between 1931 and 1935, according to factory records. The factory's average absenteeism rate of 3 percent during this period illustrates the stability of the workforce (*Kokajō* 1935, second half).

The special bonus, which was paid in cash, was given to workers who had made contributions to the factory, such as suggesting a scientific or technological invention or catching a thief. The certificate of merit was given to workers whose performance was excellent and who had contributed to the factory operation. The certificate played a role in wage increases and promotions.

Besides these regular bonuses, the company also made a special contribution based on years of continuous service to a worker's seniority bonus and retirement fund to encourage regular workers to remain at the factory. The seniority bonus was given semiannually, in January and July, to workers with five or more years' continuous service as a regular worker. Workers with 5–6 years of service received ¥5; with 7–9 years, ¥8; with 10–14 years, ¥14; with 15–19

Table 2.17
Recipients of Continuous Service Pensions
at the Sŭnghori Factory, 1935

	Years of service						
Nationality	5	7	10	15	20	25	Total
Japanese	16	8	14	7	3	3	51
Korean	53	24	37	—	—	—	114

SOURCE: *Kokajō* 1935, second half.

years, ¥25; with 20–24 years, ¥40; and with 25 or more years, ¥60 (*Ko-kajō* 1935, second half). Regular workers also had to contribute to the pension savings account, which the company held until retirement or urgent occasions. In 1935, 165 regular workers (40 percent of all regular workers) in the Sŭnghori factory received the seniority bo-nuses; of these, 114 (36 percent) were Koreans (see Table 2.17). This figure indicates that 40 percent of the 414 regular workers in the factory in that year had worked more than eight years (three years' training plus five years as regular workers) (*Kokajō* 1935, second half).

In their report for the second half of 1933, the management of the Sŭnghori plant reported to the head office that worker discipline was satisfactory and characterized by good relations between Ko-rean and Japanese workers, good conduct on the part of both Korean and Japanese workers, low labor turnover, and increasing efficiency of the workers in general. The managers had succeeded in training and keeping a stable workforce after a decade of careful effort de-spite fluctuations in the local labor market. Regular workers ac-counted for 62.4 percent, or 409 (108 Japanese and 301 Koreans) of the total of 655 workers in 1933. Despite the initially undisciplined nature of the labor force, low educational levels, and ethnic seg-mentation between the colonizer and the colonized, the modern factory system and management techniques had produced a skilled workforce from the first generation of Korean factory workers (Oh Pyŏng-Ho, pers. interview). Carefully controlled by strict rules and encouraged by both monetary and nonmonetary incentives, local boys from the neighboring villages of P'yŏngan province readily adjusted to the disciplinary requirements of mechanized industry. This suggests that worker performance was the result not only of traditional attitudes toward labor but also of Onoda's policies and commitment to labor management. Considering the low level of industrial development in the country and the relative lack of education among the new workers, and the short history of industry in Korea, the Sŭnghori workers were quite advanced in terms of their skills, efficiency, performance, and commitment.

Despite their relatively advanced status and skills, however, the Korean workers in the Sŭnghori factory found themselves in a situation that was complicated by the colonial nature of modernization in Korea. Their ability and personal ambition probably made them grasp opportunities for individual advancement in the factory, learning Japanese and modern manufacturing technology and skills under Japanese workers and undergoing long years of training and adjustment in a situation of intense competition and colonial discrimination. How and to what extent their consciousness, especially of their Koreanness, was influenced and frustrated by this experience of the dual nature of colonial modernity is a difficult question to address. The next section examines the core issues of the colonial nature of Korean modernity, such as oppression, discrimination, group-oriented social rejection, and collaboration by self-denial as well as by emulation of the colonizers' values.

Hierarchy of the Workers

Workers were divided into four hierarchical groups in the Sŭnghori factory: novice (*teikō*), apprentice (*minarai*), regular worker (*honshokkō*), and section chief and shift head (*kakarijō* and *kosazū*). The bureaus and sections were also arranged in a hierarchy, according to the complexity of skills needed for the work in each section and its importance in the production process (*Kokajō* 1927, second half).

When a recruit was hired after a simple interview with the chief of the Workers Management Section, he was assigned to any vacant position in the twenty-nine sections (see Fig. 3). The recruit had to spend a year as a novice in this assigned position, mostly running errands and watching basic operations in the section. During this period, the novice's supervisor, usually a section chief or a senior skilled worker, watched the dexterity, intelligence, and integrity of the worker and reported his observations to the Workers Management Section. A worker who received a good evaluation as well as personal recommendations as a promising novice was eligible to apply for a two-year apprenticeship to learn the basic skills and

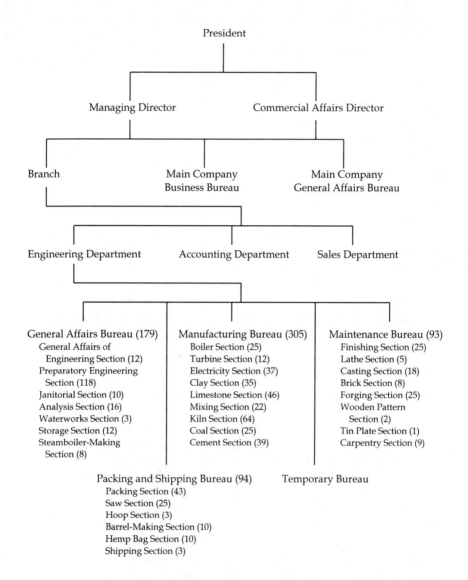

```
                            President
                               |
              +----------------+----------------+
              |                                 |
       Managing Director              Commercial Affairs Director
              |                                 |
    +---------+---------+              +---------+---------+
    |                   |              |                   |
  Branch          Main Company              Main Company
                  Business Bureau          General Affairs Bureau
    |
    +-------------------+-------------------+
    |                   |                   |
Engineering        Accounting           Sales
Department         Department           Department
    |
    +-------------------+-------------------+------------------+
    |                   |                   |                  |
```

General Affairs Bureau (179) | Manufacturing Bureau (305) | Maintenance Bureau (93)
  General Affairs of   Boiler Section (25)   Finishing Section (25)
    Engineering Section (12)   Turbine Section (12)   Lathe Section (5)
  Preparatory Engineering   Electricity Section (37)   Casting Section (18)
    Section (118)   Clay Section (35)   Brick Section (8)
  Janitorial Section (10)   Limestone Section (46)   Forging Section (25)
  Analysis Section (16)   Mixing Section (22)   Wooden Pattern
  Waterworks Section (3)   Kiln Section (64)   Section (2)
  Storage Section (12)   Coal Section (25)   Tin Plate Section (1)
  Steamboiler-Making   Cement Section (39)   Carpentry Section (9)
    Section (8)

Packing and Shipping Bureau (94)   Temporary Bureau
  Packing Section (43)
  Saw Section (25)
  Hoop Section (3)
  Barrel-Making Section (10)
  Hemp Bag Section (10)
  Shipping Section (3)

Fig. 3 Organizational chart of the Onoda Sŭnghori Factory, ca. 1925. Numbers in parentheses indicate total number of workers in bureau or section. SOURCE: *Kokajō*, second half of 1925.

knowledge required to be a skilled worker (*Shokkō kisoku*, p. 9). Novices who did not become apprentices either stayed on as novices or were dismissed from the factory. Many uneducated workers remained in this status because of the requirement that an apprentice had to have at least several years of a modern education and to understand Japanese. Promotion to apprenticeship meant acceptance as a recognized member of the factory. Apprentices received factory uniforms and could participate in the company's benefits programs, such as the savings bank, the cooperative society, and clinics (*Kokajō* 1927, second half). After these three years as a novice and an apprentice, a worker could apply for regular-worker status, which meant final acceptance as a member of the Onoda company. The skills and commitment of the worker to the company were fully recognized by this promotion (*Shokkō kisoku*, p. 9).

The most obvious colonial modification of the Japanese employment system was in the eligibility for the positions of section chief or shift head. These positions were generally filled by senior regular workers with many years of experience and the technical and supervisory skills to operate a section. In the Sŭnghori factory, these positions were reserved for Japanese workers, due to the ethnically segmented nature of the labor market until the end of the colonial period. Initially, Japanese workers brought from the main factory in Japan filled these posts. Later, some Japanese workers trained in the Sŭnghori factory were promoted to these positions (Kye and Lee interviews).

This group of Japanese workers was a peculiar product of the colonial situation. From management's point of view, control of these skilled Japanese workers was as important as control of Korean workers. First, it was not easy to persuade skilled Japanese workers to work in Korea, where living conditions were poorer and more backward from the Japanese standpoint. These workers also had to leave relatives and friends behind (*Kokajō* 1927, second half). Moreover, their jobs involved direct supervision of colonial workers, many of whom were uncommunicative, ignorant, and potentially hostile to the Japanese bosses. Because of language and social differences, Japanese office workers were reluctant to deal directly with the Korean workers. This made management even more dependent on the skilled Japanese workers. As supervisors, they acted as lower-level managers rather than as leaders of the workers in the section, as would have been the case in Japan.

In addition to emphasizing loyalty to the Onoda company, management had to provide monetary incentives to Japanese workers, who in general complained more than did colonial workers about wages and working conditions. Special post and overseas allowances raised their wages 40 percent above the daily wages at the main company. The company also provided housing. This group controlled day-to-day activities in the workshops, were responsible for merit evaluations, and enforced policies on illnesses, injuries, vacations, absences, tardies, and personal leaves for occasions such as funerals and marriages. These face-to-face dealings with the colonial workers frequently made these Japanese workers visible and adamant symbols of colonial authority. The feelings of being disliked by the colonial workers often made them nervous and obsessed with Japanese "we-ness," turning them into spiteful and vengeful bosses. Some of them made the workers' lives miserable, and created instability and hostility among subordinate colonial workers. More important, the existence of this group symbolized the dead-end careers faced by Korean workers and their position in the ethnically segmented colonial labor market. The Japanese-style seniority-oriented promotion system was applied to Korean workers only up to a certain point: they could become full-time regular workers but never shift heads or section chiefs.

As a result of this ethnic segregation between supervisors and supervisees, the number of Korean regular workers without hope of further promotion steadily increased. Many Korean workers probably accepted this system without many qualms and were satisfied with the job security, better working environment, in-company training opportunities, and other welfare benefits afforded by a large Japanese factory, such as seniority-oriented monetary bonuses and the pension plan, which were rare in the local labor market. Some workers may even have perceived themselves as a labor elite in the colony. It would not have been hard for them to rationalize their position in a situation in which better alternatives were nonexistent (interviews with Kye Chi-P'ung and Lee Kŭn-T'ae).

Nevertheless, the limited, conditional incentive system inevitably made Korean workers' commitment equally conditional and limited. It was easily broken when other opportunities came along. The high turnover rate among Korean regular workers in the Sŭnghori factory during the mid-1930s industrial boom is indicative of the dissatisfaction and frustration among Korean workers in this period (interview with Kye Chi-P'ung).

The more capable Korean workers were probably frustrated by this exclusion from promotion to more responsible jobs because of their nationality. No matter how capable he was, a Korean worker could not complain about or question a decision by a Japanese worker, even those at a lower level. Koreans, regardless of their experience or formal position, were always defined first and foremost by their Koreanness. They could not have avoided serious reflection about the social rejection and contempt they had to endure as a colonized people. Their position in the ethnically segmented colonial labor market was driven home to them on a daily basis.

Industrial relations at the Sŭnghori factory are a good example of the colonial practice of Japanese-style labor relations. Because of the shared East Asian cultural background, the Japanese-style seniority system (*nenkōsei*) was quite acceptable to the Korean workers. However, its application was incomplete, conditional, and fragmented.

In addition to the vertical hierarchy of employee classifications, there were also important differences among the sections in the factory. The wages and skills of regular workers in the 30 sections varied according to section. Certain sections in the manufacturing and maintenance bureaus had higher concentrations of Japanese and Korean workers with special skills who were paid higher wages. As Table 2.18 shows, workers in the Turbine, the Boiler, the Coal, the Limestone, and the Electricity sections in the Manufacturing Bureau as well as in all sections in the Maintenance Bureau were paid much more than workers in other sections. Even more important, workers learned special skills in the Tin Plate, Forging, Lathe, and Casting sections that were rare in the colony until the mid-1930s (*Kokajō*, 1923, 1925, second halves). On the other hand, sections handling nonproductive processes like packing and shipping or general affairs required many manual, unskilled workers. For these tasks the factory hired many Korean novices or apprentices for shorter periods at lower wages and assigned just a few regular workers to supervise these unskilled workers (*Kokajō* 1923, first half; 1925, second half).

The managers of the Sŭnghori factory did not practice a selective assignment system among the Korean recruits until 1927. During the first seven years of the factory's operation, a novice Korean worker

Table 2.18
Wage Differences by Section at the Sŭnghori Factory, 1923
(¥/*day*)

Section	Number of workers	Wages Japanese	Wages Korean
Manufacturing Bureau	305		
Boiler	25	2.35	0.86
Turbine	12	2.29	1.20
Electricity	37	2.19	0.92
Clay	35	2.07	0.88
Limestone	46	2.46	0.82
Mixing	22	2.09	0.95
Kiln	64	2.11	0.99
Coal	25	2.22	0.86
Cement	39	2.13	0.89
Maintenance Bureau	93		
Finishing	25	2.59	1.02
Lathe	5	n/a	n/a
Casting	18	2.77	1.05
Forging	25	2.99	0.88
Wooden Pattern	2	2.77	1.05
Tin Plate	1	2.92	1.30
Brick	8	n/a	n/a
Carpentry	9	2.54	1.40
General Affairs Bureau	179		
General Affairs of Engineering	12	2.18	0.67
Preparatory	118	2.25	0.80
Janitorial	10	1.95	0.91
Analysis	16	1.49	0.78
Waterworks	3	2.19	0.92
Storage	12	1.99	0.73
Steamboiler making	8	n/a	n/a
Packing and Shipping Bureau	94		
Packing	43	n/a	n/a
Saw	25	2.38	0.83
Hoop	3	n/a	n/a
Barrel making	10	1.95	0.83
Hempbag	10	n/a	n/a
Shipping	3	n/a	n/a
TOTAL	671	2.27	0.88

SOURCE: *Kokajō* 1923, second half.

was assigned to whatever post was vacant at the time of his entry and began his training while on duty. By 1925–26, as the factory began to lose many Korean workers as a result of increasing labor demand elsewhere on the peninsula, management found this training method slow, costly, and inefficient (*Kokajō* 1926, second half). This sudden increase in the turnover rate resulted in the loss of many workers trained in the factory over a period of years, and the vacancies in the more skilled positions could not be filled immediately. The concurrent expansion of the Sŭnghori factory and the opening of a second branch demanded a stable workforce. The company also had to prepare for the labor turnover anticipated in the near future (*Kokajō* 1926, second half).

To meet these needs, the Sŭnghori management adopted a new training and evaluation program for recruits beginning in 1927. A selective assignment system replaced the general assignment system. Each new recruit was given a two-month training program to introduce him to basic factory operations. The new workers were evaluated and, at the end of the orientation period, assigned to positions according to the evaluation results. The brighter or more educated workers were assigned to the more important sections, which required a common school diploma (*Kokajō* 1926, second half).

In sum, the hierarchical system in the Sŭnghori factory was typically colonial in nature during 1920–37. Although Korean workers were not allowed to rise beyond the status of regular worker, their skills, education, and seniority were reflected in their status and wages. The luckier or the brighter ones worked in sections of the factory that allowed them to learn advanced skills and upgrade their market value in the outside labor market with its increasing demand for skilled workers (Kye interview).

As mentioned above, the question of the Korean workers' response to this hierarchical system is probably the most important one for understanding colonial social psychology and the nature of colonial modernity, although it is hard to substantiate with concrete historical evidence. Naturally, there was a wide range of responses among the workers because of the complexity of personal and social interests involved in colonial life. The assertion of nationalist historians until the 1970s that, except for a tiny group of collaborators, every member of society was fighting for independence is certainly naive. In pitting a few collaborationists against the vast majority of Koreans, these historians ignored the wide range of Korean responses to social rejection and discrimination and the diverse and uneven nature of modernity in colonial Korea.[6]

The responses of the Sŭnghori workers to colonial modernity were not simply monolithic—either resistance or collaboration—but quite varied and opportunistic, reflecting the diverse identities formed in the interaction of the various historical forces at work. Jobs at the Sŭnghori factory were certainly secure and advantageous in terms of security and benefits. The workers' reactions to the differential wage scale and the limitations on advancement were affected by their relative seniority and their personal or family situations. Some accepted the status quo and worked silently; others rebelled by leaving the factory. Some enjoyed the security and advantage of jobs in a large Japanese factory whose wage level was in the upper middle range of the national average; others became distressed and infuriated by the discrimination and humiliation they felt (Kye interview).

In general, there were four types of responses among Korean workers during the initial years of their work experience. The first type corresponded to the initial years of employment, when the recruits were ardently learning their job and skills in the unfamiliar factory environment. During this training period, the workers gradually came to recognize the hierarchical dualism between Japanese and Korean workers as well as the horizontal hierarchy among the sections. Most of them came to realize that there was no way to change the system as long as Korea was under Japanese rule and that their frustration with colonial oppression and discrimination could not be dealt with through their efforts as individuals or as members of the working class (Memmi 1965: 134).

Two further responses appeared as the recruits began to achieve regular worker status. At this point they divided into two groups: one that stayed, and another that left the factory. The first group was

6. This analysis is indebted to Albert Memmi's (1967) study of Tunisian colonial society and Karl Moskowitz's (1980) case study of Korean employees in the Shokusan ginkō in colonial Korea. Moskowitz traces the formation of Korean white-collar bank employees who gained their knowledge of banking and finance under Japanese managers and clarifies the historical continuity in human capital before and after the liberation in 1945. Sŏn Chae-Won's (1996) comparative study of labor relations in the main Onoda factory and the Sŭnghori factory was also very insightful about the colonial complications.

composed mostly of those who became regular workers in the more important sections of the production process, especially in the Manufacturing and the Maintenance bureaus. These workers could perceive themselves as a select minority among Korean workers who were paid higher wages and were learning valuable skills on the job. Usually these workers had families to support, and the pressure to remain in a secure job was very strong among these workers. Gradually, they were transformed into committed and reliable employees. Management treated them almost like Japanese employees in terms of incentives. Some of them were dispatched to Ch'ŏnnaeri and Komusan to train Korean recruits there, as Japanese workers had done earlier in the Sŭnghori factory (*Kokajō* 1929, 1937, second halves).

These men had reached the top of the ladder for Korean workers under colonial rule. They were the first group of skilled Korean workers and demonstrated good performance, long service, and commitment to their work and even to the company. They remained the leading skilled workers in the cement industry after the liberation (Oh interview). Because of their advanced status, this group probably had the most complex and subtle experience of the conflict between colonialism and modernity. The essential characteristic of colonial modernity existed not only in the factory hierarchy but also in their own consciousness. Individually each was hard-working, able, and skilled and had achieved economic independence. But the price was high. Because of his pride in his work and his loyalty to his superior, he developed a commitment to his job, his coworkers, and Onoda despite his nationality. In other words, through everyday contact, he unwittingly began adopting the colonizers' modern sociocultural values. While learning the skills and technology, he unconsciously started to accept Japanese views on Koreans and things Korean. The experience of being in discord with his Korean self and of having several hybrid identities was painful. In short, he became alienated from himself. He soon realized, however, that he never would be accepted as an equal by the colonizers even after this painful process of self-denial. This collective, dehumanizing drama in colonial human relations is the subject of the next section.

The workers who left the factory tended to have only two to three years of training in the factory; typically these workers had been employed in the Maintenance Bureau or in the nonproduction and lower-level sections. Workers in this group often decided to look for better opportunities elsewhere, instead of waiting three or four years to become regular workers. The skills they learned in the Maintenance Bureau such as forging, casting, lathe operation, and wooden pattern making were in great demand in the local labor market. For some Korean workers, finding a better job was personal revenge for the frustration experienced at the Sŭnghori factory. This was especially true since there were no other channels for complaint, resentment, or anger (Kye interview).

Finally, some workers revolted against the unfair and humiliating treatment at the factory. Until recently this minority received more attention from Korean historians than the silent majority of the workers who stayed. Many young, single, radical workers identified their acts with revolt against the colonial system as a whole and refused to collaborate. They usually caused trouble in the factory either by attacking Japanese shift heads or section chiefs or by agitating among other workers for strikes. The result of these revolts was typically either arrest and imprisonment or exile abroad. Many of those who fled turned to the overseas independence movement, dedicating themselves to the nationalist or the Communist movement against Japanese imperialism (Kye interview).

Social Hierarchy in the Colonial Factory: A Collective Drama

No Korean worker, especially the veteran regular worker, could avoid incidents that reminded him that he could never be accepted as a full member of the group of Japanese regular workers. Most of these incidents happened not at the workplace but in social contacts between Korean and Japanese workers. The Japanese frequently reminded Koreans of their inferior status by social humiliation and insult. In the workshop the Koreans and Japanese were bound by common goals, but this bond seldom grew into a broader social exchange. The Japanese had a fundamental contempt for the colonized people as a collective entity. Some Korean skilled workers had to endure listening to their Japanese bosses ridiculing and insulting other Koreans; for example, "Korean workers are slow as cows when they are asked to work, but fast as airplanes when they are asked to eat" (Kye interview); this is a good example of the Japanese image of Korean workers. Such remarks brought home to Korean workers their colonial status and the collective Korean identity as a colonized people whom the Japanese despised and rejected. This attitude explains why the Japanese could not apply their labor-management system, especially the seniority-oriented promotion system, to the colonial workers.

Until the mid-1930s, however, the majority of Korean skilled workers stayed in the Sŭnghori factory, seemingly rationalizing their existence as the best possible under the circumstances because there was no better alternative elsewhere and no practical possibility of changing the system. Some displayed a passive-aggressive attitude through sabotage or deliberate laziness and inefficiency, the "weapons of the weak" to use James Scott's (1985) term, to justify to themselves that they had not yielded completely to the colonizers. It is doubtful that Japanese managers were successful in drawing maximum effort out of the colonial workers due to this lack of total loyalty or commitment to the company. It was equally doubtful that the Japanese expected this kind of loyalty and commitment.

Negative descriptions of the majority of the Korean workforce, by both Korean and Japanese managers at the time, as a group prone to irresponsible behavior, hot-tempered spontaneous violence, tardiness, and high absenteeism and turnover rates, especially in contrast to the Japanese workers, were common. These traits were seen as lowering the quality and productivity of the labor force and making adjustment to factory life difficult. The fairness of this evaluation is questionable considering the extreme gap between Korea and Japan not only in the level of capitalistic development but also in the level of elementary education. The managers of the majority of small- and medium-size factories were equally irresponsible and biased in their labor management (for a good description of the *Chōsenjinkan* [view of Koreans] of Japanese managers, see Sŏn 1996: 214–40).

According to the recollections of Kye Chi-P'ung, discrimination against Koreans was most unbearable in social and collective contact in the Sŭnghori factory. Some of the brighter and more radical Koreans experienced difficulty in accepting the atmosphere of social rejection in the factory. Compared with the humiliation Koreans experienced in social contact with the Japanese, however, the shop floor was not a major area of friction. Basically, the Japanese avoided social contact with Korean workers, and this hurt the workers and alienated them. Paradoxically, this often caused an intense aspiration to be accepted as a member of the Japanese organization. Although alienation was not uncommon among workers of other industrializing countries, including Japan during the 1910s and early 1920s, the social discrimination and collective rejection the Korean workers experienced reinforced their self-alienation in the colonial milieu (Gordon 1985: 47–82). Earlier theoreticians of colonialism such as Frantz Fanon and Albert Memmi conceptualized this complicated, split-identity formation in colonial subjects as self-alienation, historyless-ness, or identityless-ness. Among the colonial generation in Korea, the sentiment of *han* (the resentful bitterness of hearts hardened by oppression or injustice) symbolized this experience of painful self-alienation, the feeling that they never succeeded in constructing a modern identity that corresponded to their true nature.

Social life in the factory included the common daily routines of toilet and bathroom use, communal dining, recreational activities such as picnics or athletic gatherings, and housing. In all these areas, there were sharp differences in neatness and orderliness between Japanese and Korean facilities. Both Japanese and Korean workers used the same toilets, but the public baths were segregated. There were two baths of equal size, one for Japanese and one for Korean workers, even though the number of Korean workers was almost five times that of Japanese workers. Japanese workers organized an exclusive self-governing group, called the *kyōreikai* (cooperative society) and cleaned and maintained their bathrooms and smoking rooms. They openly ridiculed the dirtiness and untidiness of the facilities used by the Koreans. The Japanese also organized picnics or recreational meetings for themselves. Jogging, tennis, and bicycling were popular among the Japanese workers and their family members. Watching these exclusive social gatherings of Japanese workers, Korean workers felt envious and frustrated. Often they organized their own traditional mutual savings societies such as *kye* or social and athletic meetings separately. Out of envy and frustration, they emulated the colonizer's modern life-style in an incomplete form — the typical split identity found in colonial modernity.[7]

Japanese workers lived in neat and modern company housing. By contrast, Koreans lived in privately owned rental housing, which was often temporary, crowded, and lacking in modern conveniences. There were several Korean regular workers who qualified for company housing benefits. Their fellow Korean workers often jeal-

7. For a discussion of the effect of this envy and deprivation in creating a love-hate reaction against modernity and in engendering the "catch up with Japan" attitude of economic nationalism during the decolonization period, see Yu Yŏng-Ik 1992: 214 and Cumings 1984: 482.

ously referred to these dwellings as *"yangban* housing" (Sŏn 1996: 151).

Another example of social humiliation was discrimination at the front gate. Family members typically brought a worker's lunch to the front gate just before the lunch hour. If a family member of a Korean worker asked the gate guard to hold a worker's lunch for him to pick up, the request was usually refused, and the family member had to wait, even in the rain or snow, until the Korean worker came out at mealtime, whereas lunchboxes for Japanese workers were routinely accepted. The pretext for refusal was the bad smell of *kimch'i* (Korean-style pickled vegetables). It was said that "Chōsen no bentō wa kusai" (Korean lunchboxes are smelly). Yet often the guard himself was a Korean. Many Korean workers and their wives greatly resented this attitude, in which one can sense a small example of the collaboration found in colonial societies, the typical phenomenon of finger-pointing among the colonized people (Kye interview).

The Japanese supervisors were after all colonialists and never allowed the colonized Koreans to identify with or to penetrate their group, in either the work or the social environment. This contemptuous attitude probably generated Korean contempt for the Japanese government's Naisen Ittai (Japan and Korea as one body) assimilation policy or the Kōminka (transformation of the colonial peoples into imperial subjects) movement during the war. This experience also explains many sociopsychological characteristics and phenomena of Korean society after 1945, such as the deep sense of *han*, the national inferiority complex, the endless obsession with approval and recognition, and the xenophobic anti-Japanese nationalistic sentiments, which engendered a counter-mythology that stressed that everything Korean was pure and good and must be restored and retained.

Labor Turnover

The high turnover rate among Korean workers was one of the major complaints of Japanese managers during the colonial period. To put these criticisms in perspective, they were usually personal opinions based on comparisons with Japanese workers, who were working in a much more advanced stage of industrialization and urbanization and had a much better educational background. The behavior of Korean workers was not only a product of the socioeconomic background of the workforce but also, to an even greater extent, a product of the employers' labor-management policy and the government's labor policy, as analysis of the Sŭnghori case shows.

From the workers' point of view, moving from one job to another was a way of searching for better employment, particularly wages, in an environment in which it was not possible to struggle for improvement of labor conditions in a factory. It was, in effect, the only way, albeit a rather passive way, for colonial workers to protest against the management of a given company. Instead of striking or otherwise protesting and risking a police record as a troublemaker, not to mention dismissal or imprisonment, workers simply left (Kye interview).

The length of service of Korean workers in a factory was commonly short in comparison to the tenure of Japanese workers. The social and economic instability of the time, the low quality of the labor force, and the rural ties of the workers have generally been cited as main sources of this high turnover rate, which was particularly high among miners and female workers in the textile and other light industries. Other explanations include the workers' educational level, the nature of the work, labor conditions, manager commitment, and the labor market situation. Unfortunately, there are few substantial data on the reasons for the high turnover rate, and it is difficult to determine the exact contribution of any of these factors. Without these data, we cannot even tell whether the labor turnover involved a movement of workers among factories or between factories and the countryside.

The Sŭnghori factory demonstrates that management considered controlling the high turnover rate as serious a problem as the disciplining of workers. It took at least two years to train recruits to become disciplined workers. The loss of such workers not only immediately lowered production efficiency but also forced managers to hire more recruits and train them from the start. This was a serious drain in terms of managerial time, money, and energy. The Sŭnghori factory's success in keeping a stable labor force between 1920 and 1937, except in 1927, and even during several years after 1937, was possible only because of management's careful and strenuous efforts.

As Table 2.19 shows, the turnover of workers in the Sŭnghori factory was constant throughout the colonial period. According to company records, reasons for leaving included not only voluntary

Table 2.19
Turnover Rates of Workers at the
Sŭnghori Factory, 1920–1942

Year	Number of workers	entering (a)	leaving (b)	c= a+b	Turnover rate c÷2÷a
1920/11	823	684	346	1,030	75
1921	721	82	114	196	120
1922	593	46	78	124	134
1923	578	64	80	144	113
1924	610	102	52	154	75
1925	672	43	36	79	92
1926	n/a	160	81	199	62
1927	n/a	167	94	261	78
1928	n/a	218	177	395	91
1929	n/a	124	77	201	85
1930	1,052	59	194	253	214
1931	790	n/a	n/a	n/a	n/a
1932	703	n/a	n/a	n/a	n/a
1933	655	14	27	41	146
1935	700	78	39	117	75
1938	685	72	43	115	80
1940	690	95	112	207	109
1941	688	58	58	116	100
1942	682	94	145	239	127

SOURCES: *Kokajō* 1920, 1925, 1929, 1935, 1941, 1942, second halves.

leave but also dismissals for work stoppage, tuberculosis, violation of rules, death, and transfer. This makes it difficult to analyze the data except in terms of broad trends. The fluctuations in Table 2.19 clearly reflect both internal and external changes in labor demand. The numbers of entering workers show management responding to the changes in labor conditions both inside and outside the workshop. The large number of hirings and leavings in 1920 and 1921 reflects adjustments to the new three-shift system, which required many new workers for the third shift. Gradually the company reduced the number of workers to 578 by 1923 by recruiting fewer workers than the number who left. In 1924, new recruits again outnumbered the workers who left, probably because of the expansion of the factory that year (*Kokajō* 1923, second half).

According to the *Kokajō* for 1927 (second half), it was in that year that management became aggressive in preventing a sudden increase in the labor turnover rate. The plant required a much larger workforce for both internal and external reasons in these years. As mentioned above, the increasing external demand for workers on Nihon chissō's various projects was partially met by the colonial government's policy of transferring surplus rural labor from the south to the north. Still these projects proved attractive to many workers at the Sŭnghori plant. Internally, the expansion in Onoda's operations in Korea created a demand for more workers as well. These projects required many temporary day laborers. Beginning in 1926, the company hired many more workers (160 in 1926, 167 in 1927, 218 in 1928, 124 in 1929) than it had in previous years, and the number of workers who left was not as great as the number of new hires. Thus, management confronted the problem of how to train these newly hired workers into a stable and capable workforce as quickly as possible to fill the vacancies created by the external demand and to meet the labor force needs of the internal expansion. The new training program set up in 1927 was the response (*Kokajō* 1927, second half).

The numbers of new hires (59) and departing workers (194, of which 159 were dismissed temporary workers) in 1930 suggest that management started to reduce the number of workers as the expansion was completed. By the early 1930s, the workers hired after 1926 had had three–four years of training and had become an efficient and stable labor force. Management continued to dismiss construction or other temporary workers for the next few years (the total number of workers fell from a peak of 1,052 in 1930 to 790 in 1931 to 703 in 1932 to 655 in 1933); by 1933 the workforce was slightly smaller than it had been in 1925 (*Kokajō* 1930, 1933, second halves).

The relatively low numbers of new hires and workers who left between 1930 and 1935 (see Table 2.19) reflected the stability of the labor force in this period. In 1935, the factory had 313 skilled Korean workers. Among these workers, 114 had more than five years of service in the Sŭnghori factory and 37 more than ten years (*Kokajō* 1935, second half).

Overall, the labor turnover rate at the Sŭnghori factory before the war was not high, except in the years of high external and internal demand in the second half of the 1920s. Most of those who left or were dismissed were probably relatively uneducated workers who had no chance of becoming regular workers. Management immediately responded to this situation with more careful recruitment of common school graduates and skillful training of new recruits with selective appointments, strict rules, welfare benefits, and incentive systems. They also tried to retain experienced workers with no schooling by educating them in company training classes. Through these means, they had established a well-disciplined, stable labor force by the early 1930s.

The Onoda company's success in building and retaining a well-trained, stable labor force refutes the stereotypical picture of the Korean workers as an unstable, irresponsible, unreliable, lazy group that was hard to train. This product of the colonial prejudice of Japanese managers, which was another example of the collective group identity in the colony, was uncritically accepted by conventional nationalist narratives until the 1980s. To be sure, this kind of committed effort was limited to the large-scale modern factories, like the Sŭnghori factory, until the 1930s. When the large-scale textile and heavy industrial plants mushroomed in colonial Korea beginning in the early 1930s, the role and status of Korean labor changed and improved in diverse ways. Few Japanese managers would then be able to repeat those arrogant and irresponsible remarks about the Korean workers. This implies a close relation between, on the one hand, the size and nature of the industry and employer policies and, on the other hand, worker behavior.

Wages and Other Forms of Compensation

Throughout the colonial period, the basic compensation system of the Sŭnghori factory was composed of a daily wage (for eight hours of work) and other compensations, including limited housing benefits, bonuses (see above), and contributions to a retirement fund. Wages were paid twice a month, on the seventh or eighth and the twenty-second or twenty-third days of each month, just as at the main factory in Japan (*Shokkō kisoku*, p. 31).

The wage scales for Japanese and Korean workers differed throughout the period. As explained above, Japanese workers at the Sŭnghori branch were paid basically the same wages as workers at the main factory received, plus an overseas allowance of approximately 40 percent of the basic pay. Korean workers' wages were based on the local wage level, a practice the company had followed earlier at the Dalian branch factory (Takeda ms). In 1922, the average daily wage of workers in the main Onoda factory was ¥1.443. That same year, the average daily wage of Chinese workers at the Dalian branch factory was ¥0.68, much lower than ¥1.11 paid the average Korean worker. Temporary workers for manual work like limestone collecting or transportation were hired by subcontractors, and the Onoda company paid the subcontractor a lump sum to cover their wages (*Kokajō* 1920, second half).

The first nine months of the factory's operations were used to test worker efficiency and to determine the appropriate wages. During this period, the factory operated two shifts of 10.5 hours each. Average net pay was ¥1.72 for Japanese workers and ¥0.55 for Korean workers. In addition to the basic wage, temporary daily bonuses (¥0.35–0.20) were paid to compensate for inflation (*Kokajō* 1920, second half). (Rapid inflation began in 1917 with the economic setback following the WWI economic boom. Wages rose but could not keep pace with the soaring prices of commodities. Calculated on the basis of 100 in July 1910, the wholesale goods index in Seoul had risen to 125 by 1916 and peaked at 298 in 1919 and 292 in 1920. Thereafter prices fell until 1940, when war production again brought inflation. See Table 2.20 [Zenkoku keizai chōsa kikan rengōkai, Chōsen shibu 1939: 40; Chosŏn ŭnhaeng, Chosabu 1948: 111–45].)

Besides the inflationary pressure for wage increases, increased productivity became more and more important for the Sŭnghori factory due to the growing market for cement in Korea. As explained above, the high accident rate caused by the two-shift system led to the adoption of the three-shift system at the Sŭnghori factory on October 1, 1920. The increase in productivity and the decrease in the accident rate more than compensated for the higher wage bill (*Kokajō* 1920, second half). At the main factory, implementation of the three-shift system has lowered production costs in spite of the rise in labor costs. Along with the reduction of the workday to eight hours, a new pay scale was adopted to keep wages in line with local wages. In the revised system, the temporary bonus was discarded, and the basic wage was increased by 10 to 15 percent. A night duty bonus per shift of ¥0.10 for the second shift and ¥0.20 for the third shift was created. The average daily wage of workers increased to ¥2.40 for Japanese workers and ¥0.86 for Korean workers; these figures represented a 40 percent increase for Japanese workers and a 56 percent increase for Korean workers. The overall average daily wage at the Sŭnghori factory was ¥1.07 in November 1921 (*Kokajō* 1920, second half).

Table 2.20
Wholesale Price and Wage Indexes in Kyŏngsŏng
and the Onoda Sŭnghori factory, 1920–1944

Year	Wholesale prices (b)	Wages	Onoda wages Koreans (a)	Real Onoda Wage (a/b)
1920	100.0	100.0	100.0	100.0
1921	77.7	91.8	100.0	129.0
1922	81.5	102.3	101.2	124.0
1923	78.4	88.6	102.3	130.0
1924	80.4	89.5	100.0	124.0
1925	89.0	87.9	100.0	112.0
1926	80.1	85.5	97.7	121.0
1927	76.0	87.5	95.3	125.0
1928	73.3	87.5	93.0	127.0
1929	71.2	87.1	90.7	127.0
1930	61.6	78.1	97.7	159.0
1931	50.0	68.8	94.2	188.0
1932	45.9	57.8	97.7	213.0
1933	56.1	58.2	98.8	176.0
1934	54.8	58.2	102.0	186.0
1935	60.6	58.2	102.0	168.0
1936	65.8	68.4	103.5	157.0
1937	65.8	72.7	104.7	159.0
1938	69.9	78.5	115.0	165.0
1939	93.8	87.9	119.8	128.0
1940	106.8	91.4	127.9	120.0
1941	106.2	105.4	146.5	138.0
1942	114.0	115.2	160.5	141.0
1943	126.7	125.8	n/a	n/a
1944	142.1	136.2	n/a	n/a

SOURCES: Chosŏn ŭnhaeng, Chosabu 1948: III-145; and *Kokajō* 1920, first half; 1920, 1923–30, 1933, 1935, 1938, 1941–42 second halves.

In colonial Korea, work conditions varied by industry, factory size, composition of the workforce, and managerial experience. In the absence of factory laws, in a surplus labor market, there were no standards for work hours, no minimum wage scales, and no workshop regulations until the war brought close control of economic life. Wage scales were determined primarily by the nature and size of the industry, skill levels, sex, and age. As noted above, nationality was a

Table 2.21
Changes in Average Daily Wages at the
Mitsubishi Iron Manufacturing Company in
Kyŏmip'o, Hwanghae Province, 1918–1922
(¥/*day*)

Year	Japanese	Korean
1918	1.60	0.65
1919	1.97	0.85
1920	2.46	1.03
1921	2.46	0.95
1922	2.61	0.98

SOURCES: Mitsubishi gōshi kaisha, *Shahō*, nos. 69 (2/1/ 1919), 120 (1/31/1920), 170 (1/22/1921), 216 (12/27/ 1921), 233 (4/6/1922).

basic factor in wage determination. According to a survey by the Social Affairs Section of the Government General in 1922, the average daily wage for a Japanese male was ¥2, for a Japanese female ¥1, for a Korean male ¥1, for a Korean female ¥0.5, and for a Korean child ¥0.2 (*Andō shōmonroku* 1979: 78–79).

The wages of Korean workers at the Sŭnghori plant were comparable to local wage levels, which increased rapidly in 1919 and 1920. For example, the daily wage of a skilled worker in a knitware factory owned by a Korean in P'yŏngyang increased from ¥0.54 in 1919 to ¥0.88 in 1922 (Kajimura 1977: 178). Daily wages at Mitsubishi Steel Manufacturing Company in Kyŏmip'o, Hwanghae province, an example of a higher-paying manufacturing industry, show similar fluctuations in this period (see Table 2.21).

Increases in an individual worker's wages depended on factors such as seniority in the factory, the importance of the section in which he worked, and evaluations by section chiefs or shift heads. Bonuses, both monetary and nonmonetary, and fines also affected a worker's daily wage, although the exact method used to calculate a regular worker's wage cannot be determined from the available sources. According to Kye Chi-P'ung, the methods used to calculate wages were also unclear to workers. The reports record only average wages, and occasionally maximum and minimum wages. The system of pay raises is also untraceable in extant sources.

Table 2.22
Daily Wages of New Employees at the Sŭnghori Factory by
Age Group and Nationality, April 1921
(¥/*day*)

Skill level and Japanese-language abilities	Age		
	20–40	13–20, over 40	Child (< 13)
Koreans			
Temporary worker	0.55	0.50	0.45
Unskilled, no Japanese	0.65	0.60	0.40
Unskilled, with Japanese	0.68	0.63	0.43
Skilled, no Japanese	0.85	0.68	
Skilled, with Japanese	0.90	0.72	
Japanese			
Unskilled	1.48	1.30	0.80
Skilled	2.00	1.60	

SOURCE: *Kokajō* 1921, second half.

Wages at the Sŭnghori factory reflected larger economic fluctuations as well as the factory's reaction to those changes (see Tables 2.20 and 2.23). After the new wage system, based upon local wage levels and current inflation, became stabilized, average wages did not fluctuate much until 1933, except in 1929. Average wages stayed at the same level during the early 1920s but gradually decreased from 1926. Wages bottomed out in 1929 but started rising again after 1931 as a result of the rearmament boom following the Manchurian Incident. Wage levels at the Sŭnghori factory were in the middle range of the national averages throughout the colonial period, somewhere between the average for light industry and that for heavy industry. A 1923 survey by the Sŭnghori factory of wages and other labor conditions in five Japanese-owned factories in the P'yŏngyang area gives some idea of comparative wage levels (see Table 2.24). In terms of hourly wages, the Onoda factory paid more than the other five factories. The Sŭnghori factory also paid Korean workers the highest starting pay (¥2.09), which was probably a strong attraction, for this implied a larger potential pay in years to come. The night duty bonus of ¥0.20 was also very attractive. Most

Table 2.23
Average Daily Wages in the Onoda Factories
by Nationality, 1920–1942
(¥/*day*)

Year	Sŭnghori Factory			Dalian		
	Japa-nese	Kore-an	Aver-age	Main	Japa-nese	Chi-nese
1920/9	1.72	0.55	0.71	1.615		
1920/11	2.40	0.86	1.07	1.554		
1921	2.26	0.86		1.480	2.31	0.63
1922	2.56	0.87		1.470	2.30	0.68
1923	2.27	0.88		1.452	2.23	0.56
1924	2.29	0.86	1.11	1.460	2.35	0.55
1925	2.27	0.86	1.09	1.478		
1926	2.28	0.84	1.08			
1927	2.27	0.82	1.06	1.469		
1928	2.22	0.80	1.04			
1929	2.29	0.78	1.01			
1930	2.18	0.84	1.06			
1931	2.15	0.81	1.07			
1932	2.27	0.84	1.13			
1933	2.30	0.85	1.14			
1934	2.30	0.88	1.20			
1935	2.32	0.88	1.19			
1936	2.33	0.87	1.212			
1937	2.46	0.92	1.26			
1938	2.65	0.99	1.33			
1939	2.75	1.03	1.37			
1940	2.95	1.10	1.40			
1941	3.18	1.26	1.53			
1942	3.41	1.38				

SOURCES: *Kokajō* 1920, first half; 1920, 1923, 1924, 1925, 1926, 1927, 1928, 1929, 1930, 1933, 1935, 1938, 1941, 1942, second halves; Takeda manuscript for wages in the Dalian factory.

workers preferred longer hours if it meant more take-home pay (Kye interview).

According to a 1930 survey, wages at the Sŭnghori factory remained in the medium range in terms of nationwide average wage levels in industry (see Table 2.25). As seems apparent from the data

Table 2.24

Survey of Number of Workers, Daily Wages, and Daily Work Hours
in Five Japanese Companies in the P'yŏngyang area, 1923

| Company | Number of workers | | | Work hours |
	Japanese	Korean	Total	
Sadong Mining Company	250	100	350	10–14
Chōsen Ordnance Factory	130	70	200	10
Dai Nihon Sugar Refinery	47	106	153	12
Chōsen Electrical Company	35	55	90	10
Chōsen Commercial and Industry Ironworks	20	160	180	10
Onoda Cement Factory	107	503	610	8

| | Wages (¥/day) | | | | | |
| | Japanese | | | Korean | | |
	Max.	Min.	Aver.	Max.	Min.	Aver.
Sadong Mining Company	4.63	1.00	2.65	1.25	0.50	0.78
Chōsen Ordnance Factory	4.60	1.30	n/a	1.90	0.58	n/a
Dai Nihon Sugar Refinery	3.35	1.40	2.26	2.00	0.60	0.87
Chōsen Electrical Company	2.50	1.15	2.00	1.65	0.70	1.00
Chōsen Commercial and Industry Ironworks	2.55	0.70	2.00	1.50	0.60	0.80
Onoda Cement Factory	3.38	0.70	2.29	2.09	0.43	0.86

SOURCES: *Kokajō* 1923, first half; Takeda manuscript

presented in Table 2.25, the type of industry was the most important determinant of wage levels. The average daily wage levels for Korean male workers confirms the wage gap between heavy and light industries. The three heavy industries—machine and machine tools, metal, and the gas and electric industries—were at the top with wages of ¥1.01. The maximum wage level also shows a similar pattern; in most heavy industries maximum daily wages of over ¥3 were common. There was no legal minimum wage during the colonial period, and the lower wage levels of female workers in the textile and silk-reeling industries demonstrates the severe sex differential in the wage structure of light industries. In the early 1930s, workers whose daily pay was ¥3 or higher included autoworkers (¥3.00), furniture makers (¥3.00), shipbuilders (¥3.10), tailors/seam-

Table 2.25
Maximum and Minimum Daily Wages by Industry
for Korean and Japanese Workers, June 1931
(¥/day)

Industry	Japanese			Korean		
	Max.	Min.	Aver.	Max.	Min.	Aver.
Machine and machine tools	5.46	0.30	1.90	3.50	0.10	1.01
Metal	5.00	0.10	2.37	3.33	0.10	1.01
Gas and electricity	5.00	0.40	1.69	2.90	0.40	1.01
Printing	7.15	0.40	2.08	4.00	0.10	0.92
Miscellaneous	4.50	0.30	1.76	3.10	0.10	0.88
Lumber and wood products	5.00	0.70	2.07	3.00	0.20	0.86
Textiles (all workers)	3.30	0.70	2.40	2.60	0.40	0.80
(women only)	1.35	1.10	1.16	1.22	0.33	0.60
Cement	*3.66*	*0.76*	*2.14*	*2.20*	*0.50*	*0.80*
Food processing	6.07	0.20	1.89	4.80	0.10	0.75
Chemical	3.95	0.60	1.54	2.50	0.20	0.71
Ceramics	3.66	0.60	2.08	3.00	0.15	0.66
Silk reeling (all workers)	3.00	0.30	1.23	1.90	0.15	0.58
(women only)	1.57	0.40	0.78	1.25	0.10	0.41
TOTAL MALE	7.15	0.10	1.81	4.80	0.10	0.80
TOTAL FEMALE	1.81	0.30	0.87	2.50	0.10	0.44

SOURCE: Chōsen sōtokufu 1933: 233–43.

stresses (¥3.10), flour mill workers (¥3.30), pig iron forgers (¥3.33), general machinists (¥3.50), printshop workers (¥4.00), and rice-milling machine operators (¥4.80) (Chōsen sōtokufu 1933: 233–43).

The wage level of Korean workers at the Sŭnghori factory was in the middle of this spectrum, in terms of both average wages (¥0.80) and maximum wages (¥2.20). This may well have encouraged some skilled workers to leave Onoda to seek higher-paying jobs elsewhere when opportunities broadened later in the colonial period. In particular, jobs in machinery or metalworking factories would have attracted Korean workers with basic skills in forging, lathe operation, casting, or other skills learned in the Maintenance Bureau.

In sum, the Onoda Sŭnghori managers kept pay scales in line

with local wage levels in order to retain a stable labor force. They were successful in doing this until the mid-1930s. The wage standard was accepted by the workers with little resistance, since the alternatives for most workers were migration to overseas worksites or jobs in Korean-owned, mostly small- or medium-size, factories with lower wages, poorer working conditions, and longer hours.

After 1933 Sŭnghori managers also instituted regular wage increases in order to maintain their workforce in a period of labor-market fluctuations and high inflation. Both the labor turnover and the inflation rates increased rapidly from the mid-1930s and accelerated after the war in China began. The managers of the Sŭnghori factory began paying semiannual bonuses to cope with the wartime labor shortages and inflation (*Kokajō* 1933, 1935, second halves).

There are no data on the cost of living for a working-class family or on living standards in the Sŭnghori area that would permit reconstruction of a poverty level for Korean workers. There is no doubt that colonial workers led poor and simple lives. Most workers and their families lived in rented rooms and owned a few kitchen utensils, bedding, clothing for summer and winter, and a piece or two of furniture. That items such as clocks, books, or a Singer sewing machine were viewed as modern luxury items indicates the meager level of living standards (Kye interview; *Kokajō* 1926, 1929, second halves). In the *Kokajō* report for the second half of 1925, the Sŭnghori managers made the interesting comment that the cost of living for Korean workers was approximately one-third that of Japanese workers. Price lists of commodities normally purchased by Japanese and Korean workers allows us to compare consumption patterns (*Kokajō*, 1925, 1926, 1928, second halves).

> *Japanese workers*: rice, soybeans, Japanese sake, beer, beef, eggs, soy sauce, soybean paste (*misō*), sugar, charcoal, salt, heavy soled work *tabi* (socks), knitted cotton shirts, towels, toilet paper, socks or stockings, firewood, beancurd, soap
>
> *Korean workers*: millet, red beans, glutinous millet, Korean wine, pork, Korean soy sauce, salt, flour, noodles, kerosene, cotton cloth, dried fish, chili peppers, beancurd

A sample budget of income and expenses for a Korean worker earning ¥0.83 per day published in the *Kokajō* for the second half of 1929 provides an interesting look at the living and consumption

Table 2.26
Sample Monthly Budget for a Korean Worker
at the Sŭnghori Plant, ca. Late 1920s
(*daily wage = ¥0.83; with wife and one son*)

Income		Expenses		
Source	Amount	Item	Quantity	Amount
Wages for		Rice	3 *to*	¥4.20
28 days	¥23.24	Millet	2 *to*	2.10
Bonus for		Soybeans	1 *to*	0.70
no absences	1.68	Rent	monthly	1.50
Regular		Water	monthly	0.20
savings	-1.86	Lamp fuel	3 bottles	0.40
Fees for		Vegetables		3.00
cooperative	-0.35	Soy sauce and		
		paste	3 bottles	1.00
		Fuel		3.30
		Candies (for son)		1.00
		Bath fee		0.32
		Barber		0.30
NET INCOME	¥22.71	TOTAL EXPENSES		¥18.02

SOURCE: *Kokajō* 1929, second half.

patterns of a working-class family in Sŭnghori (see Table 2.26). These lists imply different habits and patterns of consumption and living. Relatively high-priced items such as rice, beef, eggs, sugar, charcoal, firewood, towels, socks, toilet paper, soap, and cotton knitware were in common use by the Japanese workers but not by the Koreans. Ironically, Japanese managers often used the simpler life-style of Korean workers to justify the discriminatory wage scales (see, for example, *Kokajō* 1925, second half).

The *Kokajō* for the second half of 1926 pointed out that dissatisfaction with wages was stronger among Japanese workers; the Korean workers were eager to stay on the job and did not complain. Allegedly, a Korean worker who received ¥1 a day was more satisfied than a Japanese worker paid ¥3 a day because of the higher level of expectations among the skilled Japanese workers. Moreover, the report added, many Korean workers were unsettled or migratory workers.

Basically, the Sŭnghori managers adopted the seniority-oriented wage system developed in the main company in Japan, with the critical modification of wage differentials between Japanese and Korean workers. The wages of Korean workers at the Sŭnghori plant were determined by local wage levels and fell in the middle range of the national wage spectrum. Even so, the bonus system and the regular work hours and eight-hour shifts attracted workers. The juxtaposition of Korean and Japanese workers in the same factory receiving different pay for the same work, however, inevitably gave rise to a keen sense of discrimination and unfairness. The next section discusses some responses of the Korean workers.

Labor Responses

This section addresses the Korean workers' responses to the colonial labor situation and labor relations in the factory, particularly labor organizations and labor disputes. The number of labor disputes and participants in Korea doubled during the 1920s, and the pattern of disputes became more radical and militant, despite the meager level of industrial growth and the restrictive colonial labor policy. The majority of labor disputes in the 1920s occurred in small- or medium-size workshops such as rice mills, ports, and textile factories, where labor conditions were extremely miserable due to the lack of modern management, and where police control was weak. More than half the participants in labor disputes (335 disputes, 28,291 participants) in the first half of the 1920s were mill and dock workers in rice-exporting ports such as Pusan, Inch'ŏn, Mokp'o, and Kunsan in the southern provinces. Textile workers were the third largest group, with 13.2 percent of the total number of strikers (Kim Yun-Hwan 1982: 141–48). This is a reflection on the elementary state of manufacturing and the steady growth of rice exports, which had led to the predominant position of the rice milling and textile industries in the first half of the 1920s.

During 1926–30, official statistics recorded an increase in the number of disputes to 556, with 51,531 participants. The majority of participants were non-factory workers like daily laborers or dockworkers (36.5 percent of total participants) and construction workers (14.9 percent). Factory workers accounted for only 12.2 percent; again, this is a reflection of the low level of industrial growth and the huge layer of urban informal-sector workers (Chōsen sōtokufu, Keimukyoku 1933: 146–47).

Another change in labor disputes in the later half of the 1920s was that the geographic center shifted to the northern provinces, including South Hamkyŏng and South P'yŏngan provinces, because of the construction and industrial boom and the direct and more aggressive infiltration of Communists in this area. Workers' demands became more sophisticated, and their solidarity and willingness to hold to their positions lengthened the duration of the strikes.

Two examples of this longer, more organized, and more militant pattern of disputes were strikes at Yŏnghǔng, South Hamkyŏng province, in 1928 and at Wonsan, South Hamkyŏng province, in 1929. Although in the end the workers lost in both cases, they demonstrated an unprecedented ability to organize, and their newfound solidarity helped create a tradition within the Korean labor movement (Kim Yun-Hwan 1982: 172).

The Wonsan General Strike of 1929 marked the beginning of the labor upsurge, and the frequency of labor disputes peaked during the depression years of 1930–1931. The depression hit the colonial agricultural sector hard, causing heated tenant disputes and labor friction over rapidly falling rice prices and wages for workers. Official statistics record 160 disputes, with 18,872 participants, for 1930 alone, and 201 disputes, with 17,114 participants, for 1931. Never again under Japanese rule did Korean workers rise up and strike as they did between 1929 and 1932 (Chōsen sōtokufu, Keimukyoku 1933: 143–47).[8]

Another impetus for the radical increase in labor disputes and turmoil was the sudden increase in male workers engaged in heavy industry, including chemical factories, railroads, and dam construction, in the northern provinces during this period. These industrial sites became an important target for Communist activists and Red labor union programs. According to Kobayashi Hideo's (1969: 115–22) detailed study of the Red labor union movements in the north, the Korean workers' fighting spirit was further intensified after the Wonsan General Strike when the Comintern and Propintern adopted the new extreme Leftist line after 1929, focusing on the effort to convert more laborers and farmers, who were agitated by rapidly falling rice prices and wages. The results were a soaring number of disputes among workers in the north and more militant and revolutionary

8. For a detailed discussion of the Great Depression and its impact on the Korean rural sector, especially tenant-landlord relations and the Red peasants union movements, see G.-W. Shin 1996: 58–113.

anti-imperialistic Red labor union and Red peasants union movements in the early 1930s.

The basic strategy of Communist activists was to infiltrate existing labor unions, gain control over the leadership of the organization, and channel union activities along more anti-Japanese, revolutionary lines. Their first known activity is the reorganization of a labor union in a Sinŭiju factory in October 1930; this was followed by the organization of the Hamhŭng Committee of the Chosŏn Red Labor Union in February 1931. The committee organized the Hŭngnam Chemical Red Labor Union as a subgroup. Most of the northern industrial regions, including Sinŭiju, P'yŏngyang, Hamhŭng, Hŭngnam, and Wonsan, were affected by this spurt in Red labor union organization. The colonial government was determined to eliminate any Communist elements from the north and launched an extensive anti–Red labor union campaign, starting with the arrest of the leaders of Hŭngnam Red Labor Union in 1931. Several waves of large-scale roundups of Communist activists brought the total number arrested to about a thousand by 1933 (Kobayashi 1969: 115–22).

Did the expansion of the number of factory workers and the development of a skilled workforce during the 1930s influence the class consciousness of colonial workers? Ironically, the peak of the colonial labor movement came earlier, during the late 1920s and first years of the 1930s, when the substantial industrial growth in Korea was just beginning. The fifteen years between the two world wars, which began with the 1919–20 recession after the World War I economic boom and ended with the Showa depression, was the only period when labor disputes and strikes increased and the organized labor union movement spread aggressively in colonial Korea. In addition to the economic crises, the colonial government's Cultural Policy in the 1920s and Communist infiltration of worksites are generally cited as the causes of this spurt in labor militancy and activity (S.-W. Park 1990: 43).

The Communist-oriented labor movement had an indirect, ideologically inspiring impact; for a minority of labor leaders, it provided a clarifying and forceful rationale for labor conflict even though it did little to improve actual labor conditions. Socialist study groups of young intellectuals mushroomed in the early 1920s, and the Korean Communist party was formed in 1925. These developments indirectly increased the spirit of resistance among colonial workers. This threat was sufficient to make the colonial government determined to crush Communist and radical elements. It can also be argued that the Communist movement had a negative impact on labor disputes because it intensified the government's policy of suppression. Determined to uproot Communist elements from the colony, the police indiscriminately suppressed labor leaders as Communists (Pak Hyŏn-Ch'ae 1979: 10–40).

Before 1930, the colonial government had very limited and self-serving labor control policies, which concentrated on preventing Communist agents from penetrating the factories or other industrial worksites and on supplying cheap, abundant Korean labor to large-scale Japanese factories. Japanese labor legislation like the Factory Law was not yet applicable to colonial Korea, although the Saitō government considered the full application of the Factory Law a major policy agenda under Saitō's principle of the extension of Japanese policy and cultural rule in Korea. There had been continuous debates among different government bureaus, the colonial police, businessmen, Korean nationalists represented by Korean newspaper editorials or articles, and Communist organizations on the applicability of the Factory Law to Korea in the interwar years (see Sŏn 1996: 173–204; S.-W. Park 1998). The Factory Law debates cooled down after 1934, and the effort to apply it to Korea was officially abandoned in 1936. Under these circumstances, employers had a free hand to manage Korean workers as they saw fit until the wartime government intervened in labor-management relations. Colonial workers basically had no legal protection and expressed their discontent by spontaneous strikes or more passive tactics like work stoppages, slowdowns, and frequent changes of jobs. If workers became uncooperative, the colonial police were always there to see that the employer's will was obeyed.

The image of the Korean workers' movement as anti-Japanese and anti-colonial is value-laden, nationalistic, and incorrect. Starting with the formation of the first nationwide labor organization, the Korean Workers Mutual Aid Society (Chosŏn nodong kongjehoe) in Seoul in 1921, the 1920s witnessed numerous attempts at labor organization such as the Korean Worker-Peasant League (Chosŏn nonong ch'ongdongmaeng) in 1927, and the united front organization, the Sin'ganhoe, in the same year. Non-Communist and Communist-oriented labor movements coexisted as separate forces during this period. The Communists were unable either to gain a foothold among rank-and-file workers or to penetrate workplace organizations, even though they remained a genuine threat to the colonial government (Kim Yun-Hwan 1982: 126–27).

During the entire colonial period, the Onoda Sŭnghori factory apparently had only two strikes. The first occurred on July 26, 1919, while the factory was under construction, and the second on May 7, 1931. The 1919 strike involved 38 kiln and miscellaneous day workers who demanded an immediate 50 percent raise in wages. The strike lasted one day and was settled when management promised to raise wages. The 1931 dispute was much larger. A riot involving several hundred workers broke out when a Korean worker attacked a Japanese foreman. The worker was one of many hired during the factory expansion in 1929 and 1930 who was being demoted to the temporary day-work section. The rioters accused the Japanese foremen of favoritism in selecting workers to remain in full-time factory employment. The dispute lasted several hours and was broken up when the police arrived.

The two disputes coincided with periods of labor unrest caused by economic fluctuations (Chōsen sōtokufu, Shakaika 1923: *furoku*, p. 46; *Tonga ilbo*, May 7, 1931, p. 6). Strikes were common in both these periods and broke out as a result of the high inflation after World War I and the rapid deflation and wage decreases following the Great Depression. Like the strikes at the Onoda factory, most of these were non-union outbreaks. Nationwide, the main issues were demands for wage increases due to high inflation and opposition to wage reductions or layoffs during recessions or depressions.

Collective action by Korean workers at the Sŭnghori factory was hindered by the internal segmentation of the workforce as a result of the presence of Japanese skilled laborers at the top of the structure. These Japanese workers never identified with the problems of the Korean workers under them, and they acted as low-level managers.[9] Under the circumstances, it was understandable that there were no large-scale strikes or labor disputes and no trace of union growth in the Sŭnghori factory during the colonial period.

The Sŭnghori factory, like all other large modern factories, became a target for outside agitators in the 1920s. The managers of the Sŭnghori factory were aware of increasing Communist activities in Korea. Twice, during the second half of 1925 and in the second half

---

9. Two works on the Indian industrial labor force point out the special role of foremen in the colonial factories: Lambert 1963; Morris 1965: 130–39. In India, however, Indians could become foremen.

of 1930, management reported to the main office that the labor movement was growing stronger and that Korean agitators or radical elements were present among Korean workers at the Sŭnghori factory. The *Kokajō* for the second half of 1930 emphasized that control of these radical elements in the workshop was required. It also pointed out the relationship between labor unrest and the layoffs of temporary workers hired for the expansion project. The managers responded to this threat from outside by increasing the number of security guards at each factory gate and having them patrol the factory to keep Korean workers from forming large gatherings during or after work.

These two reports suggest that the management of the Sŭnghori factory by and large was able to keep its workers isolated from outside radical agitation even though some radical elements penetrated the Sŭnghori workshop in the late 1920s. Like all other large-scale Japanese factories in Korea at the time, the Sŭnghori factory was physically a closed, isolated, and protected place. It was surrounded by a wire fence and constantly patrolled by guards. Japanese managers kept radical elements out by tight inspection, and they were fully supported in this effort by the government and the police. In the case of any agitation, the police immediately arrested the workers involved and kept them in prison on charges of violating the Peace Preservation Law (Oh and Kye interviews). The Japanese sought to use the fear of Communism to bind Koreans closer to the colonial system. As noted above, however, the results were the exact opposite. Ironically, the government authorities' tendency to see the Communists behind every dispute and every labor trouble enhanced their prestige and made them a force in the post-liberation period.

Due to the unbalanced and uneven nature of colonial industrial growth, and the totalitarian nature of the wartime emergency rule, however, the usual pattern of industrial workers leading the labor movement and increasing solidarity was not realized. The reality was quite the opposite. Labor troubles cooled down radically after 1934 and went underground completely in 1937 under the wartime emergency rule and compulsory assimilation policies. With the coming of war, unions no longer were tolerated.

Growth of a Factory Town: Sŭngho ŭp

Sŭnghori, located five miles southeast of P'yŏngyang, was transformed in one decade from a nameless village to a booming factory town, Sŭngho *ŭp*. By examining the demographic, occupational, and social changes Sŭnghori workers experienced after the coming of the Onoda factory, we can see the fascinating process of the growth of a factory town in the colonial period. This study illustrates how the lives of the workers, their family members, and other people around a large factory were influenced and transformed by, albeit with the colonial modifications, modern technology and modern values.

In terms of topography, Sŭnghori was a part of Mandal *myŏn*, and only a few dozen farm families lived there before the coming of the Onoda factory in 1917. Mandal *myŏn* was located along the southern border of Kangdong *kun* (see Map 3) and was the most populous of the twelve *myŏn* in Kangdong *kun* in 1910. Like other *myŏns* in Kangdong *kun*, the majority of the population was engaged in agriculture. Only a small portion of villagers were engaged in pre-capitalistic commerce and industrial activities.

There were few rice paddies, and the major agricultural products were millet, beans, red beans, and corn cultivated in hilly dry fields. Because of the closeness to P'yŏngyang, commercial crop cultivation was feasible, and cotton, peanuts, cabbage, and sugarbeets were grown. In addition, sericulture was well developed among farm households; since the Chosŏn dynasty the area had earned a name for producing beautiful silk and cotton fabrics (P'yŏngan namdoch'ŏng 1975: 1103).

The P'yŏngan area had abundant natural resources, including iron ore and coal, and blacksmithing and coal mining developed rapidly after the opening of the country. Kangdong *myŏn*, Samdŭng *myŏn*, and Wŏnt'an *myŏn* were the three major coal-producing areas in Kangdong *kun*. The area was also famous for production of traditional iron pots for cooking rice. *Yangban* families were relatively few, except in the P'yŏngyang area, due to the traditional discrimination against the P'yŏngan area during the Chosŏn dynasty. Commercial and industrial activities were relatively well developed. Rotating markets on a five-day schedule were opened in six places by turn in Kangdong *kun*. During the transitional period of the 1880s and the 1890s, Christianity was introduced by active Presbyterian

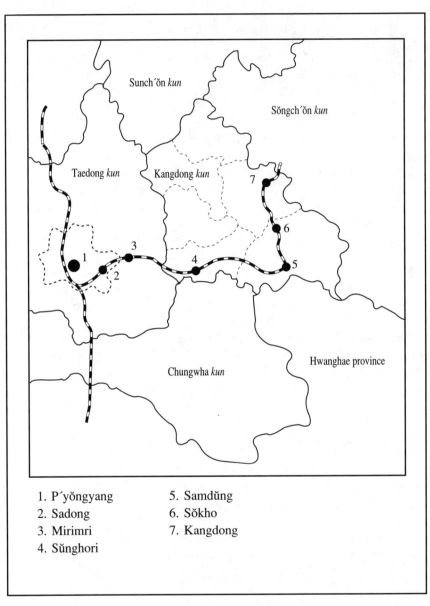

Sunch´ŏn *kun*

Sŏngch´ŏn *kun*

Taedong *kun*

Kangdong *kun*

7

6

1

3

2

4

5

Chungwha *kun*

Hwanghae province

1. P´yŏngyang
2. Sadong
3. Mirimri
4. Sŭnghori
5. Samdŭng
6. Sŏkho
7. Kangdong

Map 3 Kangdong *kun*, 1930

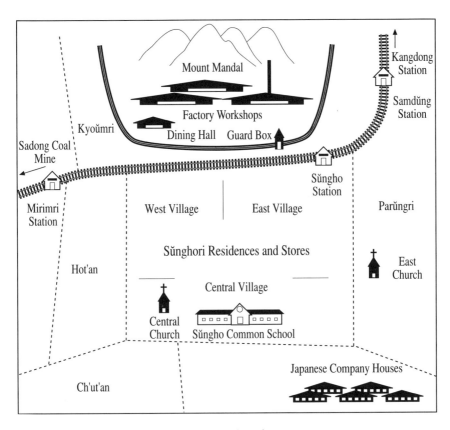

Map 4 The Sŭnghori factory

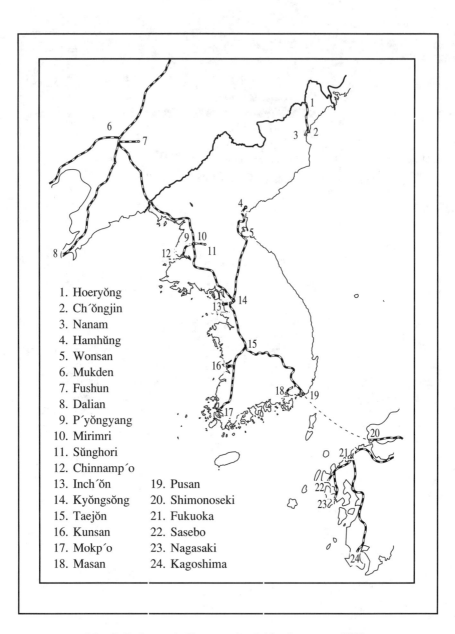

1. Hoeryŏng
2. Ch´ŏngjin
3. Nanam
4. Hamhŭng
5. Wonsan
6. Mukden
7. Fushun
8. Dalian
9. P´yŏngyang
10. Mirimri
11. Sŭnghori
12. Chinnamp´o
13. Inch´ŏn
14. Kyŏngsŏng
15. Taejŏn
16. Kunsan
17. Mokp´o
18. Masan

19. Pusan
20. Shimonoseki
21. Fukuoka
22. Sasebo
23. Nagasaki
24. Kagoshima

Map 5 Railways in Korea and neighboring areas, 1919

missionaries, and their evangelical effort was welcomed with enthusiasm. The area became the strongest Christian community in the country. Many educators and industrialists from this Christian community built a strong infrastructure of private schools and Korean-owned industries, making such things as knitware socks and rubber shoes, in this area (P'yŏngan namdoch'ŏng 1975: 1103).

The surrounding villages of Kyoŭmri, Hot'an, Ch'ut'an, and Parŭngri were mainly agricultural areas. After completion of the 11.3 km railway between Mirimri, the location of the Sadong Coal Mine, and Sŭnghori in 1917 and factory construction in 1919, many newly hired workers and their families moved in and settled in the area in front of the factory. Thus Sŭnghori rapidly developed residential and commercial areas called the East, West, and Central villages for the Korean workers and their families, which emerged as the center of activity in Mandal *myŏn*. In addition, the Onoda company housing complex was constructed in the southeast part of Sŭnghori (Kye interview; see Map 4).

The railroad from Mirimri to Sŭnghori was initially constructed to bring materials and coal for the factory construction from the Sadong Coal Mine, the largest and nearest mine in the province. By 1919, the railroad had been opened to ordinary passengers as well. An extension of this railway connected Sŭnghori to the South P'yŏngan coal mine line and the Kyŏngsŏng-Sinŭiju line, which passed through P'yŏngyang. This facilitated more frequent contact and easy access to the faster demographic, socioeconomic, and urban development occurring along the colonial railway network connecting Pusan, Kyŏngsŏng, and Sinŭiju (Andō interview; see Map 5).

Demographic Change

The sudden increase of in-migrants to the factory construction site from elsewhere in South P'yŏngan and from the surrounding provinces rapidly transformed a pre-industrial, quiet rural village into a fast-growing factory town of aggressive young people with varied backgrounds, hopes, and interests. Initially, many people from the vicinity were hired for construction work on the railway and factory facilities. Many of these day workers as well as their sons did not return to agricultural work but settled down in Sŭnghori as workers in the Onoda factory. The news of construction work and openings for day labor and factory hands spread quickly among the rural population of the province, and ambitious and intelligent young men surged into Sŭnghori looking for factory work, as well as for other work in the commercial sector that developed to support the expanding factory community (Kye interview). The census reports of the Government General for 1909, 1925, 1930, and 1935 cover only *myŏn*-level administrative units, and this makes it impossible to reconstruct demographic statistics exclusively for Sŭnghori. We can, however, make several points about population changes in Mandal *myŏn* that reflect the growth of the Sŭnghori factory in this period by comparing demographic data on Mandal *myŏn* with the five other *myŏn* in Kangdong *kun*.

During the colonial period, the local administrative institutions of the Chosŏn dynasty underwent considerable reorganization; the primary change was a reduction in the number of *kun* (counties), *myŏn* (townships), and *ri* (villages). In 1915, the Government General revised local administration into thirteen provinces (*dō*), twelve cities (*fū*), 220 *kun* (traditionally there had been 317), and 2,521 *myŏn* (a reduction from 4,322). Reorganizations continued during the colonial period to keep up with demographic changes in each unit. The number of *myŏn* in Kangdong *kun* was reduced from twelve in 1909 to nine in 1915 and to six in 1930.

Mandal *myŏn* was the most populous unit in Kangdong *kun* even before the coming of the Onoda factory in 1917, and the existence of the largest modern factory in the province at Sŭnghori and the employment opportunities there attracted more immigrants to this area in the 1920s and 1930s (see Table 2.27). The 1930 census of Korea, the only census with thorough, detailed demographic information on colonial Korea, shows a huge in-migration from other *myŏn* in the area and other provinces to Mandal *myŏn* in addition to the natural population increase. The data on birthplace of residents indicate that, in comparison to other *myŏn* in Kangdong *kun*, Mandal *myŏn* had considerably more in-migrants from other areas. The migrants were composed of an almost equal number of male and female Koreans; this implies family migration rather than the concentration of single male migrants in a factory town.

Table 2.28 also shows a concentration of foreigners, mostly Japanese and Chinese in Mandal *myŏn*. Of the 1,242 foreigners in Kangdong *kun*, 76.6 percent (951) resided in Mandal *myŏn*, probably con-

Table 2.27
Population of Kangdong *kun* and
Mandal *myŏn*, 1909–1942
(*1909 = 100*)

Year	Kangdong *kun*	Mandal *myŏn**
1909	36,604 (100)	4,928 (100) 13.5%
1925	56,396 (154)	11,312 (230) 20.0%
1930	61,873 (169)	15,319 (311) 24.8%
1935	67,267 (184)	14,599 (296) 23.6%
1942	93,268 (255)	20,221

*The percentages indicate the population of Mandal *myŏn* in relation to the total population of Kandong *kun*. By 1942 Mandal *myŏn* had been upgraded to Sŭngho *ŭp* and was no longer administratively part of Kangdong.
SOURCES: Chōsen tōkanfu 1909: 333–34; Chōsen sōtokufu 1934: South P'yŏngan *tōkeihyō*, p. 30; Chōsen sōtokufu 1935: 3; and Chōsen sōtokufu 1930–42 (1942 ed.): 36.

centrated around the Onoda Sŭnghori factory. According to Onoda's 50-year company history (Onoda semento kabushiki kaisha 1931: 521), Sŭnghori had 1,502 Korean households with a total population of 6,894 persons; and 198 Japanese households, with 658 persons. There were 42 office workers at the Onoda plant, 5 of whom were Koreans. There were 981 factory workers, of whom 193 were Japanese and 789 Korean.

Within a decade, the village had become a booming factory town with a population of over 7,000. It became a place for labor (*no-dongp'an*) where work was always available and where life was relatively better than in poor rural villages. The entire population, about 10 percent of which was Japanese, was related to the factory in one way or another. The town continuously expanded into the surrounding villages, and finally, when its population reached 20,221 (833 Japanese and 19,183 Koreans), it was upgraded to an *ŭp* (an administrative unit larger than a *myŏn* but smaller than a city, with a population between 20,000 and 50,000) during the administrative reforms of the Government General in 1941 (P'yŏngan namdoch'ŏng 1975: 1103; Chōsen sōtokufu *Tōkei nempō* 1941: 36). By 1939 there were 20 towns with populations over 50,000, and many centers had

Table 2.28
Population of Kangdong *kun* by Birthplace, 1930

	Born in South P'yŏngan province					
	Born in same *myŏn*			Born in other *myŏn*		
	Total	Male	Female	Total	Male	Female
Kangdong *kun*	38,979	21,213	17,766	18,739	7,920	10,819
Kangdong *myŏn*	5,935	3,236	2,699	2,699	1,052	1,647
Samdŭng *myŏn*	8,224	4,364	3,860	2,279	921	1,358
Mandal *myŏn*	6,130	3,349	2,781	6,807	3,391	3,416
Wont'an *myŏn*	5,965	3,246	2,719	3,321	1,516	1,805
Koch'on *myŏn*	5,905	3,226	2,679	1,644	467	1,177
Pongjin *myŏn*	6,820	3,792	3,028	1,989	573	1,416

	Born in other provinces			Foreigners			GRAND
	Total	Male	Female	Total	Male	Female	TOTAL
Kangdong *kun*	2,913	1,530	1,383	1,242	845	387	61,873
Kangdong *myŏn*	249	118	131	85	54	31	8,968
Samdŭng *myŏn*	612	276	336	17	9	8	11,132
Mandal *myŏn*	1,431	781	650	951	626	325	15,319
Wont'an *myŏn*	418	262	156	170	145	25	9,874
Koch'on *myŏn*	96	37	59	13	7	6	7,658
Pongjin *myŏn*	107	56	51	6	4	2	8,922

SOURCE: Chōsen sōtokufu 1934: 30.

been upgraded to *ŭp* status as their population passed 20,000 (Chō-sen sōtokufu 1940: 73). There were four other *ŭp* in South P'yŏngan province by 1941 (P'yŏngan namdoch'ŏng 1975: 1103). Kangdong *kun* thus had one *ŭp* and five *myŏn* by the end of 1945.

Occupational Change

The proportion of the population employed in the industrial sector grew considerably in Mandal *myŏn* as the number of workers at the Sŭnghori factory increased rapidly from 1919. A rural village where, in 1909, 87.9 percent of the population had been engaged in agriculture was transformed into a town, in which only 35.1 percent of the population was engaged in agriculture and the proportion of the population engaged in industry reached 22.2 percent by 1930 (see

Table 2.29). Since there were 789 Korean workers and 5 Korean office workers in the Sŏnghori factory in 1930, 72.6 percent of Mandal *myŏn's* industrial workers were employed by the Onoda Sŭnghori factory. The growth of the cement factory, which required support workers in related industries such as mining and shipping, created new jobs in mining, transportation, and commerce as well as administrative professional positions, drawing many people out of agriculture. Many women also became engaged in commercial, industrial, and professional work by 1930.

In the midst of this demographic boom, many modern, urban institutions and facilities were introduced into Sŭnghori society from the early 1920s. The opening of the Sŭngho Post Office in March 1924 made telegraph and telephone service available. The Sŭngho Savings Association was set up in July 1925. The Sŭngho Financial Association and the Sŭngho Consumers Association were organized in December 1930 (*Tonga ilbo*, Mar. 1, 1924, p. 1; July 15, 1925, p. 3).

A primary school was established as the population of Sŭnghori jumped to a thousand households by 1924. The colonial government had just finished its project of "one common school in every three *myŏn*" by 1922, and was on the verge of building "one common school in every two *myŏn*" at that time. In Kangdong *kun*, only two public common schools existed, in Kangdong and Samdŭng; a private school run by a Korean had been established in P'arŭngri in 1920 (P'yŏngan namdoch'ŏng 1975: 560). The Onoda management supported the plan to establish a common school by donating the money to buy land and construct a school building to the Government General, which approved the opening of a common school in Sŭnghori in 1924. A Korean in the village participated in this plan by selling the land for the school site at a minimum price. The need for education was so urgent that the Sŭngho Common School opened in November 1924 in temporary housing. The new building opened in May 1925. As noted above, the school soon became a source of Onoda company recruitment. The secondary-level Sŭngho Higher Common School was established a year later in May 1926 (*Tonga ilbo*, Oct. 4, 1924, p. 3; Nov. 1, 1924, p. 3; May 8, 1928, p. 6).

Commercial activities also grew rapidly in the early 1920s. There were three markets, one each in the East Village, West Village, and Central Village, each of which opened twice a month by turn. The three markets competed, but the central market outgrew the other two, and by 1927 it was open six days a month. Various manufac-

Table 2.29
Occupational Structure of Mandal *myŏn*, 1909 and 1930

	1909	1930 (no. of persons)	
	(households)	Male	Female
Yi official	2	–	–
Confucian scholar	2	–	–
Agriculture	847 (87.9%)	1,732 (35.1%)	1,584 (79.4%)
Commerce	67 (7.0%)	425 (8.6%)	228 (11.4%)
Industry	27 (2.8%)	1,093 (22.2%)	123 (6.2%)
Miscellaneous	16 (1.7%)	800 (16.2%)	13 (0.7%)
Day labor	3	–	–
Fishing	1	1	–
Mining	0	426 (8.6%)	9 (0.4%)
Transportation	0	328 (6.6%)	1
Bureaucrats, professionals	0	104 (2.1%)	19 (0.9%)
House servants	0	19 (0.4%)	18 (0.9%)
TOTAL	965 (100%)	4,928 (100%)	1,995 (100%)

SOURCES: Chōsen tōkanfu 1909: 333–34; Chōsen sōtokufu 1934: South P'yŏngan *Tōkeihyō*, p. 33.

tured items were sold in the market, and prices ran about 20–30 percent higher than in city markets due to the high demand and lower availability in Sŭnghori (Kye interview). Despite low wage levels, money circulated constantly because of the purchasing power of the workers, and work was available regularly in Sŭnghori in contrast to the static employment situation in other rural villages. An urban plan for Sŭnghori had been developed by the South P'yŏngan provincial government by 1931 as the village continued to expand. A system of running water and indoor faucets was expanded in 1930, and a fire station was set up in 1931 (*Tonga ilbo*, Apr. 12, 1931, p. 3; Oct. 26, 1930, p. 6). The Sŭnghori factory workers were regular consumers, with stable incomes, and belonged to the working-class community of Sŭnghori, which was being introduced to modern technology, an urban life-style, social movements, and modern values in a compartmentalized way in what was otherwise a rural area. The growth of Sŭngho *ŭp* demonstrates the uneven nature of modernity in the colony, which evolved not as a general, uniform process but with multiple possibilities unevenly spread across diverse social groups and regions in the colony.

The concentration of population, especially of the younger generation, in the confined yet booming area of Sŭnghori attracted domestic social movements such as the Presbyterian church or the educational enlightenment movement with its national independence leaders, many of whom were Presbyterians themselves (Min 1974: 182–252). These domestic independence forces had adopted a realistic, "education and industrialization" approach to their anticolonial struggle in the early 1920s after the failure of the March First movement in 1919. By 1931, two Presbyterian churches had been built, one in the East Village and one in the Central Village; both had several hundred members. These churches provided valuable places for social contact among the Korean residents. The Sŭngho Christian Youth Association was also organized in 1931 (*Tonga ilbo*, June 4, 1931, p. 3).

The youth community movement also became very active. The Sŭngho Youth Society, organized in June 1924, initiated many community activities for youths including the Sŭngho soccer team, the Sŭngho marathon team, and a night school for children of poor parents. The Sŭngho Temperance Society and the No Smoking Society were also organized among the youth as a means of improving their minds and health. Modern leisure sports like bicycling, tennis, soccer, and running were introduced by the Japanese residents and received enthusiastically by the Korean youths. The Korean residents held athletic meetings in the playground of the Sŭngho Common School in town, and these meetings became regular social events in the town. On rare occasions, Japanese and Korean players competed against each other; these events immediately became a focus of intense competition between the colonizer and the colonized groups. In 1929, the Sŭngho Boy Scout Troop was also organized (*Tonga ilbo*, July 6, 1929, p. 3).

The residence of nearly two hundred Japanese workers and their families in Sŭnghori (198 households with 658 Japanese in 1930) was as much a driving force for socioeconomic transformation as the modern factory facilities that brought modern transportation, communications, and labor control methods. Even though Japanese did not mix with Koreans socially, their higher standard of living, their different life-style, and their consumption patterns had a powerful demonstration effect on Sŭnghori. Although the impact on the villagers was undoubtedly complex in nature, the advanced Japanese standard of living was both criticized and enviously emulated (Kye interview).

The growth of Sŭngho *ŭp* is an example of the complexity of colonial modernity, which exercised a hegemonial impact on the colonial labor situation, labor relations in the factory, and workers' lives. The experience of workers in the Sŭnghori factory, where Koreans were in everyday contact with the condescending colonizers, made the situation much more complex. The mutually conflicting elements in colonialism and modernity fragmented the reaction of the Korean residents; indeed, fragmentation was the essence of the social psychology of Korean society in this period. It took many years of decolonization in the second half of the twentieth century for Koreans to undo these complex, reactive, love-hate attitudes and to accept modernity with a more positive, independent, and open-minded attitude.

THREE

The War and Korean Workers: Disintegration of the Colonial System

Wartime Changes in the Colonial Labor Force

During the last eight years of the colonial period in Korea, Japanese militarism profoundly affected the nature of both the colonial system and colonial modernity. Paradoxically, these changes were neither intended nor controllable by the Japanese policymakers, and would never have been permitted in peacetime.

Based on new empirical studies of the workforce in the colonial period, a group of scholars have come to emphasize the historical continuity between the colonial and post-colonial periods. The war, they argue, propelled diverse and intensive social change, including the greater penetration of capital in the society, rapid alteration of the occupational structure, increased urbanization, and growth of both the male and the female industrial workforce, an urban middle class, and Korean capitalists. These changes accelerated in the post-colonial period, despite the tumult of the immediate post-liberation period and the Korean War. Some historians and social scientists working on twentieth-century Korea have liberated themselves from the old historical periodization and focused on the longer period of the 1930s–1960s as a fundamental transition period for the society and economy. More research and theorization on this period will certainly lead to a better understanding of the roots of Korean modernity.

The wartime changes in the Korean labor force were significant and substantial. As noted in Chapter 1, the period witnessed the rapid absorption of surplus rural labor and urban informal-sector workers into industrial, formal-sector jobs. The colonial government actively intervened in labor mobilization and training programs. An extreme example was the organization of workers for spiritual mobilization, including the Sanpō movement and patriotic meetings. All these practices gave labor-management-government relations a different character. From the workers' point of view, although they suffered, both physically and psychologically, under the fanatical Naisen Ittai policies and the Kōminka movement, the intensive experience of some Korean workers served to make them valuable human assets in post-liberation, post–Korean War industry.

In August 1936, a year before Japan started full-scale warfare in China, Army General Minami Jirō arrived in Kyŏngsŏng as the new governor-general of Korea. He would serve until June 1942. Like his predecessor, Ugaki Kazushige, Minami was determined to mobilize the colonial economy and human resources for Japanese military expansion in China. His administration was a period of extreme struggle and suffering for the Korean people because the government authorities intervened in every aspect of colonial life, social, economic, and spiritual.

Government direction and control increased tremendously, as the economy of the colony came to be planned and controlled exclusively for the war effort. The Law for the Control of Major Industries, implemented in Japan since 1931, was extended to Korea and Manchuria in 1937, giving the Government General greater power over the expansion and establishment of war-related industries. In September 1937, the government assumed control of finance and trade through the Temporary Fund Control Law and the Temporary Regulations for Imports and Exports. From 1938 on, armament industries were subsidized by the government, through national bond drives and compulsory savings (Chŏn and Ch'oe 1978: 231–310; Kobayashi 1973: 147).

The third national-level policymaking conference, the Commission to Investigate Countermeasures for the Current Situation, organized by the Minami administration in September 1938, was charged with producing a blueprint for industrial development. The advisory report of the committee recommended (1) expansion of industries essential to the war effort, such as mining and the metalworking, machine, and machine tools industries; (2) reorganization of the Korean labor force for military purposes through the training of technicians and skilled workers and mobilization of unskilled workers; and (3) the transformation of small- and medium-size factories into subcontracting workshops for large-scale war-related industries (Kobayashi 1973: 147–48).

Accordingly, the Government General restructured colonial industry by organizing industrial associations that controlled the production, distribution, and consumption of manufactured items under the Industrial Association Law (Chōsen kōgyō kyōkairei) of September 1938. Government control was further expanded when the rationing of daily necessities such as rice, meat, fuel, rubber, sugar, and cloth was instituted in April 1941 (Kobayashi 1973: 160; Ppuri gip'ŭn namusa 1983: 87–89).

The national labor market also changed drastically. As the war progressed on the continent, the demand for natural as well as human resources increased uncontrollably from the battlefield, from factories and mines, and from construction sites inside and outside the colony. The labor surplus vanished with industrial expansion in Korea and explosive out-migration to overseas labor markets. Soon, the labor supply could not keep pace with demand. The shortage was keenly felt not only in unskilled positions but also in skilled jobs when Japanese workers, who had dominated the upper layers of most of the modern-sector job market in Korea, began to be drafted after 1939. The government's labor-related policies became more aggressive and compulsory following the inauguration of the Kōminka and the Sanpō movements.

The Government General started an aggressive official employment promotion policy (*Kan assen shokugyō seisaku*) at the national level in April 1937 to supply Korean laborers to strategic industrial projects. The National Mobilization Law, proclaimed by Prime Minister Konoe Fumimaro in Japan in March 1938, was also applied to Korea and other Japanese-ruled areas in order to control the natural and human resources of the empire. The colonial authorities appointed special officials in each province to recruit rural workers for war-related factories on the peninsula. Later recruits were sent to mines, construction sites, and factories in Japan (Hirose 1995: 132–35; Hŏ 1985: 154–65). For example, the government had to include mineworkers in the official labor mobilization program beginning in November 1938, since the Ordinance on the Korean Gold Production, promulgated in September 1937, had started a gold-mining boom. Under the program, 12,000 workers were mobilized in 1937,

20,000 in 1938, and 40,000–50,000 every year from 1939 to 1944 (Hori 1995: 98).

As noted briefly in Chapter 1, labor market fluctuations became very explosive from 1940 on as labor shortages both inside and outside Korea grew. The government's labor mobilization program became compulsory policy in 1939 with the promulgation of the Ordinance on the National Draft (Kokumin chōyōrei) and intensified in 1941 when the age of compulsory service was changed from 20–45 to 18–45, as the demand for labor became desperately urgent. The government even launched the Patriotic Labor Corps for National Support (Kinrō hōkokutai) campaign to mobilize students, women, and older males within Korea for more extensive labor (Hirose 1995: 140). These groups were frequently mobilized into such groups as the Students' Corps for National Protection (Gakudō hōkokudai), the Women's Corps for National Protection (Fujin hōkokudai), or the Industrial Corps for National Defense (Sangyō hōkokudai). Around four million persons, including women and students, were mobilized into these temporary groupings between 1942 and 1945 in both rural and urban areas for war-related work in armament factories, mines, and airport and harbor construction sites (Hŏ 1985: 197).

Besides the general labor mobilization policy, a series of compulsory regulations to control labor in every worksite were announced during 1937–1942 to stem the increasing labor turnover caused by high inflation, commodity rationing, forced labor mobilization, and deteriorating labor conditions (see Table 3.1). In March 1939, for example, the maximum work hours and wages were frozen at current levels by the Regulation on Working Hours and Wages of Workers (Shūgyōin rōdō jikan oyobi jinkin seigen torishimari rei) in order to stabilize the high turnover rate (Kwon Yŏng-Uk 1965: 204–12; Ppuri gip'ŭn namusa 1983: 89).

The shortage of skilled workers was all the more threatening because the newly established or expanded plants needed more highly skilled workers. Furthermore, the training of Korean technicians and skilled workers was essential to fill not only the new positions but also the vacancies caused by the drafting of Japanese workers. The limitations of the colonial workforce and the lack of government programs to train industrial workers were revealed clearly in this period. A skilled labor force could not be produced overnight from a labor pool whose previous experience had mostly been in simple,

Table 3.1

Wartime Industry- and Labor-Related Regulations, 1937–1942

Date	Title
1937/3	Laws for Control of Major Industries
1937/9	Temporary Fund Control Law
	Temporary Regulation on Import-Export Items
	National Compulsory Savings Association Law
1938/3	National Mobilization Law
1938/7	Establishment of Korea branch of "National Spiritual Mobilization Movement"
	Establishment of monthly patriotic day
1938/8	Inauguration of monthly air-raid drills
1938/9	Industrial Association Law
	Regulation Limiting Hiring of New Graduates
1939/3	Regulation on Working Hours and Wages
1939/6	Regulation on the In-company Training of Technicians
1939/7	National Draft Law, Special Voluntary Army Program
1939/8	Regulation Limiting Hiring of New Employees
1939	Abolition of Korean language from official usage
1940	Regulation on Employment Offices
1941	Regulation on Preventive Arrest of Thought Criminals
	Regulations on the Merger of Small- and Medium-Scale Enterprises
	Korean Labor Association Law
	Labor Control Law
	Regulation on National Labor Notebook System
	Japanization of Korean names
	Beginning of rationing of industrial materials, daily commodities such as rice, sugar, salt, meat, cloth, shoes, etc.
	Collection of war materials from the people, including daily utensils and clothes, cloth, cotton, wool, hardware items, copper, brassware, etc.
1942	Regulation on Draft at Place of Employment
	Regulation on the Compulsory Draft

small-scale workshops or who were farmers fresh from the country-side (Chōsen sōtokufu 1942: 34–35).

To meet the demand for workers, the Government General had to produce more Korean technicians and skilled workers. In 1937, it established a Skilled Worker Training Center (Jukurenkō yōseisho), in affiliation with the Chōsen Industrial Association, to promote the training of Korean technicians and skilled workers. The center had an Electrical Bureau and a Machinery Bureau and trained approximately 100–300 Korean youths every year until 1945 (An Pyŏng-Jik 1988: 172–74; Chŏng Chae-Chŏng 1989: 70–72). The government also implemented a series of labor-related laws to deal with the acute labor shortage, such as the Regulations Limiting Hiring of New Graduates (Sept. 1938), the Regulations on In-Company Training of Technicians (June 1939), and the Regulations Limiting Hiring of New Employees (Aug. 1939) (Kobayashi 1973: 158).

The Chōsen Industrial Association, organized in accordance with the Industrial Association Law of September 1938, promoted the training of skilled workers in designated factories, all of which were large-scale operations. Under the Regulation on the In-Company Training of Technicians, the designated factories were ordered to train and maintain at least 6 out of every 100 workers as skilled workers; other factories were ordered to send selected Korean youths to these designated factories for training (Kobayashi 1973: 157).

Ideological mobilization for the war was also forced on the colonial people, which made their ordeal even more complicated. The Korean branch of the National Spiritual Mobilization Movement, established by the Government General in July 1938, organized the entire country into small groups called "patriotic units" (*aikokuhan*), in every residential area (ten families as one unit), office, and factory. In the name of the Kōminka movement, the "Ideology for Imperial Subjects" was propagated in regular monthly meetings of the patriotic units. The Minami administration launched the Naisen Ittai to justify wartime hardships as an honorable sacrifice by imperial subjects for the glory of the Japanese empire. These patriotic units were later used to promote the collection of war materials such as cotton, cloth, and metals. Ration cards were distributed through these units (Ppuri gip'ŭn namusa 1983: 88–89). A series of programs including abolition of the Korean language and the Han'gŭl writing system in all official documents (1939), the closing of all Korean newspapers (1940), the Special Voluntary Draft Program (1939), the Japanization of Korean names (1941), and new educational laws (1938 and 1943) were enacted. Koreans regarded these programs as the totalitarian destruction of Korean identity. Ironically, however, many Korean elites fell into the trap of collaboration by propagating the Kōminka ideology to their compatriots (Kobayashi 1973: 159).

As the labor shortage situation grew even more urgent when the Pacific War started, the Association for Korean Labor Affairs (Chōsen rōmu kyōkai) was established in 1941 as an institute exclusively for labor mobilization. In the Government General, the Labor Affairs Section was also hurriedly established. In March 1940, the Labor Affairs Section undertook a comprehensive survey of labor resources in farm households to mobilize the remaining rural workforce; beginning in 1941 it was joined in this effort by the Association for Korean Labor Affairs. The results were published during 1941–43 as *Results of the Statistical Survey of Korean Laborers and Technicians*, and rural people were mobilized by forced draft (*kyōsei chōyō*) from 1942 on.

As of 1945, the number of compulsorily mobilized workers in Korea reached almost 720,000 (out of a total estimated population of approximately 24 million). By occupation, there were 340,000 coal miners, 200,000 factory and other miscellaneous workers, 110,000 construction workers, and 67,000 metallurgical workers. An additional 240,000 Koreans were mobilized as civilian workers for the military beginning from 1943, making almost one million men and women mobilized from Korea by force during 1939–45 (Sŏn 1996: 57; Ch'oe Chin-Ho 1981: 22).

Within Korea, 422,000 laborers were mobilized by the Government General between 1935 and 1945 into large-scale firms for armament or construction projects. Approximately 210,000 industrial workers, mostly rural recruits, were absorbed into major industrial areas such as Hŭngnam, Kyŏng-In, Sŏsŏn, and Pusan between 1937 and 1945 (Han 1963: 122–27). The outskirts of major cities in these areas became industrial and residential suburbs due to this rapid influx of rural workers (see Map 6). Thus, because of the increased openings in the expanding war economy, a large-scale interprovincial migration and a nationwide recruitment network started for the first time in the history of the colony (Ch'oe Chin-Ho: 1981: 21).

As pointed out in Chapter 1, demographic change accelerated

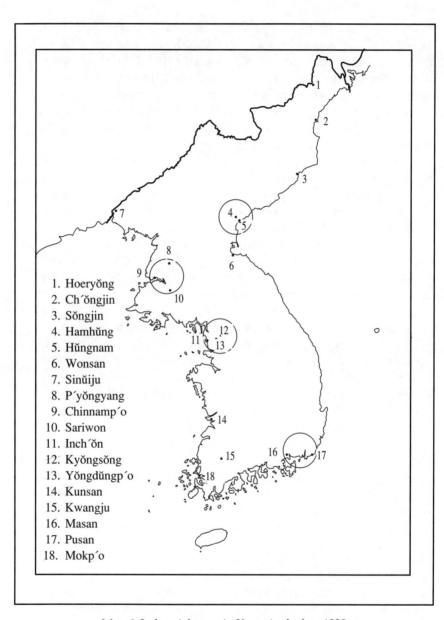

1. Hoeryŏng
2. Ch´ŏngjin
3. Sŏngjin
4. Hamhŭng
5. Hŭngnam
6. Wonsan
7. Sinŭiju
8. P´yŏngyang
9. Chinnamp´o
10. Sariwon
11. Inch´ŏn
12. Kyŏngsŏng
13. Yŏngdŭngp´o
14. Kunsan
15. Kwangju
16. Masan
17. Pusan
18. Mokp´o

Map 6 Industrial areas in Korea in the late 1930s

rapidly in the exclusive yen-bloc labor market, which integrated all the peripheral colonial labor markets. The population movements took place both to and from Korea. The explosive out-migration from Korea between 1937 and 1945 stretched throughout the wartime Japanese labor market. The number of Korean residents in Japan increased from 780,528 in 1936 to 2,100,000 in 1945, or approximately 1.32 million people (Sŏn 1996: 56–57). Emigration to Manchuria, most of which was composed of farmers from the poor southern provinces or North Hamkyŏng province, totaled 656,500 from 1937 to 1942, peaking at 167,726 in 1940. The total number of Korean residents in this region increased from 1.04 million in 1938 to 1.56 million in 1944 (Hori 1995: 116). Equally significant was the continuous influx of Japanese residents into the colonial labor market. The number of Japanese residents in Korea increased from 527,000 in 1930 to 713,000 in 1940 to 750,000 in 1945 (Hori 1995: 114–16; Ch'oe Chin-Ho 1981: 13).

As we saw in Chapter 1, the pace of rural-urban domestic migration also accelerated during the war and brought about rapid urbanization. The population of cities with more than 20,000 people increased from approximately 1.6 million (7 percent of the total population) in 1935 to approximately 4 million (14 percent of the total population) in 1945. Around two million people moved to urban or industrial areas in the last decade of the colonial period, a remarkable change compared to the previous decades (Hori 1995: 110–14). Roughly half a million people, the majority of whom had just left rural areas, were absorbed into mining, industry, and construction activities in major industrial areas between 1937 and 1943 (see Table 3.2).

Equally impressive and significant in this period was the growth of the factory workforce. Both quantitatively and qualitatively, the colonial industrial workforce grew, despite its abnormal, imbalanced nature. The number of factory employees increased from 207,002 in 1937 to 390,000 in 1944, outstripping the growth rate for the first half of the 1930s. Because of the wartime industrial policy of emphasizing the chemical, metalworking, and machine and machine tool industries, male workers were rapidly absorbed into large-scale, highly sophisticated heavy industrial factories. This in turn engendered an upgrading of the quality of the workforce in this period (Chŏn and Ch'oe 1978: 311–15; Im 1969: 51–52).

Table 3.2
Changes in Numbers of Factory, Mining, and
Construction Workers, 1937–1943

Year	Factory	Mining	Construction	Total
1937	207,002	166,568	161,499	535,069
1943	362,953	280,000	380,000	1,020,000
Increase	155,951	113,432	218,501	484,931

SOURCE: Hŏ 1985.

The composition of the factory labor force also changed, becoming oriented more toward heavy industry and dominated by males. The ratio of workers engaged in the two major light industries, textiles and food processing, decreased from 44.6 percent of the total number of workers in 1936 to 30.7 percent in 1943, while workers engaged in the chemical, metalworking, and machine and machine tools industries increased from 38.1 percent in 1936 to 42.1 percent in 1943. Most noteworthy was that growth in the number of workers engaged in the metalworking and machine and machine tools industries, as a percentage of all industrial workers, increased from 9.9 percent in 1936 to 24.6 percent in 1943 (see Tables 3.3 & 3.4).

A significant change also took place in the role and status of trained Korean workers in this period. The turnover rate among skilled Korean workers, especially in large modern factories, however, became very high as many skilled Japanese workers left for the battlefield. Many Korean workers sought better jobs, and many were lured away by the managers of newly established factories who were able to make better offers (*Kokajō* 1935, 1938, 1941, second halves; Kye, Oh, and Kamata interviews). Managers also made an effort to improve grievance-resolution mechanisms and gave regular wage increases, bonuses, and special commodity rations (*Kokajō* 1935, 1938, second halves). Workers who stayed were often given more responsibility, an indication of improved opportunities for the upper strata of the Korean factory workforce, as we will see below and in Chapter 4. In addition, workers in simple, small-scale workshops could move upward to larger factories, and in some cases rural recruits were trained intensively for a short period for skilled jobs (Kye, Lee, and Oh interview).

Table 3.3
Structural Changes in Industry and the
Industrial Labor Force, 1936–1943
(*absolute numbers*)

Industry	1936		1939		1943	
	Factories	Workers	Factories	Workers	Factories	Workers
Textiles	402	33,830	608	52,081	2,605	79,763
Metal	259	6,787	295	17,875	645	41,504
Machine and machine tools	344	7,939	613	29,579	1,354	47,821
Ceramics	366	8,269	342	15,162	1,818	36,920
Chemicals	1,425	41,972	1,618	71,673	987	63,718
Lumber	271	4,906	360	12,401	2,005	28,417
Printing	286	6,273	313	8,403	606	10,053
Food processing	2,258	32,617	2,348	48,610	2,202	31,758
Utilities	50	812	34	1,336	123	8,921
Miscellaneous	296	5,394	422	13,319	871	16,078
TOTAL	5,957	148,799	6,953	270,439	13,216	364,953

SOURCES: Chōsen sōtokufu 1930–43 (1936–39, 1943 eds.; includes all factories in Korea without regard for size of capitalization); 1943 figures from No Tong-Sang 1948: p. 24.

The correlation between the rapid growth in the size of the industrial workforce and its qualitative improvement is, however, still a matter of controversy in Korean historiography, because scholarship is in general cautious and reluctant to accept a pluralistic, more complex approach not only to the issue of the quality of the labor force but also to the evaluation and interpretation of the wartime changes. "Enclave" theorists argue that since the increase in the factory labor force was compulsory and the result of ad-hoc wartime policies, it was inevitably abnormal, temporary, and imbalanced. They also point out that upgrading human resources takes time and could not have been done in eight short years. The sudden, forced labor mobilization lowered the productivity of industrial worksites, and the quality of the workforce was diluted by a continuous influx of new rural recruits.

It is true that the majority of conscripted laborers were fresh from the countryside and some had probably never seen a modern factory. It was difficult for such recruits, who had little or no schooling

Table 3.4
Structural Changes in Industry and the
Industrial Labor Force, 1936–1943
(*as percentage of total*)

Industries	1936		1939		1943	
	Factories	Workers	Factories	Workers	Factories	Workers
Textiles	7.0%	22.7%	8.7%	19.3%	19.7%	22.0%
Metal	4.3	4.6	4.2	6.6	4.8	11.4
Machine and machine tools	5.0	5.3	8.8	10.9	10.3	13.2
Ceramics	5.7	5.5	4.9	5.6	13.7	10.2
Chemicals	24.2	28.2	23.3	26.5	7.5	17.5
Lumber	4.6	3.3	5.2	4.6	15.2	8.1
Printing	4.7	4.2	4.5	3.1	4.6	2.7
Food processing	38.0	21.9	33.8	18.0	16.7	8.7
Utilities	0.9	0.5	0.5	0.5	0.9	1.9
Miscellaneous	4.9	3.6	6.1	5.0	6.6	4.4
TOTAL	100.0	100.0	100.0	100.0	100.0	100.0

SOURCE: Calculated from data in Table 3.3.

and seldom understood Japanese, to comprehend the manufacturing process (Oh and Kamata interviews). They were trained in simple factory operations for a short period and then tasked with simple jobs that did not require much skill. The results were high accident rates, frequent absenteeism, group desertion from the workplace, and sabotage. Studies of this enclave theory group often contend that the labor force mobilized from the countryside during the war was influenced but not transformed by its experience, a "spurious" group of workers who showed little continuity in development after the end of colonial rule (see, e.g., Cumings 1984: 489–90).

Nevertheless, many recent studies of this period have discovered that the conventional enclave theory interpretations, mainly because of their politically biased, dichotomizing logic, overlook the significant historical changes Koreans experienced in the Japanese wartime empire. Revisionist historians, such as An Pyŏng-Jik, Hori Kazuo, Chŏng Chae-Chŏng, Hŏ Su-Yŏl, Soon-Won Park, and Sŏn Chae-Won, agree that although the forced mobilization created a huge group of "spurious" workers and lowered the average quality of the factory workers, the colonial workforce at the time of liberation consisted of varied groups who differed fundamentally in their attitude toward urban industrial life. Current Korean scholarship is seeking to understand the multiple characteristics of colonial society to rediscover silenced voices and overshadowed historical truth.

For example, the workforce formed before 1937 should be distinguished from temporarily mobilized, displaced peasants. Some of the former had been transformed into factory workers through at least five years of regular work experience before the war, and this group did stay in an urban industrial environment after the war, whereas the wartime draftees hoped to return to their native villages. Inevitably these two groups varied widely in their level of class consciousness and their connection with urban working-class life, depending on the time of their entry into the industrial work environment, the number of years of urban industrial life they had experienced, and their work motivation and skill level.[1] Younger historians and social scientists are searching for a new historical narrative that will illuminate the complex nature of colonial modernization in various aspects of Korean society, which evolved with multiple variations unevenly spread across diverse social groups, regions, and periods.

War and the Sŭnghori Workers

The cement industry in colonial Korea and Manchuria, where rapid industrialization was also pushed by the Japanese government and military, was treated differently from the way it was treated in Japan. In Japan, it was hit hard in 1937, when the government categorized it as nonessential industry in wartime and banned expansion of production facilities. Rationing of coal for the cement industry started in 1939, and the production of cement dropped to approximately one-third of the 1939 level after 1940. The production and distribution of cement in Japan were controlled by the government through the Cement Industry Association organized in 1940 under the Industrial Association Law (Onoda semento kabushiki kaisha 1951: 368).

The chiefs of staff of the Japanese army in Manchuria and Korea controlled production and distribution and the expansion of facili-

---

1. The question of whether these draftees returned to the countryside or stayed in urban and industrial areas after liberation remains unanswered by Korean historiography to date.

ties by dispatching production supervisors to every large, war-related factory. Army planners gave absolute priority to war industries such as chemicals, metals, machines, and machine tools, and to the mining of strategic raw materials such as coal, gold, iron, nickel, black lead, and other light metals.

Until the expansion of the war with the bombing of Pearl Harbor, the cement industry in northern Korea and Manchuria was encouraged to expand existing facilities and to build new facilities. The demand for cement accelerated with the construction of industrial sites, railroads, ports along the northern coast, and a huge hydroelectric dam on the Yalu River. From a business standpoint, Onoda's early expansion in Korea and Manchuria worked well as a counterweight to the slump in the cement industry in Japan. The Ch'ŏnnaeri factory had increased its capacity to 400,000 tons/year by 1937, outstripping the mother factory in Japan and becoming the largest Onoda factory, producing almost 50 percent of the total profits of the company (Onoda semento kabushiki kaisha 1951: 360; *Andō shomonroku* 1979: 98).

Other Japanese cement companies searching for new investment opportunities outside Japan also ventured into Korea. The Ube Cement Company set up the Chōsen Cement Company in Haeju, Hwanghae province, in 1936 and the Asano Cement Company opened its branch, Chōsen Asano Cement Company, in Sariwon, Hwanghae province, in 1937. Onoda and the other two companies organized the Cement Industry Association in 1937 and divided the market for cement in colonial Korea, with 55 percent for Onoda and 45 percent for Ube and Asano (*Andō shomonroku* 1979: 94).

The Onoda company responded to the wartime government and military intervention by expanding its operations in northern Korea and Manchuria and developing a closer relationship with the Government General. Six new Onoda factories, three in Korea and three in Manchuria, were set up during the war, giving Onoda five factories in Korea and seven in Manchuria by 1943 (see Map 1, p. xvi). The Government General sent a production supervisor to the Sŭnghori factory in 1938 to guide and control the company's plans and decisions to meet the needs of the war. In return, the Minami administration provided loans from the Bank of Chōsen and various administrative supports to establish new factories in strategic locations.

The locations of the three new factories in Korea (Komusan, Samch'ŏk, and the Yalu River or Sup'ung Dam) were selected for their strategic importance. The Komusan factory (established in 1937) was set up in North Hamkyŏng province, where metalworking and the machine and machine tools industries were rapidly developing to exploit the rich natural and mineral resources of the province for the war effort. These items were shipped directly to Japan through the northeast ports of Ch'ŏngjin, Najin, Sŏngjin, and others. The Samch'ŏk factory (established between 1937 and 1942 because of wartime difficulties in construction) was established in Kangwon province to supply cement to the southern areas, which had previously had no cement factory. The Yalu River Dam factory was set up to supply the huge demand for cement to construct the Sup'ung Hydroelectric Dam, started in 1939 as a joint venture between the Noguchi zaibatsu and the Manchurian government. Due to the urgent need for cement, the factory was fitted only with a pulverizing system by 1940, and semiprocessed cement was shipped from the Sŭnghori factory to be finished there (Onoda semento kabushiki kaisha 1951: 374, 392).

Another industrial effort undertaken by the government in support of the war was a new railway in South P'yŏngan province. The construction of the South P'yŏngan Central Railway was launched in 1939 to help develop coal mines in the northern areas of the province around Kangdong, Samdŭng, and Taesŏng to meet increased wartime demand. The Sŭngho station, which had been an isolated terminus of a branch railway line, was now connected to the cross-provincial South P'yŏngan Central Railway, which was extended to Sŏkho station in July 1939 and then from Sŏkho to Kangdong in November 1939. This was the final impetus in the urban transformation of Sŭnghori; with the in-migration that resulted, the population increased to over 20,000, and in 1941 Sŭnghori became an *ŭp*.

Another impetus for in-migration was the announcement of the Regulation on the Draft at the Place of Employment (Genchi chōyōrei) by the government in 1942. Under this regulation, Korean youth who wanted to escape the draft for forced labor in Southeast Asia or the Japanese coal mines surged into this factory town to grasp any kind of employment that would exempt them. This phenomenon occurred in all large factories in Korea (Lee interview).

The production of cement in the colonies peaked in 1939. Japan occupied most of China by 1939, and the force of the war had abated as Japan exhausted its resources. The coal supply to the cement factory was reduced considerably, and the quality of the coal that was supplied was poor. There were also shortages of other materials and machine parts. Fluctuations in the labor supply of both Japanese and Korean workers were also critical. Production was often interrupted, and productivity declined precipitously. The production of cement in Korea declined from 150,000 tons/year in 1942 to 80,000 tons/year by 1945 (Onoda semento kabushiki kaisha 1951: 387).

Finally, in 1942 the government designated the Onoda factories in Korea war-related factories to manufacture alumina clinker, a material used in fighter planes. Alum mined in North Hamkyŏng province was processed into alumina clinker using the cement-pulverizing rollers in the Onoda factories and sent to Japanese factories to make aluminum, since the supply of bauxite from Southeast Asia was blocked in 1942 (Onoda semento kabushiki kaisha 1951: 389).

With the expansion of the war following Pearl Harbor, Japan's demand for human resources finally exhausted the colonial labor reservoir. The nature of the changes in the labor force at the Sŭnghori factory during this period is revealing. First, the ratio between Korean and Japanese workers changed markedly, although the total number of workers remained constant at around 650–700. The number of Japanese workers decreased from 131 (19.1 percent) in 1938 to 83 (12 percent) in 1942, and the number of Korean workers increased from 554 (80.9 percent) in 1938 to 599 (88 percent) in 1942.

Second, the number of regular workers, both Japanese and Korean, decreased, and the number of Korean novices and apprentices increased (see Table 3.5). The drop in the number of Japanese regular workers, which started in 1934 or 1935, accelerated after 1938 when many Japanese workers were drafted. The number of Japanese draftees increased from 19 in 1938 to 20 in 1939 to 21 in 1940. These vacancies remained unfilled due to the shortage of young Japanese men, especially after the Pacific War began in 1941 (*Kokajō* 1935, second half; Sŏn Chae-won [1996: 133] points out that a small number of the Japanese draftees returned to the plant before the end of the war).

A decrease in the number of Korean regular workers was also

Table 3.5
Number of Workers by Rank and Nationality
at the Sŭnghori Factory, 1933–1942

Rank	1933	1935	1938	1941	1942
Japanese					
Regular	108	101	92	62	66
Apprentice	16	12	19	14	7
Novice	13	45	20	16	10
TOTAL	137	158	131	92	83
Korean					
Regular	301	313	255	220	248
Apprentice	162	88	111	149	159
Novice	55	141	188	227	192
TOTAL	518	542	554	596	599
GRAND TOTAL	655	700	685	688	682

SOURCES: *Kokajō* 1938, 1941, 1942, second halves.

noticeable between 1935 and 1938. A company report from the second half of 1935 recorded a concern over the rising turnover rate among skilled Korean workers due to the increasing demand for these workers from large-scale war-related industries. In particular, skilled workers in the lathe, forging, and casting sections of the Maintenance Bureau of the Sŭnghori factory were leaving for better jobs in the growing machine and machine tools, and metalworking industries because of their technical skills. The establishment of branch factories of the Ube and the Asano cement companies in Hwanghae province in 1936 and 1937 further accelerated the turnover rate of skilled Korean workers in the cement industry (*Kokajō* 1938, second half; Kye interview).

Third, frequent intra-company transfers sent skilled workers to the newly established factories in Komusan (1935–37), Samch'ŏk (1937–42), and the Yalu River Dam (1939–40). For example, the skilled workers group at the Samch'ŏk factory was composed of around twenty Japanese skilled workers and twenty Korean skilled workers transferred from the Sŭnghori, Ch'ŏnnaeri, and Komusan factories. At the same time, these new factories sent their apprentices

to the Ch'ŏnnaeri or Sŭnghori factories for several months of training (Oh interview).

The number of Korean apprentices and novices rose considerably,
from 229 in 1935 to 351 in 1942. This increase reveals the drastic
steps taken by management to cope with the high turnover rate
among regular workers and the general shortage of workers as the
war progressed. The Regulation on the Draft at the Place of Employment also provided an incentive to mobilize workers in large
Japanese factories by making conscription for unskilled jobs in the
Sŭnghori factory equivalent to the military draft. Thus, jobs in the
Sŭnghori factory became very attractive to youths who desired to
avoid the military draft. After the rationing of daily necessities
started in April 1941, workers in large, war-related factories such as
the Sŭnghori factory received rations of rare items such as rubber
sneakers, socks, and clothing. They could use these items to bargain
for rice on the wartime black market (Oh interview).

Of equal significance is the close relation between seniority and
the turnover rate of the regular workers. The number of regular Korean workers with more than five years of experience and who received the long-term service bonus increased from 114 in 1935 to 174
in 1938 (see Table 3.6). During the war, the turnover or transfer of
regular workers who had between five and seven years of experience at the Sŭnghori factory increased, although the number of
regular workers with more than ten years of seniority increased
continuously between 1935 and 1942 (see Table 3.7).

This stability among the most senior workers probably resulted
both from the workers' commitment to their job and the factory and
from management's emphasis on seniority as a guiding principle of
labor relations. Such loyalty developed not only because the individual worker had invested more than a decade of commitment in
the company but also because management had made a determined
effort to keep experienced skilled workers by giving them seniority-
oriented benefits such as regular pay increases, pensions for long
service, retirement benefits, and other bonuses (Kokajō 1938, second
half).

As for ideological mobilization, the Onoda Sŭnghori factory was
also incorporated in the National Spiritual Mobilization movement.
As a part of the Campaign for the National Protection Corps of Industrial Workers, the Onoda Sŭnghori Branch of the Federation of

Table 3.6
Number of Regular Workers by Years of Service and
Nationality at the Sŭnghori Factory, 1935–1942

Years of service	1935	1938	1941	1942	Long-service bonus (¥)*
		Japanese			
5 years	16	17	3	2	¥5
7 years	8	23	14	9	8
10 years	14	14	16	14	14
15 years	7	11	13	10	25
20 years	3	2	4	6	40
25 years	3	4	3	3	60
TOTAL	51	71	53	44	
		Korean			
5 years	53	68	22	4	¥5
7 years	24	56	63	42	8
10 years	37	39	45	63	14
15 years	0	11	30	29	25
20 years	0	0	1	5	40
25 years	0	0	0	0	60
TOTAL	114	174	161	143	
GRAND TOTAL	165	245	214	187	

*This bonus was paid twice a year; years of service include service in the Onoda
factories in Japan.
SOURCES: *Kokajō* 1935, 1938, 1941, 1942, second halves.

Table 3.7
Number of Workers with over Ten Years of Service
in the Sŭnghori Factory, 1935–1942

Nationality	1935	1938	1941	1942
Japanese	27	31	36	33
Korean	37	50	76	97

SOURCES: *Kokajō* 1935, 1938, 1941, 1942, second halves.

the National Spiritual Mobilization was organized in July 1938 to promote the spiritual education of workers by emphasizing austerity and sacrifice. All other forms of social gatherings among the workers, such as athletic meets, movie nights, or recreational nights, were discontinued. Instead, patriotic units were organized, and blackout, fire, and air raid drills, lectures, and ceremonies were held to prepare for total war and possible air raids. Every month, the factory stopped operations for several days, and all the workers had to participate in these gatherings (Komusan branch *Kokajō* 1938, second half).

Beginning in July 1938, on the first anniversary of Japan's invasion of China, a "patriotic day" ceremony was held on the first of each month. The ceremony started at 10 A.M. with bows toward the east in the direction of the Imperial Palace in Tokyo. This was followed by prayers for the Imperial Army and a silent tribute to fallen soldiers. Then the Japanese flag was hoisted, and everyone sang the Japanese national anthem. The lectures that usually followed this anthem consisted of explanations of the progress of the war, remarks celebrating victory, and statements encouraging austerity and sacrifice as hallmarks of the peoples of the Japanese empire. After the lecture, the "Patriotic Marching Song" was sung, and "The Oath of Imperial Subjects" was chanted. The meeting ended with shouts of "Banzai!" for his Imperial Majesty (Ch'ŏnnaeri branch *Kokajō* 1938, second half).

At this point, the Japanese contempt for Koreans as a colonized people began boomeranging on them. As Kim Sam-Su (1993) notes, the Japanese had to recognize Koreans as "pseudo-subjects" of the Japanese empire in order to elicit voluntary participation and sacrifice for the war effort. This was a clear denial of the entire rationale for colonialism, which was based upon discriminatory racism. In this sense, Japan was fighting a war against itself to resolve certain basic problems engendered by rapid modernization in the first half of the twentieth century: the imbalances between Japan and weaker neighbors, between Japan and the West, and, most of all, between Japan's aspirations and its actual capabilities.

Although the degree of participation in these programs by workers, especially Korean workers, or even Japanese managers is doubtful, as noted above, government-labor-management relations and labor-management practices that evolved during this period had a lasting impact in the colonies as well as in Japan. In line with the

Sanpō movement, the Onoda factories in Japan had to reorganize and expand the existing *kondankai* (round-table social gathering) to include blue-collar production workers as equal members of the company community, in addition to the original white-collar engineers and office managers, for the first time in its history. Andrew Gordon (1981: chaps. 11–15) stresses, developing Hyōdō Tsutomu's earlier work, that the wartime labor-management experience, based on mutual respect and voluntary cooperation, was instrumental in the formation of post-1945 Japanese-style labor-management systems, including paternalism, lifetime employment, and the company union system.

At the Sŭnghori factory, however, colonial circumstances once again led to a modification of practices followed in Japan. During the prewar years, the Sŭnghori management had organized the Cooperative Society exclusively for social exchanges among Japanese workers; workers did not, however, participate in decision making, even on such matters as improving working conditions and workshop productivity (*Kokajō* 1925, first half; Sŏn 1996: 164–65). The Japanese managers had accepted Korean office clerks and engineers only to the extent of including them in the Kurabu (Club) organization with other Japanese office managers and engineers.

During the Sanpō campaign, the Sŭnghori managers again avoided applying the essential part of the campaign—mutual respect and voluntary cooperation for national goals—to the Korean workers, because of the fundamental conflicts between the Sanpō idea and the nature of colonialism. There was no reorganization of the Cooperative Society at the Sŭnghori, Ch'ŏnnaeri, or Komusan factories. Instead, a more superficial, sacrificial, military-style regimentation was practiced in the name of patriotic meetings and the Sanpō; it included such activities as disciplinary lectures, patriotic meetings, and air-raid drills (Ch'ŏnnaeri branch *Kokajō* 1940, first half; Komusan branch *Kokajō* 1941, second half). In short, the essence of the Sanpō movement—acceptance of the workers as equal members of the company community—was never applied to colonial factory workers, even during the desperate times of war. The self-deceiving nature of the wartime Naisen Ittai policy was undeniable. In the colonial factory, Korean workers and Japanese managers were bound together as protagonists in a collective drama in which the unequal two were an indispensable pair.

In sum, the wartime industrialization after 1937 brought substantial changes in the labor market, labor-management relations, and state-labor relations. The colonial government's authoritarian and self-serving labor policy, which focused only on Japanese interests, had worked quite efficiently during the prewar period but began to fall apart during the war years. Many unwanted, unintentional changes happened to the Korean economy, society, and labor. These changes led to the rapid disintegration of traditional Korean society and opened up greater opportunities for the upper strata of Koreans who were participants in the colonial system. These changes became a significant colonial legacy in post-colonial Korea. The Sŭnghori case shows how these changes affected Korean workers. The upper layer of the Korean workforce learned economic drive in an intensive manner and responded to wartime industrial growth, making themselves into more responsible and skilled workers.

Nevertheless, the fundamental ethnic segmentation of the colonial labor system, indeed of all aspects of Korean society, never ended, even in the midst of the Kōminka movement. For the Japanese, acceptance of the colonized people as equals would have meant a fundamental denial of the central notion of Japanese imperialism: the Japanese deserved to rule because they were superior.

The psychological and sociocultural experiences of Koreans who lived through the war explain the deep sense of bitterness of the colonial generation and the nationalistic psyche and energy shown not only in the economic drive but also in the strong movements for self-renewal and self-rediscovery of everything Korean after the 1960s. The drive for self-assertion has been so strong and obsessive that it is often pointed out that there has been not an aggressive but a defensive racism, a counter-mythology in Memmi's term, among Koreans toward outsiders, especially the Japanese.

The model for the colonial generation was, however, Japan, and this mind-set instilled in this generation a confused love-hate attitude toward modernity in general; this distinguishes them from the following generation. By 1945, Korea had come a long way toward modernity, compared with the situation at the beginning of the colonial rule in 1910, but a free, independent view of self and a confidence in a fuller form of modernity were still a long way away. Chapter 4 examines the equally dramatic changes in Korea in the post-liberation period by looking at the Onoda Samch'ŏk branch factory and its workers.

FOUR

Workers in Liberated Korea: The
Onoda Samch'ŏk Factory

What happened to the Onoda Sŭnghori factory when the colonial regime dissolved abruptly in August 1945 and the Japanese left the factories? And what happened to the Korean workers in the plant? Unfortunately, the lack of access to sources in North Korea makes it impossible to answer these questions in detail. We can, however, glimpse the connection between the colonial legacy of technological skills and the reopening of the factory in the immediate post-liberation period, based on interviews with former managers, engineers, and workers from both the Sŭnghori and the Samch'ŏk factories now living in South Korea or Japan.

According to Andō Toyoroku (pers. interview), manager of the Sŭnghori factory in 1945, the factory was immediately taken over by a "self-governing council" (*chach'i kwalli wiwonhoe*) organized by Korean office and factory workers on the day of liberation, August 15, 1945. Andō had gone to P'yŏngyang that morning, unaware that Japan had surrendered, to attend a meeting of factory managers organized by the governor of South P'yŏngan province. At the meeting, he heard the news that the war had ended, and hastened to return to the factory. When he arrived at the Sŭngho train station, he found the railroad already under the control of the Korean staff, who demanded that passengers not speak Japanese, saying, "Only in Korean . . . ."

The self-governing council had already taken over the factory when Andō arrived at the plant. In retrospect Andō believes that the Koreans had anticipated an eventual Japanese surrender and set the council up much earlier. The council's representative asked Andō to hand over the cash and gold in the office, saying, "Everything in the plant will be done by Koreans from now on." Andō said his house was later used as the official residence of the Soviet lieutenant who took charge of the Sŭnghori factory. All the Japanese employees of the plant hurriedly prepared to return to Japan, fearing violent treatment by Koreans or Soviet soldiers. The repatriation of ordinary Japanese workers at the Sŭnghori factory by chartered boats continued for a year and was not completed until September 1946 (Andō interview).

Andō and approximately three dozen engineers were, however, detained for the next three years by the Soviet military, which used them as technical supervisors and trainers for Korean managers and workers. The final return of Japanese engineers to Japan took place during November 1947–June 1948. Another Sŭnghori factory engineer, Ikeda Yoshihisa, remembered this period vividly. He arrived at Sŭnghori in December 1944, as the chief engineer of the Brick Section, and stayed until June 1948. Ikeda was interviewed in January 1949 and described in detail what happened after the liberation. According to him, the Sŭnghori factory was taken over by the Soviet Occupation Army on August 29 as a nationalized industry and resumed operations on October 15 under the supervision of the Soviet military. Four months later, in February 1946, the Japanese detainees began making plans, as industrial and technical advisors to the Soviet military, to resume operations on a small scale at other factories. Andō and Ikeda and the other engineers, who were now treated with special care and protected by the occupation authorities, visited many major factories throughout northern Korea, including the Hwanghae Steel Mill at Kyŏmip'o, the Haeju Cement Factory, the P'yŏngyang Ceramics Factory, and the former Onoda cement factories at Ch'ŏnnaeri and Komusan, advising on operational, technical, and planning matters (Morita and Nagata 1980: 474–80).

The Japanese were ordered to teach industrial planning to young technicians and engineers recruited in the P'yŏngyang area. The occupation authorities also ordered them to start a one-year technical school, first called the Sŭngho Ceramics Industry Technical School (Sŭngho yŏŏpkisul hakkyo) in 1946 and then renamed the Ceramics Industry Higher Technical Center (Yoŏp kodŭngkisul hakkyo) in 1947, when the school accepted 40 middle-school graduates as students. Initially, the Japanese engineers taught four classes in technical and engineering subjects: cement, firebrick, ceramics, and glass manufacturing. Koreans taught classes in English and politics. As the Japanese engineers were gradually repatriated, their numbers were reduced to three by 1948 (Morita and Nagata 1980: 474–80).

By the end of 1948, the newly established Democratic People's Republic of Korea (DPRK) authorities, led by Kim Il Sung, had taken over the management of all major industrial facilities, and the Soviet occupation forces withdrew. The Sŭnghori area has been developed and expanded as a major industrial complex on the outskirts of P'yŏngyang, although the details of development are not available. The modern transformation begun in the late nineteenth century abruptly bifurcated into two totally different paths in the second half of the twentieth century.

The changes in management and employment at the Onoda Samch'ŏk factory, the only Onoda plant in what became South Korea, can be traced in more detail from available written sources and through personal interviews. This chapter examines the reconstruction process at the Samch'ŏk factory in the post-liberation era and in the 1950s and then addresses some larger historical questions related to the colonial legacy from the point of view of labor and the characteristics of the members of the colonial generation. The legacy of colonial modernity—a complex self-view, self-alienation from their Korean selves, and the view that they were a new generation—could not be erased overnight and deeply affected the history of post-colonial Korea.

The Onoda Samch'ŏk Factory in 1945

The 1980s were a major turning point for socioeconomic historical studies and interpretations not only of the colonial period but also of the 1950s in South Korea. Many iconoclastic studies criticized work done during the 1960s and 1970s as politically biased reflections of the nationalistic issue of the "independence of the national economy." These critics argued that, as with the works of the enclave theory school of the colonial period, the perspectives of Japanese Marxist economists and Korean nationalist historians had dominated earlier scholarship. Nationalist historians have viewed the socioeconomic changes of the 1950s with a fixed and negative image of "monopoly capitalism," or sometimes "economic imperialism," which was heavily dependent on the international dynamics of the capitalist world. Their portrait of Koreans in this period was, inevitably, negative, focusing on the "distortion," "imbalance," and "victimization" of the Korean economy, the "severe sacrifice" of agriculture, the "concentration and monopoly of power" in the few economic giants (the *chaebŏl*), and the "severe political abuses" of the ruling Liberal party (for representative examples of nationalist histories, see An Rim 1954; Kajimura 1965; Hwang 1966; Pak Hi-Bŏm 1968; Pak Hyŏn-Ch'ae 1978; Chŏng Yun-Hyŏng 1984; Kim Tae-Hwan 1981). Labor was depicted as cheap, abundant, exploited, potentially volatile, and politically anti-government.

The new empirical studies that appeared during the 1980s reexamined these views and criticized them for focusing on historical discontinuities and the impact of external factors to the neglect of the internal dynamics of the Korean people and society and the historical legacy and socioeconomic continuity, which began unfolding fully with the new industrialization of the 1960s. Like the revisionist energy directed at the enclave interpretation of colonial industrial growth, these studies attacked the economic imperialism model of the 1950s as totally ignoring the complex political and military relations between Korea and the United States in this period, when Koreans were much more independent historical actors. To be sure, South Korea's success as a model newly industrializing country restored national self-confidence to some degree and made observers, both inside and outside the South Korean academic community, probe Korean capitalist growth from a more objective historical perspective. In this context, the new studies emphasized historical continuity with the colonial period, as well as the Korean War and reconstruction periods, as the foundation of the rapid industrial growth and social change in the 1960s, although they also admit the reality of dependency in South Korea's economic development (see, e.g., Yi Tae-Kŭn 1987; Yi Pyŏng-Ch'ŏn 1987; Kim Chin-Yŏp 1985; and Yi Sang-Ch'ŏl 1989).

With these larger historiographical trends in mind, the guiding questions in the examination of the reconstruction of the Samch'ŏk Cement Factory are: What was the legacy of the "colonial labor experience" for post-1945 Korean labor history? To what extent did the patterns of labor mobilization and control of the 1960s and later differ from those of the colonial period? What was the relationship among the state, business, police, and workers in this period? What did the colonial birth of the workforce mean for the history of Korean labor in the twentieth century? To what extent did the colonial period represent a break with Korea's past and establish a new pattern of labor relations and state-society interaction? What was distinctive about Korea's labor force as it developed in this period, compared with that of Japan or the West during their respective periods of formation of a modern labor force?

The Samch'ŏk factory, Onoda's fourth branch factory in colonial Korea, was established in Sajik-ri, Samch'ŏk *kun*, Kangwon province, in 1937. Because of the difficulties of obtaining machinery and materials during the war, construction of the factory was not completed until five years later, in June 1942. The operation experienced difficulties from the beginning due to wartime coal rationing and an insufficient supply of machine parts for maintenance. The factory, with a capacity of 84,000 tons/year, usually operated below that level.

In terms of labor organization within the factory, the Samch'ŏk factory was organized into a General Affairs Bureau and an Engineering Bureau, with employees divided into two groups: office workers and production workers. The General Affairs Bureau was composed of eighteen office workers, including two Korean clerks and two Korean engineers. The Onoda main office sent seven newly recruited engineers, including one Korean, to the newly opened factory to supervise production in February 1942. These seven were recruited by the Onoda main office along with 45 other new graduates of professional engineering colleges or universities in December 1941 (the graduation date had been advanced three months in order to alleviate the wartime shortage of technicians and engineers). The six Japanese engineers were drafted into the Japanese army over the next two years, leaving only the Korean engineer, Oh Pyŏng-Ho. The vacancies were not filled, and older Japanese engineers who were not drafted because of their age took over their functions. In addition, several elderly, trusted skilled Korean workers were given more responsibilities (Oh interview).

During the remaining three years of the colonial period, Oh transformed himself into a thoroughly knowledgeable cement industry engineer. Oh's career is a good example of the rapid advancement open to the upper layer of the Korean labor force in modern-sector jobs in schools, companies, banks, factories, stores, and even government offices. In 1942, Oh was 22, an unmarried white-collar worker living in company housing, fresh out of the Ube Professional Engineering College in Japan. He worked long hours, due to the increased demand for his time given the vacancies in many engineering positions. Consequently, he was able to learn all the production processes in the factory by spending several months in rotation in the various sections of the Engineering Bureau, under the special guidance of his Japanese supervisor. The head of the Engineering Bureau, Kusagawa Shintarō (?-1989), was a second-generation colonialist who graduated from the Keijō Technical Professional School (Keijō kŏgyŏ senmon gakkō) and later from the faculty of engineering of Meiji University. After graduation, he was hired by the Onoda main office in Tokyo and sent to Sŭnghori in 1928. He worked there until he was sent to Samch'ŏk when it started operations in 1942.[1] Oh was able to learn all aspects of cement manufacturing by the end of World War II. Thus, this eldest son of a landlord in Chinju, South Kyŏngsang province, became the only experienced cement industry engineer in South Korea at the time of liberation. His knowledge became immensely valuable at the time of the reconstruction of the Samch'ŏk factory as the Tongyang Cement Company in 1957.[2]

The factory workshop, which was under the Engineering Bureau, had approximately 40 skilled workers and around 160 new recruits. About two-thirds of the skilled workers were Koreans transferred from the Sŭnghori, Ch'ŏnnaeri, and Komusan factories; the rest were Japanese sent from the other three Korean branches or from the main factory in Japan. Most of the Japanese workers were senior employees who were not liable to the draft because of age, and they were invited to Samch'ŏk as section chiefs to supervise the production and to manage Korean laborers (Oh, U, and Ha interviews).

The unskilled workers were young Koreans, mostly recruited from the Samch'ŏk area. Many of them came to the factory to escape the overseas draft. Among these new recruits, the younger and better educated were sent to Sŭnghori and Ch'ŏnnaeri for several months of training in cement manufacturing. Under these circumstances, many Korean youth were able to accumulate valuable skills

1. Due to the close master-apprentice relationship that developed between Kusagawa and Oh in these intense three years, Oh later invited Kusagawa to Korea in the 1960s, when he had established himself as the chief cement engineer in South Korea (Oh interview).

2. Oh worked at the Tongyang Cement Company after 1957 as director of engineering and during the 1960s trained many of the key engineers of such present-day giants as the Ssangyong, Hyundai, and Hanil cement companies (Tongyang shiment chushikhoesa 1967: 107-12).

through intensive training at a much faster pace than they would have in peacetime (Oh interview).

I was able to trace and interview two of these Korean workers in 1985. U Chin-Hong, born in 1920 in Samch'ŏk and still a resident there in 1985, entered the Samch'ŏk factory as a skilled worker in 1941. He had gone to Keijō after graduation from Samch'ŏk Common School to study at the Senrin Commercial Higher Common School, but had had to quit after two years. He then entered a Japanese-owned machinery plant and worked there five years, transforming himself into a skilled worker. When he heard of the opening of the Samch'ŏk factory, he applied and was hired as a skilled worker in the Engineering Bureau. Two years later, at the time of liberation, he was a section chief in the Engineering Bureau.

The other interviewee was Ha T'ae-Ick, also born in 1920, who began work at the Samch'ŏk factory in 1941 as a new recruit. His life and career pattern were somewhat different from that of U Chin-Hong. He was born into a farm family in South Ch'ungch'ŏng province; his family moved to Samch'ŏk when his father went bankrupt and had to leave their hometown in 1938. Ha was 18 years old, fresh out of a common school, when he arrived in this booming wartime industrial town. He was immediately hired by the Mitsui Fat and Oil Company and worked two years there until he moved to the Onoda factory in 1941.

The managers of the Samch'ŏk factory enjoyed an advantage in recruitment during this time of acute labor shortage because some jobs at the Samch'ŏk factory were designated as draft-exempt in 1942 and instantly became sought after among Korean young men. Good personal connections were needed to get a job in factories in which employment exempted one from the military or forced labor draft. U and Ha remembered that many secondary school graduates, who would not have taken such jobs in peacetime, came to Samch'ŏk or other Onoda factories as office clerks to evade the draft.

At the time U and Ha were interviewed in 1985, both former Samch'ŏk factory workers were presidents of small cement-related concerns. Both emphatically recollected that during the war, skilled workers in large war-related factories were increasingly viewed as *kisulja* (engineers). These positions were seen as modern, promising, and well-paid jobs for young men. Skilled workers in war-related factories were paid relatively well. U remembered that his first pay envelope contained ¥2.20; in two years he was earning ¥3 per day, higher than the initial salary of many college graduates at the time. Ha remembered that he initially earned ¥0.90 a day. The status of artisans or handicraftsmen, traditionally quite low, was increasingly upgraded throughout the colonial period. Like the other Onoda factories, the Samch'ŏk factory was designated as a war-related factory in December 1944 and started to produce alumina clinker with its limestone pulverizers. After the liberation, it was the only cement factory in South Korea until the Munkyŏng Cement Company was established in 1957 (Tongyang shiment chushikhoesa 1967: 14–15).

From Self-Governing Council to Government Management

Like the Sŭnghori factory in the north, the Samch'ŏk factory was taken over immediately after liberation by a self-governing council organized by the two remaining Korean engineers and around 100 factory workers, including the skilled workers transferred from the northern factories. Oh and one other office worker and around a dozen veteran skilled workers emerged as leaders in protecting the factory from outsiders and in resuming operations (Oh interview).

The self-governing council's first task was to control and assist the repatriation of the Japanese working in the plant. Unlike the situation in the north, no Japanese engineers were detained for technical advice. By September 1945, most of the Japanese in the Samch'ŏk factory, including both office and factory workers and their family members, had left for Japan. Oh recollected that around twenty Japanese engineers, office workers, and skilled workers and their families were returned to Japan on two specially chartered ships by September 12. Some twenty or so skilled Korean workers who had come from the northern factories went back to their hometowns, although some stayed at the Samch'ŏk factory during this initial stage. By this time, many Koreans recruited to work in the factory at the time it began had become regular, skilled workers. Many of these were immediately promoted to leadership positions. For example, U became head of the Engineering Bureau.

Three days after the repatriation of the Japanese and less than a week after the arrival of the U.S. Army in Seoul, the U.S. Occupation Forces arrived at Samch'ŏk, because of its importance as the largest industrial complex and port on the eastern coast of the southern half of the peninsula.[3] The unit in charge of the Samch'ŏk region, commanded by a Captain Chapman, visited the Onoda Samch'ŏk factory and announced that the Samch'ŏk area was under the command of the U.S. Military Occupation Government and that every important decision should be reported to him in advance. He also ordered Oh and others to let him use the Onoda Company housing facilities as his headquarters (Oh interview).

Oh went to Seoul in September 1945 as the representative of the self-governing council to ask the U.S. Military Government for financial support to keep the factory going. He met Yu Han-Sang, the chief of the Commerce and Industry Bureau of the Occupation Government in Seoul, and asked for funds to pay wages and resume operation of the factory. The request was accepted, and money was transmitted to the Samch'ŏk factory's self-governing council through the government of Samch'ŏk *kun*. On October 1, 1945, the factory resumed operations with Korean engineers and workers. Under Oh's leadership, many of the young skilled workers trained at Sŭnghori and Ch'ŏnnaeri and the older workers transferred from those places in 1942 played important roles in this operation. But this attempt turned out to be only a symbolic act lasting less than a few months. Operations could not be sustained amid the political turmoil outside the factory (Oh interview; Tongyang shiment chushikhoesa 1967: 395).

In addition to problems caused by the lack of capital, maintenance difficulties, and the absence of committed top management, the factory environment was soon shattered by the political struggles for a national identity between left and right that enveloped the country between late 1945 and late 1948. During the next several years of turmoil and disorder, the factory ceased operations — proof of the importance of political stability for sustained economic activities.

A big turning point in the power struggle came in the winter of 1945. In November 1945, left-wing groups initiated an aggressive national labor movement by organizing the Chosŏn National Council of

3. Oh, U, and Ha said that Samch'ŏk was famous for its strong leftist tendencies. All three remembered Communist leanings among the skilled workers sent from the northern factories. There were six large Japanese factories in Samch'ŏk in 1945: the Onoda Samch'ŏk Cement (200 employees), Mitsui Fat and Oil (more than 1,000), Pukp'yŏng Steel Mill (100), Mikka Iron and Steel (200), Hokusan Chemical (150), and Tokai Development (specializing in railroad construction).

Labor Unions (hereafter called Chŏnp'yŏng, an abbreviation of Cho-sŏn nodong chohap chŏn'guk p'yŏng'ŭihoe), with a claimed membership of 400,000. The Communist groups, which had gone underground during the war, resurfaced in this period and organized workers at the factory level. In the same month, a Samch'ŏk branch of Chŏnp'yŏng was organized. This political mobilization was followed the next month by the decision of the U.S.-USSR Joint Commission at a meeting in Moscow to advocate trusteeship status for liberated Korea under the supervision of the four great powers.

Beginning in November 1945, workers in the Samch'ŏk cement factory divided into left-wing and right-wing groups. The left-wing workers participated in mass rallies organized by Chŏnp'yŏng. Factories all over the southern half of Korea became sites of confrontation between the left-wing and the right-wing and often became gathering places for unemployed leftist workers or repatriated Koreans from overseas (Oh interview). According to the recollections of Oh, U, and Ha, about 70 percent of those working in the factory were left-wingers, and regional background strongly influenced political groupings at this stage. They remembered that many of the skilled workers from Sŭnghori or Ch'ŏnnaeri were leftists, due to their early exposure to the Communist movement in the north, where Communist agitation had been more prominent. Workers from the Samch'ŏk area tended more to join the nationalist right. These assertions are, however, hard to substantiate with written evidence.

Each group tried to dominate the other and seize control of the factory. The Chŏnp'yŏng group participated in many mass rallies in Samch'ŏk, attacking the U.S. Military Government with slogans such as "Long Live Chŏnp'yŏng," "Down with the U.S. Military Government," and "Pro-Trusteeship." These demonstrations frequently escalated into physical violence and stone throwing. The factory stopped operations, and the facilities themselves were in jeopardy. Left-wing workers also organized strikes against the management of the factory, demanding payment of delayed wages and guarantees of food for the workers (Tongyang kŭrup 1987: 14–16).

The U.S. Military Government took two important steps to cope with this Communist onslaught. In December 1945, it promulgated Ordinance No. 33, which prohibited workers' self-governing councils and announced the official takeover of all former Japanese-owned public and private properties as the Occupation Government's vested properties (*kwisok chaesan*). Accordingly, the Samch'ŏk Cement Factory became a government business under the direct supervision of the Commerce and Industry Bureau of the U.S. Military Occupation Government. Within several months, the Military Government began appointing managers for the major vested properties (Tongyang kŭrup 1987: 14–16).

This move made the self-governing council at the Samch'ŏk factory meaningless by early 1946. Conventional studies of this period, especially nationalist-oriented labor studies, tended to interpret the period as one of a class-oriented labor movement led by Chŏnp'yŏng. Recent studies, however, have shown that this was an overstatement and redefined these industrial movements as the natural reaction of workers and engineers confronting a power vacuum after the Japanese left the country. As Pak Chi-Hyang (1992: 130–35) has pointed out, it is more accurate to characterize the labor movement at each industrial site as a spontaneous attempt to protect the workshop from violence and destruction and to maintain it for future operations rather than as a Marxist, class-oriented labor movement led by Chŏnp'yŏng.

The year 1946 marked the peak of Chŏnp'yŏng activities, before it was outlawed and destroyed by the U.S. Military Government. The Chŏnp'yŏng leadership succeeded in organizing a series of general strikes and numerous riots/rallies that year, including the Tongyang Textile Company strike at Inch'ŏn in June, the railway workers' general strike in September, and the Taegu riots in October. The U.S. Military Government decided to crush these leftist movements, with assistance from the rightist nationalist groups. The nationalist groups organized the Korea National Labor Union Association (hereafter "Taehan noch'ong"; abbreviated from Taehan min'guk nodong chohap ch'ong'yŏnmaeng), in March 1946, to counter the left-wing political movement of Chŏnp'yŏng. The Taehan noch'ong launched counter-rallies to block Chŏnp'yŏng activities and to draw the masses into the anti-Communist struggle. The Military Government authorities began their counterattack in December 1946 by closing the Chŏnp'yŏng organ *Haebang ilbo* (Liberation daily) and outlawing north–south travel. They finally outlawed Chŏnp'yŏng and arrested its chairman, Hŏ Sŏng-T'aek, and 51 other leaders during the annual convention in Seoul in February 1947 (Yang 1989: 197–98).

Samch'ŏk Cement as a Government Enterprise

Under Ordinance No. 33, the U.S. Military Government took over approximately 3,000 properties and began appointing managers to the most important, largest, and most urgently needed strategic enterprises and institutions. In September 1946, Lee Sŏn-Kŭn, a historian, nationalist leader, and a close friend of Yu Han-Sang, the Commerce and Industry Bureau chief of the Military Government, was appointed the first manager of the Samch'ŏk factory, which was renamed the Samch'ŏk Cement Manufacturing Company. Lee, who was an absentee manager, lasted only a year. In July 1947, as his replacement, the newly established South Korean Interim Government in Seoul appointed Han Ch'ŏl, a former construction contractor with the Onoda Samch'ŏk factory. He lasted two years, and in September 1949, a third manager, Kim Mun-Ki, was appointed. Kim was soon replaced by Hong Ki-Won, in April 1951, during the Korean War.

All these appointments came about through personal connections to powerful persons in the governments in power. All were absentee managers, uninterested in investing capital or entrepreneurial effort into the factory. Most of these men had no knowledge or experience of factory management. They were interested in the ownership of the factory primarily for its future political and economic potential and for its utility in building connections with the U.S. Military Government and later with the ruling parties, the Korean Democratic party (Han'guk minjudang) and later the Liberal party (Chayudang), and thus with the Rhee Syng-Man government (Tongyang kŭrup 1987: 17–18).

The second manager, Han Ch'ŏl, was a leader of the extreme rightist group in the Samch'ŏk area and ran a successful construction business. In appointing him, the Interim Government hoped to eliminate Red elements from the factory. At this time, the authorities arrested around 30 leftist leaders in Samch'ŏk, which included the leaders of the Samch'ŏk branch of Chŏnp'yŏng and representatives of the self-governing councils of every major factory in Samch'ŏk. Oh Pyŏng-Ho was arrested as the representative of the Samch'ŏk Cement self-governing council. Around a dozen skilled workers who had come from the Onoda factories in the north returned home, sensing the government's impending anti-Communist campaign. The Samch'ŏk-born workers and several office workers who remained tried to protect company property, as workers fought each other inside and outside the main factory buildings demanding jobs, food, and wages. Without qualified management, however, the workers went unpaid and no money was spent to repair damaged facilities or machines (Oh interview; Tongyang kŭrup 1987: 396).

Under Han's management, many unemployed people or repatriates were brought into the factory to counter the leftist mob and to end the frequent strikes and rallies inside the workshop. This surplus labor situation in the factory continued until it was privatized in 1957. U Chin-Hong and Ha T'ae-Ick remember that the left-right ratio in the workshop gradually reversed during this period until about 70 percent of the workers were rightists. Traditional feelings of regionalism appear to have been a factor underlying the political dynamics.

After the establishment of the Republic of Korea in August 1948, a semblance of stability returned to the Samch'ŏk cement factory. The new Rhee government appointed the third manager, Kim Mun-Ki, in September 1949. He arrived with a new managerial staff and tried to manage more aggressively by firing 200 of the 800 workers whose political orientation he found suspicious and by reorganizing management. The demand for cement increased as the new government started its economic reconstruction program. At this stage, the technology and operations were based on the colonial legacy, even though the quality of the products and the productivity of the operation were much lower than they had been in the colonial period. There was as yet no technological influence from the United States. Some veteran skilled workers could manage the operation using facilities and materials left from the colonial period. For example, U Chin-Hong became a leading engineer in these years, and Ha T'ae-Ick was promoted to an engineering position by 1949. A recent study of the onetime Japanese oil refinery in Ulsan and its reconstruction after 1945 confirms the continuity in technological know-how and human capital in the post-1948 era (Kim Tong-Uk 1989: 188–89).

This stabilizing trend was shattered when the Korean War broke out on June 25, 1950. The North Korean army invaded Samch'ŏk on June 29. The plant was bombed by North Korean planes at this time, and some of the machinery and cranes were destroyed. The factory workshop was immediately occupied by the North Korean army. Many left-wing workers who had been dismissed returned and seized power in the workshop. Managers, engineers, and workers who opposed the Communists had to flee south, leaving all the facilities, materials, and documents behind. Those who were not able to evacuate were killed by the North Korean army as anti-Communists. The factory was once again transformed into a gathering place for the training of villagers and workers in communist ideology (Tongyang kŭrup 1987: 102–4).

At the end of September 1950, the South Korean army recaptured Samch'ŏk after the successful Inch'ŏn landing and the taking of Seoul. North Korean soldiers remaining in Samch'ŏk pushed the South Korean army back once more but were driven out again by October 1950. Several key managers, including Oh Se-Ung and Pae Sŏk-Chi, returned to the factory to survey the destruction caused during the invasion but had to re-evacuate two months later when the Chinese People's Volunteer Corps invaded from the north in January 1951. This time, the managers and workers in the Samch'ŏk factory buried the important remaining machinery and equipment inside the plant to prevent damage. The North Korean army seized Samch'ŏk again for three months until the final Communist retreat in April 1952. When the armistice meetings began in P'anmunjŏm in the summer of 1951, the evacuated managers and scattered workers started returning to the Samch'ŏk factory (Tongyang kŭrup 1987: 102–4).

The Privatization of Samch'ŏk Cement

The agreement of the U.S.-Korean Joint Economic Committee Concerning Economic Reconstruction and Financial Stabilization, often called the "Paek-Wood agreement" and signed in May 1953, two months before the Armistice Treaty, was an important turning point in the economic recovery of Korea. This agreement guaranteed not wartime aid but a full-scale U.S. aid program for economic rehabilitation and reconstruction. Approximately U.S.$1 billion in aid, including funds from the United Nations Korean Reconstruction Agency (UNKRA), the Foreign Operation Administration (FOA), and the government dollar/whan currency reserves, was poured into the Korean economy, not in unassigned cash grants but in allotments to pay for specific budgeted items between 1953 and 1956. The Rhee government allocated this aid to the three most urgent areas of economic rehabilitation: the construction of industrial infrastructure and facilities; the import of industrial materials and consumer goods; and the supply of aid goods (roughly in a 50:45:5 ratio). Each fund controlled different areas of rehabilitation. The goal was to put the Korean economy back on an independent, aid-free footing by 1959 (Chang 1992: 84–87).

The reconstruction of the cement industry received the full attention of policy planners from the beginning of the economic rehabilitation period as the backbone of the producer goods industry along with two other major industries, fertilizers and electrical generation. The government appointed Kang Jik-Sun the fifth manager of the Samch'ŏk factory, in February 1953, to lead this recovery work.[4] A full-scale revamping was begun at the Samch'ŏk factory in March 1953 using government funds. A loan from the Bank of Korea and U.S.$631,500 in UNKRA funds were allocated to this project. Much of the limestone, coal, iron ore, and other materials had been stolen during the war, and the main crane for moving material had been destroyed. Reconstruction of the factory by the private sector would have been difficult at this stage because of the lack of capital, electricity, coal, and managerial personnel (Tongyang kŭrup 1987: 104). In previous scholarship, the severe destruction of most industrial facilities and infrastructure during the Korean War has been used as evidence to deny the colonial legacy and to emphasize the discontinuity between the colonial and the post-colonial periods. The reconstruction of the colonial industrial facilities at the Samch'ŏk factory certainly offers a contrary example and indicates the biased nature of this interpretation and its deliberate ignoring of historical continuity by emphasizing the element of discontinuity.

A new electrical generator with a capacity of 2,300 KW was built at the factory, and the factory produced 61,195 tons of cement in 1954, all the cement produced in South Korea that year. The government also initiated a survey of a limestone mine in Munkyŏng, North Kyŏngsang province, as a potential site for a new and larger cement factory that could meet the increasing demand for cement. Cement imports increased rapidly from 1951 to meet the demand from the construction boom after the war, but dropped drastically after 1958, an indication of the success of the government's import-

---

4. Kang Jik-Sun was deputy minister of the Ministry of Postal Communications at the time. He was a career bureaucrat from the Japanese colonial period and had risen in the Ministry of Postal Communications in the new government from the position of head of the post office to the ministership. He had no business experience and sought the job when he learned through his connections with the Liberal party of the impending privatization of government properties.

substitution industrial policy in this period (see Table 4.1) (Yi Tae-Kŭn 1987: 151–62; Tongyang kŭrup 1987: 105).

As expected, the Samch'ŏk factory was sold to Kang by the government for 700 million whan in 1956. This was the result of the government's decision to sell most of the major government enterprises to private industrialists, as called for in the Paek-Wood agreement. This privatization provided the foundation for the rapid growth of the so-called three "white" industries (cotton textiles, flour, and sugar) and the rapid accumulation of capital in the hands of a few industrialists, who became leaders of the *chaebŏl* (Kim Yang-Hwa 1990).

Many studies of the 1980s approached this post–Korean War industrial reconstruction through case studies of the cotton textile, woolen textile, and flour industries, which were important industries at the time (as were sugar, brewing, cement, and glass), and of the medium-size rubber and knitware industries. These studies divided the reconstruction period into two different stages: pre-1957 industrial development—a period of monopoly and commercial capital accumulation based on the foreign aid–dependent three "white" consumer goods industries of cotton textiles, flour, and sugar processing; and post-1957 industrial development—a period of light industry–oriented producer goods industries, such as cement, glass, fertilizer, and parts for cars, textile machinery, and electrical goods. They see these years of import-substitution industrial growth as laying the foundation for the 1960s export-oriented industrialization (see, e.g., Kim Chin-Yŏp 1985; Yi Sang-Chŏl 1989; Kim Yang-Hwa 1990; and Suzuki 1985). In short, these revisionist economic historians highlighted the inner dynamics of the Korean people and the energy they had accumulated for industrial growth despite a heavy dependence on foreign aid and technology at the time. These scholars continue to uncover and reconstruct Korea's modernization to clarify the complexities of this period when historical continuities and discontinuities interacted and intertwined.

When the production of Samch'ŏk Cement stayed at the 50,000 tons/year level even after the repair work, the managers identified the fundamental problems as (1) the deterioration of facilities and frequent breakdowns of machinery, which hampered operations and increased production costs drastically; (2) high transportation and distribution costs because of the remote location of Samch'ŏk;

Table 4.1
Supply and Demand of Cement
in the Republic of Korea, 1954–1959
(*metric tons*)

Year	Demand (A)	Domestic supply (B)	Imports (C)	B/A (%)	C/A (%)
1954	74,888	62,235	12,653	83%	17%
1955	188,959	56,257	132,702	30	70
1956	62,629	46,564	16,065	74	26
1957	288,886	95,427	193,459	33	67
1958	566,610	258,180	307,881	45	55
1959	461,371	419,821	41,550	91	9

NOTE: The Tongyang Cement Company manufactured all the domestic supply of cement prior to 1957, the year in which the Munkyŏng Cement Company began production. In 1957, the Tongyang Cement Company produced 78,103 MT of the total domestic production, and in 1958, 88,244 MT of the total.
SOURCE: Tongyang kŭrup 1987: 106 (the percentages shown for 1955 and 1957 and the total demand for 1958 have been changed from those shown in the source).

(3) high labor costs because of an excess number of workers (around 600), many of whom had returned to the factory claiming jobs as former workers; (4) a labor movement that became very aggressive after the promulgation of the three labor-related laws in August 1953; and (5) a huge donation to the ruling Liberal party (Tongyang kŭrup 1987: 106–7). Among these, the labor problem was the toughest challenge and demanded equally tough and committed managerial decision making. The Korean National Assembly passed three basic labor laws in August 1953 giving labor unions the rights to organize, to bargain collectively, and to strike. The Labor Standards Law, passed several months later, gave workers leverage in their struggle with management. The Samch'ŏk Cement Factory labor union was organized by the end of 1953 and became very active, using strikes and demonstrations to demand unpaid back wages, regular wage payments, and stable food supplies. The newly passed labor laws made workers more aggressive (Tongyang kŭrup 1987: 107).

Senior workers who had worked in the Onoda Samch'ŏk factory during their early twenties took leadership roles in the labor union at the Samch'ŏk factory. Most of these men had been classmates at the Samch'ŏk Industrial School (secondary level) during the colonial period, and this school connection strengthened union solidarity (Oh interview). All three interviewees, Oh Pyŏng-Ho, U Chin-Hong, and Ha T'ae-Ick, remembered the militancy of the labor movement in the Liberal party period and during the short-lived post–April 19th liberal period, especially when compared with the situation in the Park and Chun eras, demonstrating, among other things, the different levels of government intervention in labor affairs and labor-management relations among these regimes.

After the privatization of Samch'ŏk Cement, labor-management relations became even more complex and difficult. Initially workers had welcomed private management and the influx of capital for reconstruction. They hoped management would pay back wages and guarantee stable work. Soon, however, workers became disappointed by the frequent slowdowns in operations, by delays in payment of wages of days and even months, and by the inability of management to cope with these problems (Tongyang kŭrup 1987: 106). The workers even replaced good machine parts in a kiln with old parts and buried the good parts in the nearby mountains to sell and make up for back wages. Labor strife in the factory substantially reduced productivity.

In comparison with the colonial period, this post–Korean War labor situation reflected many new elements in Korea's modernity. The physical change was visible. There were too many workers in the factory and too few managers and engineers. Although the Japanese managers and Japanese workers had left, they were not replaced immediately by Korean entrepreneurs and middle-level managers. A more significant change was the legalization of the workers' movement. Another new element was anti-Communism, which became the national ideology of South Korea during the Cold War confrontation between the two Koreas. On paper, at least, the government's approach to labor affairs was heavily influenced by the American model of economic trade unionism. In reality, however, the Rhee government's labor policy was anti-Communist and politically manipulative, and often overpoliticized any issues relating to labor organization and action. For example, the national labor union organization, the Taehan noch'ong, was a top-down government-sponsored organization and a handmaiden of the ruling party rather than a representative of rank-and-file workers. Many politicians from the ruling Liberal party served as managers in the

Samch'ŏk factory. These party members were concerned more with donating political funds to the Liberal party than with renovating the factory's personnel or management systems.

By the end of 1956, a workers' strike had been under way for four months at the Samch'ŏk Cement Factory; the chief demand was for payment of back wages, which management was unable to meet. Under Kang Jik-Sun, the company faced many serious problems and recorded a huge loss in 1956. In December 1956, the company was sold to three newly emerging entrepreneurs: Yi Pyŏng-Ch'ŏl, Yi Yang-Ku, and Pae Tong-Hwan, who also jointly owned the Tongyang Sugar Manufacturing Company. The Tongyang Sugar Manufacturing Company had grown rapidly from its origins in Pusan during the Korean War. As a wartime rear-area industry, it began manufacturing sugar out of raw materials brought to Pusan as wartime U.S. relief for Korea. The three joint owners renamed the Samch'ŏk factory the Tongyang Cement Company and held it for six months in 1957. They then decided to sell the company after realizing that without a huge investment, it would be impossible to make a profit because of its old and damaged facilities, constant labor disputes, and high production costs (Tongyang kŭrup 1987: 90–92, 106).

Inauguration and Success of the Tongyang Cement Company

It was at this stage, in late 1957, that Yi Yang-Ku took over the factory using his own capital.[5] The factory finally regained its health for

5. Yi Yang-Ku's life is a good example of the high-speed careers of many Koreans from 1930 to 1960 and of the further transformation of a few into major *chaebŏl* leaders in the 1970s. He was born in Hamju, South Hamkyŏng province, in 1916 into a poor family headed by his mother. He graduated from Hamhŭng Common School in 1931 and immediately started working as an errand boy at a Japanese-owned food wholesaler, which supplied various Japanese-made food products to markets in South Hamkyŏng province (60 employees, including 20 Korean employees). Within three years Yi became a regular store clerk, and in another three years he turned himself into a managerial-level senior clerk in the company, learning all the ins-and-outs of food distribution. In 1938, he started his own business, but it was closed by the government in 1941. After the liberation, he came down to Seoul alone in 1947, and using his entrepreneurial talent, he started to flourish again with a cookie distribution business. During the Korean War, he went to Pusan and got into the sugar distribution and candymaking

the first time in the eleven years since liberation. Under Yi's determined entrepreneurial efforts and a newly organized management
and engineering team, the company started a thorough examination
of the production process, its machines and facilities, the labor-
management situation, the distribution and transportation of its
products, and its marketing system. After a full investigation, three
tasks were singled out: improvements in production capacity by re-
pairing old facilities, training of workers and engineers, and a reduction of the workforce (Tongyang kŭrup 1987: 107–12).

While reorganizing management and reducing production costs
by rebuilding existing machinery, laying off workers, and stabilizing
labor tensions, Yi also tried to renovate the engineering team. He
initially looked for former Onoda engineers and skilled workers
who had left the factory during the previous decade of chaos and
disorder. He particularly searched for Oh Pyŏng-Ho, who was sup-
posedly the only competent cement engineer in post-colonial South
Korea. At the same time, he recruited graduates of university engineering departments each spring to train them as a new generation
of engineers, a reflection of the lifetime employment approach to labor-management relations that he had learned from the Japanese in
the colonial period (Tongyang kŭrup 1987: 107–12).

Oh, who had left the Samch'ŏk factory in July 1947 when Han
Ch'ŏl was appointed manager, was found in Yŏngdŭngp'o, an industrial suburb of Seoul, working as an engineer in the P'unghan
Textile Company. After three months in prison because of his role in
the self-governing council, he was released and spent a year teaching middle school in his hometown of Chinju. He moved to Seoul in
1949, looking for a suitable job as a cement engineer. During this period, he met an entrepreneur-capitalist named Kim Yŏng-Ku in
Seoul, who was collecting competent engineers to establish a cement
factory. Around 30 engineers, most of them, like Oh, graduates of
Japanese professional technical colleges or universities, gathered
around Kim, hoping Kim's capital would enable them to start a cement industry. According to Oh, there were not enough jobs for engineers between the late 1940s and the Korean War, due to the lack

---

business. His Tongyang Confectionary Manufacturing Company made him
a fast-rising commercial capitalist and earned him the nickname "Sugar
King" by 1953. After continuous growth from 1953 to 1955, he transformed
himself into a bolder industrial capitalist and bought Samch'ŏk Cement with
Yi Pyŏng-Ch'ŏl and Pae Tong-Hwan.

of private industry. Oh and other engineers had discussed the formation of a new cement factory in Tanyang, Kangwon province, in 1949, but their plan was never realized because of the outbreak of the war. Oh had subsequently worked for Kim at other plants, including the P'unghan Fermentation Company and the P'unghan Textile Company in Yŏngdŭngp'o since 1952 (Oh interview).

Oh accepted the invitation of Yi Yang-Ku to return to the cement industry and to his old workplace in Samch'ŏk after ten years. He became head engineer of the Tongyang Cement Company and supervised the technological part of the reconstruction of the company. He recruited and trained several machine engineers, and they became key engineers in the cement industry in the 1960s. Today, Oh remains the pioneer engineer in the South Korean cement industry (Cho Ki-Jun 1987: 154–56).

Once back on its feet in 1959, the company launched a thorough repair of old facilities and machines. This project was financed with 70 million whan of Tongyang Cement Company capital and U.S.$670,000 of foreign aid. From January to April 1958, four German engineers from the Polysius Company in Germany, which had originally planned and built the Onoda Samch'ŏk factory in 1942, visited the construction site. By the end of the project, the production capacity of the factory had increased from 78,000 to 180,000 tons/year, creating a solid foundation for the growth of the Tongyang Cement Company over the next two decades (Tongyang kŭrup 1987: 397).

The management resolved the constant labor disputes by paying the back wages of the striking workers and then firing many workers to reduce the high labor costs, one of the main reasons for high production costs. Compared to the Munkyŏng Cement Company, established in December 1957 with UNKRA subsidies, which had a production capacity of 200,000 tons/year, with up-to-date technology and factory facilities, Tongyang Cement Company paid three times more in wages but produced only one-third as much. In 1957, 125 employees were dismissed from a workforce of approximately 630. The dismissal of workers continued over the next two years — 160 in 1958 and 66 in 1959 — bringing the number of workers at the factory to 284 in 1959. Naturally, these dismissals caused strikes and demonstrations by the workers. Workers with little seniority were fired initially, and many veteran regular workers trained in the Sŭnghori, Ch'ŏnnaeri, or Samch'ŏk factories before the liberation remained as the nucleus of the workforce under Oh's guidance (Tongyang kŭrup 1987: 121, 123; Oh interview).

Following this reduction of the workforce, the managers started systematic recruiting and training programs for higher-level employees and engineers, which followed the seniority-oriented employment model of the Onoda recruiting system. From spring 1958, the recruitment exams were open exclusively for new graduates of engineering colleges or industrial high schools each year; this became the regular labor recruitment and training procedure.

The Samch'ŏk Industrial High School supplied most of the new recruits. Many of these graduates were the sons of former Onoda Samch'ŏk Cement workers. Oh still remembers with pride that every new cement company started in the 1960s, including Munkyŏng, Ssangyong, Hyundai, and Hanil, received one regular engineer sent by him after being trained in cement manufacturing at the Tongyang Cement Factory. In addition, each company sent around 30 employees to the Samch'ŏk factory to receive hands-on experience. Again, these practices are reminiscent of Japanese recruiting and training systems; they were instituted by Yi Yang-Ku and Oh Pyŏng-Ho, who had firsthand experience of Japanese-style labor relations in colonial times (Tongyang kŭrup 1987: 124). Many U.S., Japanese, and German engineers were also invited to Samch'ŏk to teach the workers, and many employees were sent to German cement factories and even Japanese factories after the normalization of relations with Japan in 1965.

The management made an equally important breakthrough in its labor-management system in January 1958, when it established a comprehensive system of detailed occupational classifications and job grades for all employees (see Table 4.2). All employees were divided into the two occupational categories of white collar and blue collar, and the jobs were divided into six grades. A retirement system for each job grade was set up, and a cooperative-society store was opened for the workers. The resemblance between the labor-management methods common in Japan and this system, which unfolded in the post-colonial era through the memories and experiences of the colonial generation of businessmen, engineers, and workers, is striking.

Workers at the Tongyang Cement Company became the first generation of skilled workers in the cement industry of South Korea in

Table 4.2
Occupational Classifications and Job Grades of
Employees at the Tongyang Cement Company

Grade	General staff	Engineering staff	Position
1	Councilor (*ch'amsa*)	Head engineer (*kichŏng*)	Office chief (*pujang, siljang*) Bureau chief (*ch'ajang, kwajang*)
2	Secretary (*chusa*)	Regular engineer (*kisa*)	Section chief (*kyejang*)
3	Clerk (*sŏgi*)	Assistant engineer (*kisu*)	Regular clerk (*sawon*)
4	Assistant clerk (*sŏgibo*)	Assistant engineer (*kisubo*)	Regular clerk (*sawon*)
5	Employee (*kowon*)		Regular clerk (*sawon*)
6	Employee (*yongwon*)	Factory employee (*kongwon*)	Worker (*kongwon*)

SOURCE: Tongyang kŭrup 1987: 124.

the late 1950s and early 1960s until a better-educated second generation of skilled workers, including their own sons, emerged in the
1960s. Approximately two-thirds of these second-generation workers, generally called the "Liberation Generation," joined the company after finishing secondary-level schooling at Samch'ŏk Industrial High School (formerly the Samch'ŏk Industrial School during
the colonial period). Both generations of workers actively participated in the labor union movement in the late 1950s and the early
1960s, until the Park military junta revised the labor laws in 1963
and instituted tight control of the labor movement to support its
five-year economic plan in 1962 (Tongyang kŭrup 1987: 124).

Three new companies—Ssangyong, Hyundai, and Hanil—were
established under the Park government's economic development
plan in the early 1960s. Tongyang, Munkyŏng, Ssangyong, Hyundai,

and Hanil remain the five major cement companies in South Korea today. The cement industry of South Korea grew much faster in the 1970s, in parallel with the second and third five–year economic plans. A construction boom, starting with the Kyŏngbu Highway and including the Saemaŭl rural village movements, roads, ports, and factory and apartment housing construction, demanded huge amounts of cement. Production increased from 10 million tons/year in 1975 to 25 million tons/year in 1985. By 1982, Korea had become the world's fourth largest cement exporter, behind Spain, Japan, and Greece, and in 1985, one-third of production was exported.

The Samch'ŏk case illuminates the complex overlapping of the colonial legacy and the new historical forces in Korea in the first fifteen years after liberation. The changes that took place in Korea between 1945 and 1960 deeply affected the modern transformation of the two Koreas in the second half of the twentieth century. In contrast to the rather abrupt and swift political, economic, and institutional changes and adjustments, however, the sociocultural changes and adjustments made by the Korean people were slower and the process was more complicated and gradual, as we saw through the experience of the Samch'ŏk managers, engineers, and workers. They had to adapt to the vastly more open, new entrepreneurial, technological, and labor opportunities. Yet they could not change overnight. The colonial experience lingered and affected Korea in the second half of the twentieth century. It took many years for Koreans to fully overcome the colonial experience and move with more unity and wholeness toward modernization.

The greatest irony of the decolonization experience for Koreans is that the historical pendulum swung back, after two decades of total rejection of the colonial period and anything related to Japan. Although there was no formal contact with Japan until 1965—a telling indication of the complete rejection of the former colonizer—history often repeated itself through the experiences and memories of modernity that the members of the colonial generation carried with them when they became the main historical actors in the decolonization period. The colonial legacy, in terms of people's lives, values, and communities, played an important role in both Koreas, especially after 1965 in South Korea, when intensive business and economic exchanges resumed between South Korea and Japan.

As for labor relations at the Tongyang Cement Company, in terms of patterns and styles, they were influenced by the colonial experience and practice. The overpoliticization of labor issues, the company union system, the labor-management council system, strong government intervention in labor relations (based on the excuse of national security and anti-Communism), and police suppression were all inheritances from the colonial period. Yet they were practiced within the new American-oriented legal framework of labor affairs (see Ch'oe Jang-Jip 1989; and Ogle 1990 for labor relations under the Park and Chun regimes). This intertwining of different historical forces and the consequent hybrid identity of Koreans were part of the painful, exhausting, and often delayed process of decolonization and marked the movement toward a more independent, uniform, and thoroughgoing modernization in South Korea in the second half of the twentieth century.

Conclusion

This book has tried to portray the growth of the colonial generation of Korean factory workers within the larger historical context of the early stages of industrialization and modernization. By examining the experiences of workers at the Onoda Sŭnghori and Samch'ŏk factories in the first half of the twentieth century, we have seen how the sometimes conflictual interactions of colonialism, industrialization, modernity, nationalism, communism, and militarism worked in colonial society. Contrary to the emphases of traditional studies of this period, the present study has shown that these forces did more than generate a political, anti-imperialist movement; rather, the emerging colonial modernity fostered a more complex process of change in social, economic, and cultural values.

The starting point of this discussion was a re-examination of the nationalist-oriented views of colonial industrial growth as an example of enclave-style development and of colonial labor as a cheap, abundant, unskilled, and anti-Japanese labor force. The experiences of the Onoda Sŭnghori workers confirm that the image of a passive, victimized colonial labor force exploited in enclave-style war-related industries is a nationalist, value-laden, binary historical concept that ignores the complexities of the colonial society. Despite hardships, frustrations, fragmentation, and alienation, the colonial generation of workers were active players in their society. Their history enables us to rediscover and redefine the characteristics of early industrial growth, as well as colonial modifications in it, and the equally complicated characteristics of labor and the social structure in colonial Korea.

When the Sŭnghori plant was established in South P'yŏngan province in 1919, many ambitious Korean youth left their agricultural communities and entered this Japanese-owned modern factory. Initially, the contractually based and impersonal factory environment must have been stressful for them, because it was so different from the traditional community-focused environment and personalized social relationships they had grown up with. Despite their lack of skills and modern education, however, entry into a large Japanese company became a shortcut to social and economic advancement. In other words, for some, colonial modernization provided opportunities for social mobility. By the end of the colonial period, a number of Koreans had established themselves as responsible, independent, and skilled workers and reached the top layer of the labor hierarchy open to Koreans.

In the colonial factory, methods and practices developed in Japan, such as strict rules, the incentive system, a company welfare system, an in-company training system, and a seniority system for wages and other forms of compensation, were applied with modifications. Managers had to create separate systems for the Korean and the Japanese workers. This selective adoption and modification process inevitably reflected, as well as caused, discriminatory practices in the workshop and complicated labor-management relations in terms of economic compensation, career tracks, and social recognition. As the Sŭnghori case demonstrates, labor-management relations were modified in four areas in the colonial factory: (1) the organization was segmented by nationality, (2) skilled Japanese workers functioned not as leaders of the workforce but as lower-level managers of Korean workers, (3) the seniority system was modified to prevent promotion of Korean workers to supervisory positions, and (4) Japanese workers discriminated against Korean workers socially. Because of shared social values, this seniority-oriented labor-management system worked well for disciplining and training both Japanese and Korean recruits and retaining them as a stable labor force in the Sŭnghori plant. Moreover, the colonial government's willingness to protect the system through police action helped the Sŭnghori managers enforce the colonial management system and cope with the political dimensions of colonial labor affairs: labor disputes, worker organizations, and Communist penetration.

As Korean workers gained more experience and skills, reaching higher positions as regular workers and having more interpersonal contacts with Japanese workers and managers, they inevitably confronted the most subtle, yet essential characteristic of colonial modernity—the conflict between colonialism and modernity. For Korean workers, modernization was conditional and allowed only up to a certain point and in a fragmentary, filtered, incomplete way. Korean workers eventually had to confront the inescapable dead-end nature of their careers and to realize their position in the ethnically segmented colonial labor market.

Several ambiguous, segmented identities—individual, collective, class, and national—were entwined within the consciousness of skilled colonial workers. They were actors in a collective drama in which the frustrations that grew out of oppression and discrimination would never be settled through their efforts as individuals or as class members. Earlier theoreticians of colonialism such as Frantz Fanon and Albert Memmi conceptualized this complicated, split-identity formation in colonial subjects as self-alienation, historyless-ness, or identityless-ness. The Korean sentiment known as *han* was probably a symbolic term to characterize the resentful bitterness resulting from the difficult experience of constructing a modern identity.

More recently, post-colonial writers and theorists, including Gayatri Spivak and Homi Bhabha, have begun speaking of "hybrid identities" formed in "colonial modernity." Focusing on time lags, in-betweenness, and transitional gradations in the modernization process in colonial and post-colonial societies, they argue that the merger of colonialism and modernity created a condition of ambiguity and contingency for existing identities, and that this is an essential element of colonial modernity. In this context, Gi-Wook Shin, Michael Robinson, and others have argued, in their pathbreaking studies on the Korean colonial period, for a concept of colonial modernity that is a useful and comprehensive conceptual tool, certainly much more so than the politically biased, nationalist perspective of previous scholarship. This concept of colonial modernity gives us a more accurate picture of the complex diversity of Korean modernity and shows that it was spread unevenly across diverse social groups and regions and varied considerably by period.

The responses of the Sŭnghori workers to social rejection and discrimination in the workshop are good examples of the diverse and uneven nature of modernity in colonial Korea. The workers responded not simply with monolithic resistance or collaboration but in quite varied and opportunistic ways, reflecting the diverse identities formed by the interactions of the historical forces of colonialism, nationalism, industrialization, modernization, and Communism at work in Korean society. Some workers accepted the status quo and established themselves as regular skilled workers; others revolted against the discriminatory situation either individually or in groups in the workshop, or by revolting against the colonial system by leaving the factory and joining national independence or Communist groups overseas. Still other workers simply left the company after gaining some technical training and joined other companies in an attempt to improve their economic and social status in the labor market.

Another historical force that significantly affected the nature of colonial modernity in Korea was the Japanese militarism that emerged in the early 1930s and lasted until the end of World War II. The wartime changes in the Sŭnghori and Samch'ŏk plants show how the totalitarian wartime policies and industrialization engendered many unexpected, unintended, yet very substantial changes in the Korean economy, society, and labor. These changes propelled a qualitative leap in the nature of colonial modernity in general and the colonial labor force in particular. The period of war mobilization brought increased penetration of capital, rapid changes in the occupational structure, quick urbanization, and the growth of both the male and the female industrial workforce, the urban middle class, and Korean capitalists. These changes accelerated after the liberation.

The number of Korean industrial workers, mostly rural outmigrants, increased rapidly from the early 1930s and exploded after 1939. These workers learned economic drive and experienced rapid social changes in an intensive, firsthand manner in this period. In terms of the quality of workers, the Sŭnghori and Samch'ŏk factories illuminate how the upper layer of Korean workers responded to the new opportunities opened up by wartime industrial growth and lifted themselves up. This upward movement was not limited to the workforce in factories, mines, and construction sites but was widespread in other modern-sector jobs in schools, companies, banks, and even government offices. Although the fundamental ethnic segmentation of the colonial labor system never completely disappeared, even in the midst of the Kōminka movement, the changes during the war years were a significant foundation for Korea's modern transformation in the long run. The wartime crisis had unintended effects in both colonial society and the Japanese empire as a whole. Despite the human suffering, both physical and psychological, caused by the Naisen Ittai policies and the Kōminka movement, some Koreans gained intensive work experience that made them into valuable human assets in liberated Korea.

As demonstrated by the experiences of the Samch'ŏk managers, engineers, and workers, the post-liberation period was even more dramatic and stressful than the late colonial period. In place of the Japanese model of colonial days, the two Koreas adopted heavily American-oriented and Soviet-oriented models of modernity in the course of an abrupt and swift process of political, economic, and institutional changes and adjustments. Nevertheless, the sociocultural characteristics of the colonial generation—a complex self-view, untraditional ways of thinking, self-alienation, and the feeling of being a new generation—deeply affected Korea in the second half of the twentieth century. The colonial legacy played an important role in both Koreas after the 1960s, especially after 1965 in South Korea, when intensive business and economic exchanges resumed between South Korea and Japan.

As we saw in Chapter 4, in many aspects labor-management relations at the Tongyang Cement Company bore a striking resemblance to the colonial wartime practices. The overpoliticization of labor affairs, the company union system, the labor-management council system, strong government intervention in labor relations on the side of business, based on the excuse of national security and anticommunism, were all reflections of the colonial legacy during the painful, exhausting, and often delayed decolonization process in South Korea in the second half of the twentieth century.

Labor historians of Korea generally agree that the sense of being the first generation of Korean labor—urban settlers uprooted from the rural sector—disappeared in the late 1970s and the 1980s. South Korean society then witnessed the emergence of a second generation of industrial workers, more self-conscious, confident, and urban, with different values, outlooks, and models. These workers have a more balanced self-view and are at peace with their Koreanness, accepting their hybrid identities, with fewer illusions that everything Korean is good, pure, and positive and must be retained.

From the psychological and sociocultural perspectives, the concept of colonial modernity also explains the strong and almost obsessive drive for self-renewal and self-assertion and the movements to essentialize Koreanness after the 1960s. This tendency was so strong and obsessive that it is often pointed out that there has been a defensive racism—a counter-mythology, to use Memmi's term— among Koreans toward outsiders, especially the Japanese. The model for modernity for the colonial generation was Japan, but their ambivalent attitude toward modernity was colored by their rejection of things Japanese in the post-colonial period. In this, they differ from the following generations.

Finally, in a larger historical sense, the growth of skilled workers in colonial and post-colonial factories illuminates Korea's paths to modernity in the modern century. Like the concepts of history, nationalism, and human communities, the concept of modernity has undergone a profound process of redefinition in recent academic thinking. Contrary to the earlier argument that societies develop along the line of Western modernity, each modernizing society is now seen as following a different path to modernization. Korean modernity can be categorized as a form of East Asian modernity, which is, as Tu Wei-ming points out, the result of a conscious response to the challenge of the modern West. Korea's reception of modernity was, however, complicated because it was mediated by the filtering mechanism of colonial domination by modern Japan. The entangled intrusion and influence of both Japan and the West as models for modernity and Korea's response to this challenge are the sources of Korea's "colonial" modernity.

What we need now are not only new definitions and theories but also new questions and research to rediscover and rescue the silenced historical subjects of the colonial past, such as peasant farmers, ordinary city dwellers, nameless colonial administrators, male and female workers, rural and urban parents and children, wartime draftees, the marginal poor, and migrants, and their lives in families, classrooms, offices, markets, and worksites. Rather than just examining the politics of anti-imperialism, we need to look at the more complex ecological processes of change in social, economic, and cultural values within colonial modernity.

Reference Matter

Works Cited

Primary Sources

Interviews

Andō Toyoroku
Former manager of the Onoda Sŭnghori factory; seventh president of the Onoda Cement Company. 9/30/1982.

Ha T'ae-Ick
Worker in the Onoda Samch'ŏk factory, 1941–78. 11/20/1985.

Kamata Shōji
Office worker at the Nihon chissō hiryō kabushiki kaisha, 1941–45. 7/31/1982, 8/5/1982, 8/12/1982.

Kim Ku-Tŭk
Textile worker, 1940–45.

Kye Chi-P'ung
Worker at the Onoda Sŭnghori factory, 1932–34. 8/20/1983, 8/28/1983.

Lee Kŭn-T'ae
Office worker at the Onoda Sŭnghori factory, 1942–45. 9/5/1983.

Oh Pyŏng-Ho
Engineer at the Onoda Samch'ŏk factory, 1942–46; director of engineering at the Tongyang Cement Company until 1987. Since retirement in 1987, he has resided in Taejŏn, Korea. 11/1/1982, 11/20/1985, 4/1/1993.

Song Ki-T'aek
Textile worker at Chōsen Textile Spinning Company, Pusan, 1925–51. 2/10/1982.

U Chin-Hong
Worker in the Onoda Samch'ŏk factory during 1941–72. 11/20/1985.

Archival Collections

Onoda semento, Hyakunenshi hensaniinkai shiryō shitsu (Onoda Cement, Records Office for the Compilation of the Centennial History of the Onoda Cement Company), Onoda Cement Company headquarters, Edō Ku, Tokyo.

1. Personnel Records

Kōmuka kokajō (Personnel records for the Engineering departments of the Onoda Sŭnghori, Ch'ŏnnaeri, and Komusan factories).

Sŭnghori Factory
  1920 ge (second half), 1923 jō (first half) and ge, 1924 jō and ge, 1925–30 ge, 1933 ge, 1935 ge, 1938 ge, 1941 ge, 1942 ge.
Ch'ŏnnaeri Factory
  1927 ge, 1929 ge, 1930 ge, 1933 ge, 1938 ge, 1941 ge, 1942 ge.
Komusan Factory
  1938 ge, 1941 ge.

2. Pamphlet

Shokkō kisoku (Rules for workers; published 12/1/1926 by Onoda Cement Company).

3. Public Hearing

Andō Toyoroku shōmonroku (Printed transcript of testimony by Andō Toyoroku in 1979 for five professors who were writing the *Onoda semento hyakunen shi*). 1980.

4. List of Office Workers

Onoda shokuinroku (List of Onoda office workers) (Onoda: Onoda Cement Company, 1923–45).

5. Company History

Onoda semento kabushiki kaisha. 1931. *Onoda semento gojūnen shi* (History of Onoda Cement on its fiftieth anniversary).
———. 1951. *Onoda semento shichijūnen shi* (History of Onoda Cement on its seventieth anniversary).
———. 1981. *Onoda semento hyakunen shi* (Centennial history of the Onoda Cement Company).

U.S. National Archives, Suitland, MD, Branch Records shipped from North Korea by U.S. military during the Korean War.

Periodicals and Newspapers

Chōsen
Chōsen doboku kenchiku kyōkai kaihō (Chōsen Civil Engineering and Construction Association newsletter)
Chōsen keizai zasshi (Chōsen economic magazine)
Chōsen rōmu (Chōsen labor)
Chōsen sōtokufu chōsa geppō (Monthly survey of the Government General of Korea)
Chuō kōron (Central forum)
Gendaishi (Modern history)
Mitsubishi gōshi kaisha, *Shohō* (Staff newspaper of the Mitsubishi Company)
Panghyŏp wŏlbo (Monthly magazine of the Textile Association)
Shakai seisaku jihō (Social policy newsletter)
Shokugin chōsa geppō (Monthly survey report of the Shokusan Bank)
Sin Tonga (New East Asia)
Teikoku daigaku shinbun (Imperial University newspaper)
Tonga ilbo (East Asia daily)

Secondary Sources

An Pyŏng-Jik. 1986. *Nihon teikokushūgi to Chōsen minshū* (The Korean people and Japanese imperialism). Trans. Miyajima Hiroshi. Tokyo: Ochanomizu shōbō.

―――. 1988. "Nihon chissō ni okeru Chōsenjin rōdōsha kaikyū no seichō ni kansuru kenkyū" (Study of the growth of the Korean working class in the Japan Nitrogen Fertilizer Company). *Chōsenshi kenkyūkai ronbunshū*, no. 25: 157–92.

―――. 1990. "Shikminji Chosŏn ŭi koyongkujo e kwanhan yŏn'gu" (Study of labor relations in colonial Korea). In Nakamura Tetsu, Kajimura Hideki, An Pyŏng-Jik, and Yi Tae-Kŭn, eds., *Kŭndai Chosŏn ŭi kyŏngje kujo* (Economic structure of early modern Korea). Seoul: Pipong ch'ulp'ansa.

―――. 1993. "'Kokumin shokugyō nōryoku shinkokurei' shiryō no bunseki" (An analysis of the employment capacity of the people based on registration data). In Nakamura Tetsu and An Pyŏng-Jik, eds., *Kindai Chōsen kōgyōka no kenkyū* (Studies of the industrialization of early modern Korea). Tokyo: Nihon hyōronsha.

An Rim. 1954. *Tongranhu ŭi Han'gukkyŏngje* (The Korean economy after the Korean War). Seoul: Paekyŏngsa.

Anderson, Benedict. 1983. *Imagined Communities: Reflections on the Origin and Spread of Nationalism*. London: Verso.

Andō Ryoō, ed. 1979. *Kindai Nihon keizaishi yōran* (Economic history of modern Japan). Tokyo: Tokyo University Press.

Bhabha, Homi. 1994. *The Location of Culture*. New York: Routledge.

Chang Ha-Chŏng. 1992. *Manch'u hoesangrok* (Memoirs of Manch'u). Seoul: Pakhomunhwasa.

Charterjee, Partha. 1986. *Nationalist Thought and the Colonial World: A Derivative Discourse?* Minneapolis: University of Minnesota Press.

Cho Ki-Chun. 1987. "Han'guk shiment kongŏp ŭi chŏn'gae wa Ssangyong yanghoe" (The Ssangyong Cement Company and the development of the cement industry in Korea). *Kyŏngyŏngsahak* (Journal of management history), no. 2.

Cho Kyong-Man. 1987. "Nong'ŏpnodong hyŏngt'ae ŭi Saengt'aekyŏngjejŏk maekrake kwanhan Ilgoch'al: 1940 nyŏn chŏnhu Yang-rirŭl Chungshim ŭro." *Han'guk munhwa illyuhak*, no. 19: 141–58.

Cho Sŏng-Won. 1993. "Shokuminchi Chōsen mensaku mengyō no tenkai kōjō" (The development of the cotton textile industry in colonial Korea). Ph.D. diss., Tokyo University.

Ch'oe Chin-Ho. 1981. "Han'guk ŭi kuknae in'guidong e kwanhan yŏn'gu" (Studies on domestic population movements in Korea). M.A. thesis, Seoul National University, 1981.

Ch'oe Jang-Jip. 1989. *Labor and the Authoritarian State: Labor Unions in South Korean Manufacturing Industries, 1961–1980*. Seoul: Korea University Press.

Chŏn Sŏk-Tam and Ch'oe Yun-Kyu. 1978 [1959]. *Chōsen kindai shakai keizaishi* (Socioeconomic history of early modern Korea). Trans. Kajimura Hideki. Tokyo: Ryuke shōsha.

Chŏng Chae-Chŏng. 1989. "Chosŏn ch'ongtokbu ch'ŏltokuk ŭi koyongkujo" (Labor relations in the Railway Bureau of the Government General of Chōsen). In Nakamura Tetsu, Kajimura Hideki, An Pyŏng-Jik, and Yi Tae-Kŭn, eds., *Kŭndae Chosŏn ŭi kyŏngje kujo* (Economic structure of early modern Korea). Seoul: Pipong ch'ulp'ansa.

Chŏng Yun-Hyŏng. 1984. "Kyŏngjesŏngchang kwa tokjŏmchabon" (Monopoly capital and economic development). In Cho Yong-Bŏm and Chŏng Yun-Hyŏng, eds., *Han'guk tokjŏmchabon kwa chaebŏl* (The *chaebŏl and monopoly capital in Korea*). Seoul: P'ulbit.

Chōsen shōkō kaigishō. 1935. *Chōsen ni okeru shinkō jūyō kōgyō ni tsuite* (Important new industries in Korea). Keijō: Chōsen shōkō kaigishō.

———. 1936. *Chōsenjin shokkō ni kansuru ichi kōsatsu* (Investigation of Korean factory workers). Keijō: Chōsen shōkō kaigishō.

Chōsen sōtokufu. 1930–43. *Tōkei nempō* (Annual statistical report). Keijō: Chōsen sōtokufu.

———. 1933. *Kōjō oyobi kōzan ni okeru rōdō jōtai chōsa* (Survey of labor conditions in factories and mines). Keijō: Chōsen sōtokufu.

———. 1934. *1930 nen kokusei chōsa hōkoku* (1930 census). Keijō: Chōsen sōtokufu.

———. 1935. *Shisei nijūgonen shi* (History of 25 years of administration). Keijō: Chōsen sōtokufu.

————. 1938. *Jikyoku taisaku chōsakai shimontō shinsho* (Final report of the Commission to Investigate Countermeasures for the Current Situation). Keijō: Chōsen sōtokufu.

————. 1940. *Shisei sanjūnen shi* (History of 30 years of administration). Keijō: Chōsen sōtokufu.

————. 1941. *Chōsen ni okeru jinkō ni kansuru shotōkei* (Comprehensive statistics on the population of Chōsen). Keijō: Chōsen sōtokufu.

————. 1942. "Nōson rōmu chōsei jōkyō" (The state of control of agricultural labor). *Chōsa geppō*, no. 4.

————. 1944. *Chōsen kōgyō no sūsei* (Trends in the mining industry in Chōsen). Keijō: Chōsen sōtokufu.

Chōsen sōtokufu. Gakumukyoku. 1941. *Chōsen ni okeru kyōiku no gaikyō* (A summary of education in Chōsen). Keijō: Chōsen sōtokufu.

Chōsen sōtokufu. Keimukyoku. 1933. *Saikin ni okeru Chōsen chian jōkyō* (Recent security conditions in Chōsen). Keijō: Chōsen sōtokufu, 1933.

Chōsen sōtokufu. Rōmu kyōkai. 1941, 1942, 1943. *Chōsen rōdō gijutsu tōkei chōsa hōkoku* (Results of the statistical survey of Korean laborers and technicians). Keijō: Chōsen sōtokufu.

Chōsen sōtokufu. Shakaika. 1923. *Kaisha oyobi kōjō ni okeru rōdōsha no chōsa* (Survey of workers in companies and factories). Keijō: Chōsen sōtokufu.

————. 1933. *Kōba oyobi kōzan ni okeru rōdō jōkyō chōsa* (Survey of working conditions in factories and mines). Keijō: Chōsen sōtokufu.

Chōsen sōtokufu. Tetsudō kyōkai. 1929. *Chōsen ni okeru rōdōsha sū oyobi bumpu jōtai* (The condition and distribution of workers in Chōsen). Keijō: Chōsen sōtokufu.

Chōsen tōkanfu. 1909. *Minseki tōkeihyō* (Population registration statistics). Keijō: Chōsen tōkanfu.

Chosŏn ŭnhaeng. Chosabu. 1948. *Chosŏn kyŏngje nyŏnbo* (Annual report on the Korean economy). Seoul: Chosŏn ŭnhaeng.

Chou Wan-Yao. 1996. "The Kōminka Movement in Taiwan and Korea: Comparisons and Interpretations." In Peter Duus, Ramon Myers, and Mark Peattie, eds., *The Japanese Wartime Empire*. Princeton: Princeton University Press.

Chu Ick-Chong. 1994. "Iljeha P'yŏngyang meriyasukongŏp e kwanhan yŏn'gu" (A study of the P'yŏngyang knitting industry in colonial Korea). Ph.D. diss., Seoul National University.

Cumings, Bruce. 1981. *The Origins of the Korean War*. Princeton: Princeton University Press.

————. 1984. "The Legacy of Japanese Colonialism in Korea." In Peter Duus, Ramon Myers, and Mark Peattie, eds., *The Japanese Colonial Empire, 1895–1945*. Princeton: Princeton University Press.

Duara, Prasenjit. 1995. *Rescuing History from the Nation*. Chicago: University of Chicago Press.

Duus, Peter; Ramon Myers; and Mark Peattie, eds. 1996. *The Japanese War-time Empire, 1931–1945.* Princeton: Princeton University Press.

Eckert, Carter. 1991. *Offspring of Empire: The Koch'ang Kims and the Colonial Origins of Korean Capitalism.* Seattle: University of Washington Press.

———. 1996. "Total War, Industrialization, and Social Change in Late Colonial Korea." In Duus et al. 1996.

Evans, Peter. 1987. "Dependency and the State in Recent Korean Development: Some Comparisons with Latin American NICs." In Kim Kyong-Dong, ed., *Dependency Issues in Korean Development: Comparative Perspectives.* Seoul: Seoul National University Press.

Foucault, Michel. 1971. *The Order of Things.* New York: Pantheon Books.

Gann, Lewis. 1984. "Western and Japanese Colonialism: Some Preliminary Comparisons." In Ramon Myers and Mark Peattie, eds., *The Japanese Colonial Empire, 1895–1945.* Princeton: Princeton University Press.

Geller, Ernest. 1983. *Nation and Nationalism.* London: Verso.

Giddens, Anthony. 1990. *The Consequences of Modernity.* Stanford: Stanford University Press.

Gordon, Andrew. 1981. "Workers, Managers, and Bureaucrats in Japan: Labor Relations in Heavy Industry, 1853–1945." Ph.D. diss., Harvard University.

———. 1985. *The Evolution of Labor Relations in Japan.* Cambridge: Harvard University Press.

Han In-Su. 1963. "Han'guk ŭi kongŏpjidae hyŏngsŏng" (The formation of industrial areas in Korea). *Inch'ŏn kyodae nonmunjip* (Journal of Inch'ŏn Teachers College), no. 12.

Han'guksa yŏn'guhoe, ed. 1995. *Kŭndae kungmin minjok munje* (Modern nation-state and the national question). Seoul: Chisik sanŏpsa.

Harris, Nigel. 1990. *National Liberation.* London: Pluto.

Hashiya Hiroshi. 1990. "1930, 1940 nendai no Chōsen shakai no seikaku o megutte" (On the nature of Chōsen society in the 1930s and 1940s). *Chōsenshi kenkyūkai ronbunshū*, no. 27: 129–54.

Hirose Seizan. 1995. "Shokuminchiki Chōsen ni okeru kan assen doken rōdōsha: dōgai assen o chūshin ni" (Construction workers mobilized by the government in colonial Korea: out-of-province mobilization). *Chōsen gakuhō*, no. 155.

Hisama Ken'ichi. 1932. "Rōdōtai seido to koshitai seido" (The labor corps system and the *koshitai* system). In *Suigen kōtō nōrin gakkō sōritsu nijūgo shōnen kinen ronbunshū* (Commemorative volume in honor of the 25th anniversary of the founding of the Suwon Higher Agricultural School). Suigen: Suigen kōtō nōrin gakkō.

Hŏ Su-Yŏl. 1985. "Chosŏnin nodongryŏk ŭi kangjedongwon ŭi silch'e" (The reality of Korean forced labor). In Ch'a Ki-Pyŏk, ed., *Ilje ŭi Han'guk shikmin t'ongch'i* (Japan's colonial administration in Korea). Seoul: Chŏngŭmsa.

————. 1994. "Shikminchi kyŏngjekujo ŭi pyŏnhwa wa minjokjabon ŭi tonghyang" (Structural change in the colonial economy and trends in Korean capital). In Kang Man-Kil et al., eds., *Han'guksa* (Korean history), no. 14, *Shikminjisigi ŭi sahoe kyŏngje II* (Society and economy of the colonial period, 2). Seoul: Han'gilsa.

Hobsbawm, Eric. 1990. *Nations and Nationalism Since 1780*. London: Verso.

Hobsbawm, Eric, and Terence Ranger, eds. 1983. *Invention of Tradition*. Cambridge: Cambridge University Press.

Hori, Kazuō. 1993a. "Nihon teikokushugi no shokuminchi shihai shi shiron: Chōsen ni okeru honganteki chikuseki no ichi sokumen" (A preliminary theory on colonial rule under Japanese imperialism: one aspect of substantial capital accumulation in Korea). In Nakamura Tetsu and An Pyŏng-Jik, eds. *Kindai Chōsen kōgyōka no kenkyū* (Studies of the industrialization of early modern Korea). Tokyo: Nihon hyōronsha.

————. 1993b. "1930 nendai Chōsen ni okeru shakaiteki bungyō no saihensei: Keikidō, Keijō fu no bunseki o tsujite" (Restructuring of the social occupation structure in Chōsen in the 1930s: the cases of Kyŏnggi province and Seoul). In Nakamura Tetsu and An Pyŏng-Jik, eds., *Kindai Chōsen kōgyōka no kenkyū* (Studies of the industrialization of early modern Korea). Tokyo: Nihon hyōronsha.

————. 1994. "Shokuminchiki Keijō fu no toshi kōzō" (The urban structure of Seoul during the colonial period). *Keizai ronsō*, nos. 154–56.

————. 1995. *Chōsen kōgyōka no shiteki bunseki: Nihon shihonshugi to shokuminchi keizai* (Korean industrial growth in historical perspective: Japanese capitalism and the colonial economy). Tokyo: Yubikaku, 1995.

Hwang Pyŏng-Jun. 1966. *Han'guk ŭi kong'ŏp kyŏngje* (The industrial economy of Korea). Seoul: Korea University, Asia Institute.

Im Chong-Ch'ŏl. 1969. "Iljemal Han'guk ŭi kongŏphwa e kwanhan ilgoch'al" (Study of the Industrialization of Korea at the end of the colonial period). *Seouldae kyŏngje nonjip* (Economic journal of Seoul National University), 7, no. 2.

Kajimura Hideki. 1965. "Fusei chikuzai seiri to Chōsen no eisokuteki dokusen shihon" (Cleaning up the illegally accumulated wealth and permanent monopoly capital in Korea). *Chōsen kenkyū*, no. 31.

————. 1977. "Heijō meriyasu kōgyō" (The knitting industry in P'yŏngyang). In Kajimura, *Chōsen ni okeru shihonshugi no keisei to tenkai* (Formation and advancement of capitalism in Korea). Tokyo: Ryūkei shōsha.

————. 1981. "Higashi Ajia chieki ni okeru teikokushugi taisei e no ikō" (The movement toward imperialism in East Asia). In idem and Tomioka Nobuō, eds., *Hatten tojō koku keizai no kenkyū* (Studies of the economies of NICs). Tokyo: Sekai shōin.

Kang Ih-Su. 1991. "1930 nyŏndae myŏnbang taekiŏp yŏsŏngnodongja ŭi sangt'ae e kwanhan yŏn'gu: nodongkwajŏng kwa nodongt'ongje rŭl chungshim ŭro" (A study of female workers in large-scale cotton textile enterprises in the 1930s: focusing on labor relations and control). Ph.D. diss., Ewha Women's University.

Kang Man-Kil. 1987. *Ilje shidae pinmin saenghwalsa* (History of the poor in colonial Korea). Seoul: Ch'angjaksa.

Kang Man-Kil et al., eds. 1994. *Han'guksa* (Korean history), vols. 13–14, *Shikminchigi ŭi sahoe kyŏngje* (Society and economy of the colonial period). Seoul: Han'gilsa.

Kang Tong-Chin. 1979. *Ilje ŭi Han'guk chibae chŏngch'aeksa* (History of Japanese colonial policy in Korea). Seoul: Han'gilsa.

Keijō shōkō kaigishō. 1943. *Keijō ni okeru kōjō chōsa* (Survey of factories in Seoul). Keijō: Keijō shōkō kaigishō.

Kim Chin-Yŏp. 1985. "Han'guk komukong'ŏp ŭi chŏnkaekwachŏng e kwanhan yŏn'gu" (A study of the development of the rubber industry in Korea). M.A. thesis, Seoul National University.

Kim Kyŏng-Il. 1987. "Iljeha komunodongja ŭi sangt'ae wa nodong undong" (Labor conditions and the labor movement among rubber industry workers in colonial Korea). *Han'guk sahoesa yŏn'guhoe nonmunjip*, no. 9.

———. 1992. *Iljeha nodong undongsa* (History of the labor movement in colonial Korea). Seoul: Ch'angjak kwa pip'yŏngsa.

———. 1994. *Yi Chae-Yu yŏn'gu* (Study of Yi Chae-Yu). Seoul: Ch'angjak kwa pip'yŏngsa.

Kim Nak-Nyŏn. 1994. "Shikminji Chosŏn ŭi kong'ŏphwa" (Industrialization in colonial Korea). In Kang Man-Kil et al., eds., *Han'guksa* (Korean history), vol. 13, *Shikminchigi ŭi sahoekyŏngje* (Society and economy of the colonial period). Seoul: Han'gilsa.

Kim Sam-Su. 1993. *Kankoku shihonshugi kokka no seiritsu katei: 1945–1953 nen seiji taisei, rōdō undō, rōdō seisaku* (Establishment of the Korean capitalist state, 1945–53: the political system, labor movement, and labor policy). Tokyo: Tokyo University Press.

Kim Tae-Hwan. 1981. "1950 nyŏndae Han'guk kyŏngje ŭi yŏn'gu" (A study of the Korean economy in the 1950s). In *1950 nyŏndae ŭi inshik* (Understanding the 1950s). Seoul: Han'gilsa.

Kim Tong-Uk. 1989. "Haebang'ihu kwisokkiŏpch'e ch'ŏrikwachŏng e kwanhan yŏn'gu: Chosŏnsŏkyuchushikhoesa ŭi sarye" (Study of the management of the vested properties after the liberation: the Chōsen Petroleum Company). *Kyŏngje sahak*, no. 13.

Kim Yang-Hwa. 1990. "1950 nyŏndae chechoŏp taechabon ŭi chabon ch'ukchŏk e kwanhan yŏn'gu" (Study of capital accumulation in large-scale manufacturing enterprises in the 1950s). Ph.D. diss., Seoul National University.

Kim Yun-Hwan. 1982. *Han'guk nodong undongsa* (History of the labor movement in Korea). Seoul: Ch'ŏngsa sinsŏ.

Kobayashi Hideo. 1969. "1930 nendai zenhanki no Chōsen rōdō undō ni tsuite: Heijō gomu kōjō rōdōsha no zenesuto o chūshin ni shite" (The labor movement in Korea during the first half of the 1930s: the P'yongyang rubber industry workers' general strike). *Chōsenshi kenkyūkai ronbunshū,* no. 6.

———. 1973. "1930 nendai Chōsen kōgyōka seisaku no tenkai katei" (The policymaking process for Korean industrialization in the 1930s). *Chōsenshi kenkyūkai ronbunshū* 3, no. 10.

Kwon Hyŏk-T'ae. 1991. "Nihon teikokushugi to Chōsen no sanshigyō: shokuminchi tokushitsu to shite no nijū kōjō" (Japanese imperialism and the Korean silk-reeling industry: the colonial characteristics of dual structures). *Chōsenshi kenkyūkai ronbunshū,* no. 28.

Kwon Tu-Yŏng. 1979. "Han'guk ǔi sanŏphwa wa nosakwankye yŏn'gu" (Studies of industrialization and industrial relations in Korea). Ph.D. diss, Korea University.

Kwon Yŏng-Uk. 1965. "Nihon teikokushūgika no Chōsen rōdō jijō: 1930 nendai o chūshin ni" (Labor conditions in Chōsen under Japanese imperialism: focusing on the 1930s). *Rekishigaku kenkyū* 303.

Lambert, R. D. 1963. *Factories, Workers, and Social Change in India.* Princeton: Princeton University Press, 1963.

Lee Hyo-Chae. 1980. *Yŏsŏng ǔi sahoeǔishik* (Women's social consciousness). Seoul: P'yŏngminsa.

Masahisa Kōji. 1941a. "Chōsen ni okeru nōmin isōn" (Peasant out-migration in Chōsen). *Shokugin chōsa geppō,* no. 3.

———. 1941b. "Senjika Chōsen no rōdō mondai, ge" (Wartime labor problems in Chōsen, part 2). *Shokugin chōsa geppō,* no. 38.

Mason, Edward; Mahn Je Kim; Dwight H. Perkins; Kwang Suk Kim; and David C. Cole. 1980. *The Economic and Social Modernization of the Republic of Korea.* Studies in the Modernization of the Republic of Korea, 1945–1975. Cambridge: Harvard University, Council on East Asian Studies.

Matsumura Takao. 1970. "Nihon teikokushugika ni okeru Manshū e no Chōsenjin idō ni tsuite" (Migration of Koreans to Manchuria under Japanese imperialism). *Mita gakkai zasshi* 63, no. 6 (June): 69–76.

Matsunaga Susumu. 1991. "1930 nendai Chōsen nai rōdōryoku idō ni tsuite" (Study of changes in labor within Korea in the 1930s). *Keizai ronso* 147, nos. 1–3.

McNamara, Dennis. 1990. *The Colonial Origins of Korean Enterprise, 1910–1945.* Cambridge: Cambridge University Press.

Memmi, Albert. 1967. *The Colonizer and the Colonized.* Boston: Beacon Press.

Min Kyŏng-Bae. 1974. *Han'guk minjokkyohoe hyŏngsŏngsaron* (Formation of the nationalistic church in Korea). Seoul: Yonsei University Press.

Miyake Seiki. 1937. *Shinkō kontserun dokuhon* (Textbook on the new concern). Tokyo: Shunshūsha.

Morita Yoshio and Nagata Kanako, eds. 1980. *Chōsen shūsen no kiroku* (Records of the end of the war in Korea). Sources, vol. 3. Tokyo: Gennandō.

Morris, Morris. 1965. *The Emergence of an Industrial Labor Force in India: Bombay Cotton Mill, 1854–1947.* Berkeley: University of California Press.

Moskowitz, Karl. 1980. "Current Assets: The Employees of Japanese Banks in Colonial Korea." Ph.D. diss., Harvard University.

Nakamura Tetsu. 1991. *Kindai sekaishijō no saikōsei: Higashi Ajia no shiten kara* (Re-imaging modern world history: an East Asian perspective). Tokyo: Nihon hyōronsha.

Nakamura Tetsu, An Pyŏng-Jik, Yi Tae-Kŭn, and Kajimura Hideki, eds. 1988. *Chōsen kindai no rekishijō* (Historical image of modern Korea). Tokyo: Nihon hyōronsha.

Nam Chun-Ho. 1991. "T'ankwangŏp tŏkdaeche e kwanhan ilgoch'al" (Study of the *tŏkdae* system in the coal-mining industry). *Han'guk sahoesa yŏn'guhoe nonmunjip*, no. 28.

Nihon rōmukan, ed. 1987. *Nihon rōmukan rekishi shiryōshū*, vols. 1–2, *Kōba hō* (Collected materials on the history of the Japanese Bureau of Labor, vols. 1–2, Factory law). Tokyo: Gosandō shoten.

Nippon teikoku gikai. 1943. *Dai hachijūgokai teikoku gikai setsumei shiryō* (Summary report on the 85th session of the Imperial Diet). In *Chōsen kindai shiryō kenkyū shūsei* (Collection of historical materials on early modern Korea), vol. 1.

No Tong-Sang. 1948. "Chosŏn nodongja kekŭp kwa nodong munje" (Labor problems and the working class in Korea). *Chosŏn kyŏngje* (Korean economy), Jan.: 18–26.

Ogle, George. 1990. *South Korea: Dissent Within the Economic Miracle.* London. Zed Books.

Ōno Ken'ichi. 1936. *Chōsen kyōiku mondai kanken* (Educational problems in Chōsen). Keijō: Chōsen kyōikukai.

Pak Chi-Hyang. 1992. "Han'guk nodong undong kwa Mikuk, 1945–1950" (The Korean labor movement and the United States). *Kyŏngje sahak*, no. 16.

Pak Hi-Bŏm. 1968. *Han'guk ŭi kong'ŏp kyŏngje* (The industrial economy of Korea). Seoul: Korea University, Asia Institute.

Pak Hyŏn-Ch'ae. 1978. *Minjok kyŏngje ron* (Studies of the Korean economy). Seoul: Han'gilsa.

———. 1979. *Kankoku no rōdō undō* (The labor movement in Korea). Trans. Lee Sŭng-Ok. Tokyo: Shakai hyōronsha.

Park, Soon-Won. 1985. "The Emergence of a Factory Labor Force in Colonial Korea: A Case Study of the Onoda Cement Factory." Ph.D. diss., Harvard University.

———. 1990. "The First Generation of Korean Skilled Workers: The Onoda Cement Sŭnghori Factory." *Journal of Korean Studies*, no. 7.

———. 1993. "Haebanghu Samch'ŏk shiment kongjang ŭi chaekŏnkwachŏng, 1945–1960" (Reconstruction of the Samch'ŏk Cement Factory after the liberation, 1945–60). *Kyŏngje sahak*, no. 17 (Dec.).

———. 1998. "Making of the Colonial Policies in Korea: The Factory Law Debate, the Peace Preservation Law, and the Land Reform Laws in the Inter-war Years." *Korean Studies* 22: 41–61.

Ppuri gip'ŭn namusa. 1983. *Han'guk ŭi palkyŏn* (Discovery of Korea). Seoul: Ppuri gip'ŭn namusa.

P'yŏngan namdoch'ŏng. 1975. *P'yŏngnam doji* (History of South P'yŏngan province). Seoul: P'yŏngan namdoch'ŏng.

Ri Kuk-Sun. 1960. "Hŭngnam piryokongjang rodong jadŭri kŏrŏon sŭngli ŭi kil" (The victorious path of factory workers in Hŭngnam). *Ryŏksa nonmunjip*, no. 4.

Robinson, Michael. 1988. *Cultural Nationalism in Colonial Korea, 1920–1925*. Seattle: University of Washington Press, 1988.

Scott, James. 1985. *Weapons of the Weak*. New Haven: Yale University Press.

Shin, Gi-Wook. 1996. *Peasant Protest and Social Change in Colonial Korea*. Seattle: University of Washington Press.

Shin, Gi-Wook, and Michael Robinson, eds. 1999. *Colonial Modernity in Korea*. Cambridge: Harvard University Asia Center.

Shin Yong-Ha. 1982. "Han'guk kŭndaesayŏn'gu ŭi sŏngkwa" (The accomplishments and problems of modern Korean historiography). In *Hyŏndae Han'guk yŏksahak ŭi tonghyang, 1945–1980* (Trends in modern Korean historiography, 1945–80). Seoul: Ilchokkak, 1982.

———. 1987. "Dure kongdongch'e wa nongmin munhwa" (The *dure* community and peasant culture). In Sŏuldae sahoe hakhoe, ed., *Hyŏndae chabonchuŭi wa kongdongch'eiron* (The community theory and modern capitalism). Seoul: Han'gilsa.

Shin Yŏng-Hong. 1984. *Kindai Chōsen shakai jigyō shi kenkyū* (Studies of the history of public welfare programs in modern Korea). Tokyo: Ryokuin shobō.

Sŏ, Alvin Y. 1990. *Social Change and Development: Modernization, Dependency, and World-Systems Theories*. Newberry Park, Calif.: Sage Publications, 1990.

Sŏn Chae-Won. 1996. *Shokuminchi to koyō seidō: 1920, 30 nendai Chōsen to Nihon no hikakushiteki kōsatsu* (The colonial labor system: a comparative history of Korea and Japan in the 1920s and 1930s). Ph.D. diss., Tokyo University.

Spivak, Gayatri Chakravorty. 1993. *Outside in the Teaching Machine*. New York: Routledge.

Sueji Isoya. 1949. *Shokuminchi no goku* (The colonial prison). Tokyo: Kyōdō shobō.

Suh, Sang-Chul. 1978. *Growth and Structural Changes in the Korean Economy, 1910–1940*. Cambridge: Harvard University, Council on East Asian Studies.

Sumiya Mikio. 1964. "Nihon ni okeru rōmu kanri no keisei" (Formation of labor relations in Japan). In Sumiya, *Nihonno rōdō mondai* (Labor problems in Japan). Tokyo: Tokyo University Press.

Suzuki Yoshinori. 1985. "1950 nyŏndae Han'guk kyŏngje ŭi sŏngchang kwa kong'ŏphwa." In Suzuki, *Han'guk kyŏngje ŭi kuzo* (The structure of the Korean economy). Seoul: Hakminsa.

Takeda Haruhitō. N.d. Unpublished manuscript on wages in the Dalian branch of the Onoda Cement Company.

Togliatti, Palmiro. 1979. *On Gramsci and Other Writings*. London: Lawrence & Wishart.

Tongyang kŭrup. 1987. *Tongyang kŭrup 30 nyŏnsa* (History of the 30 years of the Tongyang Group). Seoul: Tongyang kŭrup.

Tongyang shiment chushikhoesa. 1967. *Tongyang shiment 10 nyŏnsa* (History of the first decade of Tongyang Cement). Seoul: Tongyang shiment chushikhoesa.

Yang Ho. 1989. "Migunchŏnggi nodong chohap ŭi chŏngch'ihwaldong" (Political activities of labor unions during the U.S. Military Occupation period). *Sankyŏng nonjip*, no. 5.

Yi Hong-Rak. 1994. "Shikminchigi ŭi sahoekujo" (Social structure of the colonial period). In Kang Man-Kil et al., eds., *Hanguk'sa* (Korean history), vol. 14, *Shikminchigi ŭi sahoekyŏngje* (Society and economy of the colonial period). Seoul: Han'gilsa.

Yi Jeong-Ok. 1990. "Iljeha kongŏpnodong e issŏsŏ ŭi minjok kwa sŏng" (Nation and gender in Korean factory labor during the colonial period). Ph. D. diss., Seoul National University.

Yi Kwang-Ho and Chŏn Myŏng-Ki. 1994. "Shikminji kyoyuk kwa minjokkyoyuk" (Colonial education and nationalistic education). In Kang Man-Kil et al., eds., *Hanguk'sa* (Korean history), vol. 14, *Shikiminchigi ŭi sahoekyŏngje* (Society and economy of the colonial period). Seoul: Han'gilsa.

Yi Pyŏng-Ch'ŏn. 1987. "Chŏnhu Han'guk chabonchuŭi palchŏnkwachŏng ŭi kich'okwachŏng" (Foundation of the capitalistic development in postwar Korea). In Yi, *Chiyŏksahoe wa minjok undong* (Regional communities and the nationalist movement). Seoul: Han'gilsa.

Yi Sang-Ch'ŏl. 1989. "Han'guk meriyasu kong'ŏp ŭi chŏnkaekwachŏng e kwanhan ilyŏn'gu" (A study of the development of the Korean knitting industry). M.A. thesis, Seoul National University.

Yi T'ae-Jin. 1989. "17–18 segi hyangdochojik ŭi munhwa wa dure palsaeng" (The emergence of *dure* and rural community culture during the seventeenth and eighteenth centuries). *Chindanhakpo*, no. 67.

Yi Tae-Kŭn. 1987. *Han'guk chŏnchaeng kwa 1950 nyŏndae ŭi chabonch'ukjŏk* (The Korean War and capital accumulation during the 1950s). Seoul: Kkach'i.

Yoshio Eisuke. 1929a. "Chōsen ni okeru rōdōsha no juyō" (The demand for labor in Chōsen). *Chōsen doboku kenchiku kyōkai kaihō*, no. 1.

———. 1929b. *Chōsen no gojaku kanshū* (Customs in tenant farming in Chōsen). Keijō: Chōsen sōtokufu.

Yoshioka Kiichi. 1962. *Noguchi Jun* (Biography of Noguchi Jun). Tokyo: Fuji International Consultant, Shuppanbu.

Yu Yŏng-Ick. 1992. *Han'guk kŭnhyŏndaesaron* (A study of the modern and contemporary history of Korea). Seoul: Ilchokkak.

Yun Su-Jŏng. 1990. "Han'guk nong'ŏpsaengsan e itssŏsŏ ŭi nodongchojik ŭi pyŏnhwakwajŏng'e kwanhan yŏn'gu" (Study of changes in labor organization in agricultural production in Korea). Ph.D. diss., Seoul National University.

———. 1991. "Mŏsŭmchedo e kwanhan ilyŏn'gu" (A study of the *mŏsŭm* system). *Han'guk sahoesa yŏn'guhoe nonmunjip*, no. 28.

Zenkoku keizai chōsa kikan rengōkai, Chōsen shibu. 1939. *Chōsen keizai nenkan* (Economic yearbook for Chōsen). Tokyo: Kaizōsha.

Index

Harvard East Asian Monographs
(* out-of-print)

Harvard East Asian Monographs

Harvard East Asian Monographs

Harvard East Asian Monographs

Harvard East Asian Monographs

107. Roy Bahl, Chuk Kyo Kim, and Chong Kee Park, *Public Finances during the Korean Modernization Process*

108. William D. Wray, *Mitsubishi and the N.Y.K, 1870–1914: Business Strategy in the Japanese Shipping Industry*

109. Ralph William Huenemann, *The Dragon and the Iron Horse: The Economics of Railroads in China, 1876–1937*

110. Benjamin A. Elman, *From Philosophy to Philology: Intellectual and Social Aspects of Change in Late Imperial China*

111. Jane Kate Leonard, *Wei Yüan and China's Rediscovery of the Maritime World*

112. Luke S. K. Kwong, *A Mosaic of the Hundred Days:. Personalities, Politics, and Ideas of 1898*

113. John E. Wills, Jr., *Embassies and Illusions: Dutch and Portuguese Envoys to K'ang-hsi, 1666–1687*

114. Joshua A. Fogel, *Politics and Sinology: The Case of Naitō Konan (1866–1934)*

*115. Jeffrey C. Kinkley, ed., *After Mao: Chinese Literature and Society, 1978–1981*

116. C. Andrew Gerstle, *Circles of Fantasy: Convention in the Plays of Chikamatsu*

117. Andrew Gordon, *The Evolution of Labor Relations in Japan: Heavy Industry, 1853–1955*

*118. Daniel K. Gardner, *Chu Hsi and the "Ta Hsueh": Neo-Confucian Reflection on the Confucian Canon*

119. Christine Guth Kanda, *Shinzō: Hachiman Imagery and Its Development*

*120. Robert Borgen, *Sugawara no Michizane and the Early Heian Court*

121. Chang-tai Hung, *Going to the People: Chinese Intellectual and Folk Literature, 1918–1937*

*122. Michael A. Cusumano, *The Japanese Automobile Industry: Technology and Management at Nissan and Toyota*

123. Richard von Glahn, *The Country of Streams and Grottoes: Expansion, Settlement, and the Civilizing of the Sichuan Frontier in Song Times*

124. Steven D. Carter, *The Road to Komatsubara: A Classical Reading of the Renga Hyakuin*

125. Katherine F. Bruner, John K. Fairbank, and Richard T. Smith, *Entering China's Service: Robert Hart's Journals, 1854–1863*

126. Bob Tadashi Wakabayashi, *Anti-Foreignism and Western Learning in Early-Modern Japan: The "New Theses" of 1825*

127. Atsuko Hirai, *Individualism and Socialism: The Life and Thought of Kawai Eijirō (1891–1944)*

Harvard East Asian Monographs